T0106650

city
Secrets

BOOKS

THE ESSENTIAL INSIDER'S GUIDE

MARK STRAND
EDITOR

ROBERT KAHN
SERIES EDITOR

FANG DUFF KAHN PUBLISHERS
NEW YORK

First Published in the United States of America
Fang Duff Kahn Publishers
611 Broadway, floor 4
New York, NY 10012
www.fangduffkahn.com

2009 2010 2011 2012 / 10 9 8 7 6 5 4 3 2 1

Editor: Mark Strand
Design: Ingrid Bromberg Kennedy, In-Grid Design
Printed in China through Asia Pacific Offset

978-0-7893-1839-8
Library of Congress Number: 2009902795

Distributed by Universe, a Division of Rizzoli International
Publications, Inc.

TABLE OF CONTENTS

PREFACE

By recommending a book to someone, we extend its life. If the book has been neglected or forgotten, we save it from sure oblivion. It is easy, therefore, to imagine this collection of short personal essays as a kind of rescue operation. Books that most of us probably haven't read, or known about, become suggested reading, their virtues presented in various ways—sometimes casually or anecdotally, sometimes studiously, but always with conviction. Unlike the assigned reviews that one encounters in the media, these essays usually bespeak a long and positive relationship with their subject, and treat it affectionately. This is the key to how *Books: The Essential Insider's Guide* should be read—as though we were being introduced to someone's old friend. The range of books discussed is so wide that the chances of not discovering at least one that would appeal or even become a touchstone are slim. There is something here for everyone.

MARK STRAND

New York City, June 2009

A book is not only a friend, it makes friends for you. When you have possessed a book with mind and spirit, you are enriched. But when you pass it on you are enriched threefold.

—HENRY MILLER

INTRODUCTION

As this remarkably varied compilation took shape, I marveled at the number of contributors who chose to share books that profoundly affected their lives—books that somehow changed them, filled a need, and informed their future. It came as something of a surprise to me, having expected that "unknown" or "underappreciated" books would perhaps have offered their readers more marginal experiences. It was a great reminder of the unique, subjective joy of reading, and of the ways that we experience the books we come to value, as if they were waiting just for us to open them to their fullest understanding.

This is an extensive compilation, recommending books for every mood: from the lighthearted, comic, informative, inpiring, and uplifting, to the deeply disturbing. Just about every genre is included, in every manner of fiction and non-fiction, including history, biography, autobiography, memoir, humor, nature, crime writing, war reportage, and science fiction. Some of the titles recommended were once well-read, only to be forgotten with the passage of time; others were for some undeterminable reason immediately cast aside, perhaps overshadowed by events or victimized by changing trends; a few are simply difficult reads, either in subject matter or complexity of style. I am pleased to say that they cover much of the globe, touching nearly every continent and culture, and were written over a period of more than one thousand years. But despite this diversity, *Books* reveals the universal joy of connecting with a subject or a story and the satisfaction of finding another who has shared the experience.

My knowledge of literature has been forever expanded, as I hope yours will be, by our contributors' insight, knowledge, and love for the written word.

Robert Kahn
New York City, June 2009

BOOKS A-Z

A

All God's Dangers: The Life of Nate Shaw

By Theodore Rosengarten

1974

Theodore Rosengarten was a young Harvard graduate student, a native of Brooklyn, New York, when he traveled to Alabama in 1969 to conduct research on Southern sharecroppers' unions of the 1930s. There he came across an eighty-four-year-old African-American man, Ned Cobb, who had been a member of a communist-originated union. As he probed Cobb with questions about his union involvement, he realized that this illiterate man had a remarkable capacity to recount the details and events of his life.

In 1971, Rosengarten returned to his subject with equipment to begin recording Cobb's life story. The transcription, edited down from fifteen hundred pages of material, became a six-hundred-page book entitled *All God's Dangers: The Life of Nate Shaw*, published by Alfred Knopf in 1974. (Rosengarten changed Cobb's name in the book as a safety precaution.)

All God's Dangers earned immediate praise. *The New York Times* said that " . . . Rosengarten, the student, had found a black Homer, bursting with his black Odyssey and able to tell it with awesome intellectual power, with passion, with the almost frightening power of memory in a man who could neither read nor write but who sensed that the substance of his own life, and a million other black lives like his, were the very fiber of the nation's history."

Paul Gray, in *Time*, called the book "astonishing," and noted that "Miraculously, this man's wrenching tale sings of life's pleasures: honest work, the rhythm of the seasons, the love of relatives and friends, the stubborn persistence of hope when it should have vanished. *All God's Dangers* is most valuable for its picture of pure courage."

Several reviews noted the "Faulknerian" quality of the narrative of Shaw—who was born twelve years before Faulkner and died ten years after him—and the *Baltimore Sun* commented that "Nate Shaw spans our history from slavery to Selma, and he can evoke each age with an accuracy and poignancy so pure that we stand amazed." In 1975 *All God's Dangers* earned the National Book Award.

The book has remained in print over the past thirty years, long a Vintage paperback and presently available from the University of Chicago Press. During that time, roughly the same as my own as a bookseller, I have been asked countless times to answer the same question, which always more or less comes in the form of "What one book would you say best explains the South?"

I have always answered it—usually standing right amidst the canon of Faulkner, O'Connor, Welty, and Wolfe, all in their beauteous Library of America editions, and in paperback aplenty, and *To Kill a Mockingbird*, *All the King's Men*, *Black Boy*, or *Let Us Now Praise Famous Men*, not to mention the book of a personal hero, Walker Percy, author of the first great postmodern novel by a Southerner, need I say it, *The Moviegoer*, or the work of several notable writers who are also friends, Larry Brown, Ellen Douglas, and Barry Hannah among them, and even a few newcomer gems such as *Serena* by Ron Rash or *The Missing* by Tim Gautreaux—I have always answered the question with the title whose mere utterance never fails to give a little thrill: *All God's Dangers: The Life of Nate Shaw*.

This question—What one book best explains the South?—usually begs the next: Why? Lots of reasons, many of which I have suggested, but in case not: the strength of the narrative and its epic story, the sheer beauty and honesty in the language, the uncanny detail about agriculture and animal husbandry, about *mules*, for heaven's sakes, about the economy of farming and of Shaw's time, including the Depression, about labor, class, and race—about race in a way that takes the reader to the heart of America's great, vexing issue—about family, power, and truth, and, perhaps most of all, about human dignity.

Though I do it all the time, I am sometimes annoyed to see "Southern literature" subcategorized, when doing so somehow seems to minimize its importance. *All God's Dangers: The Life of Nate Shaw*—let there be no misunderstanding—is a great American work of deep universal relevance and, for its readers, invariably, a source of astonishment and, indeed, reassurance that literature—even from an illiterate—is a thing of unsurpassing satisfaction.

RICHARD HOWORTH

Richard Howorth is the owner of Square Books in Oxford, Mississippi, the bookstore he began in 1979. He served two terms as mayor of Oxford and is a former president of the American Booksellers Association. In 2008 he received the Authors Guild Award for Distinguished Service to the Literary Community.

Allegra Maud Goldman

By Edith Konecky

1976

About twenty years ago, the Jewish Publication Society published a series entitled "Gems of Jewish American Literature," reissuing four wonderful but little-known American Jewish novels in paperback: *Wasteland*, by Jo Sinclair, *Coat upon a Stick*, by Norman Fruchter, *Leah*, by Seymour Epstein, and *Allegra Maud Goldman*, by Edith Konecky. In spite of JPS's efforts, these works remain mostly forgotten, but I would recommend them all.

My particular favorite is *Allegra Maud Goldman*, a small jewel of a novel about growing up Jewish and female (and feminist). Although not entirely neglected (the Feminist Press published a special twenty-fifth-anniversary edition in 2001), the book is not widely read and rarely given serious consideration in any discussion of American Jewish fiction.

The voice throughout is that of Allegra, a precocious thirteen-year-old Jewish girl coming of age in pre-World War II Brooklyn. She is funny, irreverent, strong, independent, and insightful. In other words, she is the type of young woman who drives her parents and teachers to distraction. Her disdain for the adults in her life and everything associated with them is palpable. Intellectually curious, Allegra attends P.S. 193 (now named Gil Hodges) in Brooklyn, where she is subjected to a principal who silences her inquisitive nature by telling her, "Ours not to reason why"; a teacher who is preoccupied with "etiquette"; and a home-economics instructor whose curriculum includes the proper making of toast ("I already know toast," Allegra complains).

The novel is often labeled "comic," and there are many laugh-out-loud scenes, especially for those of us who grew up in Brooklyn and who can recall concrete school yards where the game of choice was often a rudimentary form of dodgeball: "A useful lesson in cruelty," according to Allegra, "meant . . . to prepare us for the day when we would want to join our fellow townsfolk in stoning the village idiot to death." Complaining about home economics, Allegra's fellow student Melanie asks, "If they're preparing us to be housewives and mothers, why don't they teach us something really useful like sexual intercourse?" To which Allegra responds: "That's the kind of girl she was. Brainy."

However, for Allegra the novel is not merely comic, and in spite of her wiseass quips she is mostly alone and lonely, alienated from her mah-jongg-playing mother, her overworked and indifferent father, her nerdy and neurotic brother, and her rather dull teachers. Allegra's great moment finally arrives when a poem of hers is accepted for publication. But her father, always the pragmatic garment merchant, is interested only in the letter of acceptance and the enclosed ten-dollar payment, not the work itself.

And yet Allegra does not succumb to her environment. She eventually manages to overcome her many disappointments. At the novel's conclusion we feel along with her a sense of hope and expectation. Allegra may never reach her fullest potential, but neither will she become like her mother or teachers. She has learned to love and to accept life's absurdities. This is, after all, a portrait of the artist as a young girl—and a compelling one at that.

STEVEN J. RUBIN

Steven J. Rubin is Dean of the College of Arts and Sciences and Professor of English at Adelphi University. He is the author of a critical biography of Meyer Levin and the editor of three anthologies of American Jewish literature.

America Is in the Heart

By Carlos Bulosan

1946

"I came to know afterwards that in many ways it was a crime to be Filipino in California," wrote Carlos Bulosan in his autobiography, *America Is in the Heart.* Part of a wave of immigrants arriving in the 1930s from the Philippines—America's experiment in colonialization—the illiterate Bulosan came, his age only seventeen, his grasp of English weak, his hopes, however, unflinchingly high. He was intent on finding work so he could send money home to alleviate the poverty of his rural peasant family. What he found, instead, was racism, the hardships of the itinerant laborer's life, the Great Depression.

In Bulosan's work, a little-known past is remembered. Signs on restaurant doors declared "No dogs or Filipinos." Empty freight train cars carried men up and down the Pacific states as they pursued the cauliflower season, the asparagus season, the rumors of work canning salmon in Alaska. In cities and larger towns, Asian districts were filled with brothels and gambling dens run by Chinese gangsters, bootleggers, and settled Filipinos exploiting countrymen who'd just stepped off the boat. In such places, workers would blow newly paid wages in a night—on cards, on drink, on a few moments of "pawing at women." Bulosan and his friends, who wanted to escape such corruption, were barred from renting accommodations in better areas, told to move on, victimized by police. Filipinos were beaten when seen with white women. When whites and browns fell in love, they lived surreptitiously.

Bulosan's decade as a hotel dishwasher, cannery worker, produce picker, professional gambler, and occasional, reluctant thief put him in direct contact with the lowest members of American society. No, correct that: by his accounts, they weren't even part of American society. Fed up with that strife, and caught up in the zeitgeist, Bulosan became a labor leader and union organizer. His early efforts failed when disunity allowed strikes to be brushed aside, or when Mexican or Japanese workers were imported as scabs. As Bulosan learned to organize more effectively, his reputation grew and brought danger. He slept with a gun beneath his pillow, kept on the move. His enemies finally caught up with him one night. He and two friends were forcibly taken from a restaurant by five men, brought to the forest, tied to trees, and beaten savagely. "Monkeys!" the men cried as they hit them. When the assailants paused to attend to a bottle of whiskey, Bulosan escaped. He was hidden in the home of a white woman who happened upon him. How could some be so cruel, Bulosan asked himself, yet others so kind? The beating left Bulosan with a permanent limp.

The hard years, too, took their toll. Hospitalized for tuberculosis and confined to a ward for over a year, Bulosan had half his ribs and one lung removed. During that time, he took it upon himself to read a book a day. The visits of an educated white woman who had become fond of him provided him with all manner of books. Thusly, Bulosan began his self-education.

What is extraordinary about Bulosan's story is that his failing health pushed him to develop his mind. In the 1940s, he became one of the more visible writers in America. His stories appeared in *The New Yorker*. His poetry received acclaim. A novel followed. President Franklin D. Roosevelt commissioned an essay from him, "Freedom from Want," part of a series on the *Four Freedoms of America*, which appeared in the *Saturday Evening Post*. The exiled Philippine president, Manuel Quezon, asked to meet Bulosan in Washington, D.C.; Quezon was so impressed that he asked Bulosan to write his biography. In 1946, Bulosan's own autobiography was published by the prestigious Harcourt, Brace & Co.

But Bulosan's literary career was cut short. Charges of plagiarism—later refuted by *The New Yorker*, which had published the story in question—followed by the zealousness of the McCarthy-era FBI, curtailed Bulosan's aspirations. Blacklisted, he could no longer publish. His body half broken, he could no longer do physical work. Poverty and illness led to his death, in 1956. His writing, tinged red with left-wing ideologies, fell into obscurity. Interest was not revived until the 1970s, when Asian-Americans began their search for identity. Bulosan was proclaimed the Filipino Steinbeck and is now considered one of the first Asian-American writers.

There is, though, an unevenness to *America Is in the Heart*, with its occasional polemical exclamations and almost naïve faith in the American Dream. Yet there are shining moments of utter poetry; his recollections and anecdotes are so heartbreaking and raw that a reader cannot help but be constantly moved. Even the book's roughness adds to its power—this is a simple man telling his own un-simple story. In many ways—perhaps in every way—it is also the story of America.

MIGUEL SYJUCO

Manila-born Miguel Syjuco's debut novel, Ilustrado, won the 2008 Man Asian Literary Prize, as well as the Palanca Award, the Philippines' highest literary honor. Part of the peripatetic millions-strong Filipino diaspora, he currently lives in Montreal.

Anniversaries: From the Life of Gesine Cresspahl

By Uwe Johnson

Translated from the German by Leila Vennewitz

1970–83

Because it's enormous, not many people read this book, but I've been recommending it to people for years. I once even taught a class on it just because I wanted an excuse to read it again. Uwe Johnson's magnificent *Jahrestage: Aus dem Leben von Gesine Cresspahl* is a chronicle of life in the United States—and specifically New York City—between August 1967 and August 1968, a year that saw the murders of Robert Kennedy, Che Guevara, and Martin Luther King, as well as continued U.S. military involvement in Vietnam. The book is divided into 366 dated sections (it was a leap year)—the "Jahrestage" of the title are both "anniversaries" and "days of the year"—and many of them begin with the news stories reported each morning in *The New York Times*. But, even more, it is a book about Germany. The novel's protagonist, thirty-four-year-old Gesine Cresspahl, has fled East Germany with her eleven-year-old daughter, Marie, and is working at a New York bank. Marie is quickly becoming an American, but Gesine wants her to understand where she comes from, and so spends most of the book telling her stories of her own childhood in the German Democratic Republic and her father's childhood in Germany under the National Socialists, along with stories about Marie's father, who happens to be the protagonist of Johnson's first published novel, *Mutmassungen über Jakob* (*Suppositions About Jakob*). The result is a luminous web of interconnected stories that zigzag back and forth through history and across an ocean. These stories, the book tells us, must be preserved for future listening: at one point, Marie says she's afraid she won't remember them all and asks her mother to record them.

> On paper, with the date and the weather?
> On tape, like phono-mail.
> For when I'm dead?
> Yes. For when you're dead.

Uwe Johnson left East Germany in 1959, at the age of twenty-five, when *Suppositions* was published by Suhrkamp, a West German house. In 1966, he accepted an invitation from the legendary editor Helen Wolff to spend a year in New York as an employee of Harcourt, Brace & World. The novel that resulted from his love affair with the city eventually filled four fat volumes totaling nineteen hundred pages in the German original. The first installment appeared in 1970; the last in 1983, just one year before his death, in Sheerness-on-Sea, England, where he had lived reclusively since 1974. *Anniversaries* was published in English, in two volumes totaling 1150 pages, (with Walter Arndt as a collaborator on the translation of the second volume). The book in English is much shorter, but the cuts were made—some slight consolation—by Johnson himself. Still, reading the abbreviated novel in English might make you want to learn German to read the rest.

Johnson is one of the most stunning describers of the universe I've ever encountered. He has written the finest account in all of literature of how to fold a newspaper for reading on the subway. Whether he is describing waves crashing on the Jersey shore (they're hunchbacked, and you can see the strands of muscle on their backs), the mysterious sounds emanating from the steam pipes in a New York apartment building, or the lake-studded countryside of Mecklenburg, Johnson's prose is supple, graphic, brawny, and addictive.

SUSAN BERNOFSKY

Susan Bernofsky is the translator of a dozen volumes of modernist and contemporary German prose and the author of Foreign Words: Translator-Authors in the Age of Goethe.

Any Human Heart

By William Boyd

2002

If a reader is a voyeur, and a journal keeper an exhibitionist, then *Any Human Heart*, the novel in journal form written by the very talented William Boyd, is an utterly satisfying experience. It's both panorama and peep show. Logan Mountstuart, Boyd's Uruguayan-British journal writer, chronicles his life, beginning in Montevideo in 1906 and ending in France in 1991, with a disarming candor that compels the reader with its easy entrée into what promises to be an intimate and often uncomfortable journey through the twentieth century by way of the life of a man who confesses to not always having behaved well.

As a privileged man keeping company with interesting, creative, and well-connected people, Mountstuart encounters dozens of the artistic and literary stars of the century. He counts Picasso, Joyce, Hemingway, Martha Gellhorn, Virginia Woolf, and Ian Fleming as friends and acquaintances. He manages to thoroughly displease the Duke and Duchess of Windsor, not a wise or healthy move on his part. Mountstuart sometimes waltzes but more often stumbles and crashes through major events in the century. He is a man who often finds himself at the mercy of circumstances mostly out of his control, sometimes initiated by his work, sometimes by politics, and, not infrequently, by his penis; excuse me, I mean his heart.

In the section of the novel called "The New York Journal," Mountstuart paraphrases a list of his virtues, as observed by his ex-stepdaughter from his third wife: "English, works in the art world, knows all the groovy artists, has lived all over the place, has written novels, has been in prison. Even I begin to think what a tremendous fellow I am." Well, perhaps not. Soon after, in "The Second London Journal," you find him in his dog-food days.

Why do I want to slap this man and say, "Please think a little harder before you act"? That's the beauty and brilliance of the novel. Mountstuart never quite comes to terms with his life. He's endearing and enduring. His accomplishments, sorrows, and blunders are so very real. Logan Mountstuart's chronicled life demonstrates what it means to be fully human, sometimes behaving well, and sometimes less so.

CATHY LANGER

Cathy Langer is the lead buyer for the Tattered Cover Book Store in Denver, Colorado. She is a former President of the Mountains

and Plains Independent Booksellers Association and is on the
board of the American Booksellers Association.

The Armada

By Garrett Mattingly

1959

Garrett Mattingly's masterwork, *The Armada*, has just celebrated its fiftieth anniversary. Published in 1959, it is the only scholarly work on sixteenth-century Europe to have made its way on to *The New York Times* best-seller list. And it thoroughly deserves the distinction.

Mattingly was one of the most eminent historians of the twentieth century. He spent virtually his entire teaching career at Columbia University, where he trained a distinguished generation of political historians. None, however, matched his command of graceful prose or his eye for the telling anecdote. He brings us right into the action, for example, when he describes King Henry III of France ordering the assassination of the Duke of Guise, and then, as he is brought to the scene to view the body laid out on the floor, remarking, "I had not thought he was so tall."

When he took on the daunting task of evoking a year of international crisis, Mattingly had already written the standard work on the beginnings of modern diplomacy in the Renaissance and a moving biography of Catherine of Aragon. What drew him to this particular subject, he said, was his experience of watching England in similar grave danger in June 1940. The task he faced was to turn the maneuverings among Europe's powers in 1588, the very slow unfolding of a naval campaign, and the often dry minutiae of politics into a gripping and dramatic story.

That he succeeded beyond all expectation is clear from the opening pages, which follow a modest clerk, Robert Beale (regularly referred to as Mr. Beale), through the process that led to the execution of Mary, Queen of Scots.

Great events are made vivid and human as we meet the ordinary and not-so-ordinary people who shaped the constant flow of change during a remarkable year. What is so striking is the way that the famous and the obscure are brought to life by Mattingly's pen as he helps us to see an almost theatrical scenario unfold through the eyes of its players. He brings us to every crucial moment, but always in the company of an individual who becomes our companion. The result is a can't-put-it-down narrative filled with memorable characters and colorful set pieces.

That *The Armada* received a Pulitzer Prize was only appropriate. To this day, it remains a superb example of a work of history that is not only engaging and beautifully written but also penetrating and instructive in its exploration of the motivations and actions that drive political affairs.

THEODORE K. RABB

The principal historian for the Emmy-nominated PBS series "Renaissance," Theodore K. Rabb, Emeritus professor at Princeton University, has lectured widely and has also taught at Stanford, Harvard, and other universities. He has published dozens of articles, reviews, and books, and has long campaigned to strengthen historical literacy in America's schools.

Army of One, by Janet Sarbanes

see p. 304

On Broadway

Act One: An Autobiography

By Moss Hart

1959

"No one has ever seen the skyline of the city from Brooklyn Bridge as I saw it that morning," a twenty-six-year-old Moss Hart recalled in the afterglow of his first Broadway triumph, *Once in a Lifetime*, in 1932.

That glorious taxicab ride from Broadway to Hart's Brooklyn apartment—with the morning papers' raves folded beneath his arm—ended the first act of an extraordinary life that from then on would be forever changed. Hart would go on to a prolific career in the theater—*You Can't Take It with You*, *The Man Who Came to Dinner*, *My Fair Lady*, *Camelot*—and in show business. But, for me, he remains most redolent as a writer and an unabashed rake in constant progress.

Reading his autobiography, *Act One*, as a young man in Canada, I was captivated by Hart's romantic fascination with this city, not yet my own. It becomes a character in his book—as it was in his life—with all the theatrical pomp and bustle and energy of a Gershwin symphony. Had Hart lived to see the opening sequence of Woody Allen's *Manhattan*, he may have felt as if he had already written it himself.

It is with cruel irony that Hart died suddenly only two years after the publication of *Act One*. He was a mere fifty-seven. The third act of his life had yet to begin.

GRAYDON CARTER

The editor of Vanity Fair since 1992, Graydon Carter has won seven National Magazine Awards. Previously, Carter was the editor of The New York Observer, the co-founder and co-editor of Spy, and a staff writer for both Time and Life magazines.

Assignment America: A Collection of Outstanding Writing from the *New York Times*

Edited by Gene Roberts and David R. Jones

1974

Assignment America is a collection of stories from *The New York Times* in the late 1960s and early '70s. In selecting the pieces, the editors ignored major events—no Nixon here, not much Vietnam—in favor of stories about the lives of everyday Americans who both embodied their time and transcended it. Instead of the president, we read about a twelve-year-old boy who overdosed on heroin in Harlem. We meet an elderly couple who live in the Bronx in their 1966 Dodge, working odd jobs and eating steamer clams dug from Long Island Sound. One reporter rides the Illinois Central train line from Chicago to New Orleans with black expatriates headed home for Christmas; another visits a potato farm in northern Maine and writes an obituary for a dying industry. And the account of a group of wholesome little old ladies in Dubuque will make you laugh. ("Miss Trenk doesn't like long hair on boys because 'it's so effeminate,' but concedes that 'Thomas Jefferson had a long wig, so I suppose it's all right.' Her definition of a hippie is a drug addict.")

The small miracle of this book is that there's nothing nostalgic about it. The pieces don't feel moldy or of another time. They grip, delight, and sadden. They're told by newspapermen who wandered from their beats and found truth, honor, tragedy, humor, and wonder in the mundane goings-on of the everyday.

The stories—none of which is more than a few pages—are enlightening because they're about more than their subject. They're about religion and football and food and the prom and the Fourth of July, motels, hillbillies, racists, soldiers, untimely deaths, unnoticed heroes, and the senior-citizen dating scene in Miami Beach. It's the kind of news no one announces, the kind that reporters piece together. As the editors write in the introduction, "[*Times* reporters] have learned that many, and perhaps most, major stories do not break; they trickle, seep, and ooze." This book taught me a lot about reporting and storytelling—how to show, not tell, as English teachers say. The journalists here have appropriate dispassion but also—because they're describing human beings rather than tax policy or space shuttles—unmistakable personal interest. It's as much a lively chronicle of a few forgotten years in our country's history as it is a collection of the kind of stories people tell each other in bars, on long car rides, and around the dinner table.

RYAN D'AGOSTINO

Ryan D'Agostino is an editor at Esquire and the author of Rich Like Them. His work has appeared in The New Yorker, Money, Ski, The New York Times, The Wall Street Journal, The New York Observer, New York, and other publications.

B

A Bad Boy's Diary

By Walter Gray (Metta Victoria Victor)
1880

Metta Victoria Victor was into multiples. She had more pseudonyms than Arthur Daley, gave birth to nine children, and wrote more than a hundred books. On top of that, she wrote the first full-length detective novel—*The Dead Letter*—and raised thousands of dollars for the antislavery cause with her novel *Maum Guinea*. If that wasn't enough to keep her busy, she and her husband also invented the American dime novel—the first paperbacks. Despite all these endeavors, she fell out of the public gaze and now seems ready for rediscovery.

My first encounter with *A Bad Boy's Diary* came when my mother read to me from it. She would cry with laughter, and so would I. She had inherited the book from her own mother, who had been given it by her parents, who had bought it in 1900 (fifteen years after Mrs. Victor's death) from a tinker's cart that came up the County Down mountains once a month with supplies such as sugar and flour. If you can imagine how many American novels the tinker carried among his groceries and vitals, you begin to get the picture of how popular Mrs. Victor once was.

Georgie Hackett is the titular bad boy, and he predates *Just William* and Adrian Mole by many years. However hard Georgie tries, he cannot stay out of trouble. He shoots the vicar, is involved in a kidnapping, and accidentally becomes a burglar.

All of his adventures are written in his own attempt at sophisticated spelling.

"Do you kepe dogs?" sez the visitor.

"Nary a dog," sez Pa.

"I thought there mite be one under the table," sez he.

"O no," sez Pa.

"Will you have calfy o lay?" sez mama, "or calfy nowar?"

"Calfy nowar," sez Prim. He's frightfully fashionable.

Just then I cot him by the caff of the leg with the pincers, an' I give 'em a good squeeze.

"Ouw, wow, wow!" sez he a-jumpin' up.

The cup went smash inter the glass pickle dish, the coughy spilt on to the tablecloth, the cup and sawcer as' dish wur broke—such a time! I know I turned pail.

A Bad Boy's Diary was the best-selling book of 1880, and Georgie Hackett successfully went on to his own series—including *A Bad Boy Abroad*, in which he arrives in Liverpool during a Fenian bomb attack and visits London and Paris, with inevitable results—but nothing is as good as this first book.

Fidelis Morgan

Fidelis Morgan is an actress and writer. Her books include biographies, dramatic collections, and the Countess Ashby de la Zouche series of novels, from Unnatural Fire *to* Fortune's Slave.

Bai Ganyo: Incredible Tales of a Modern Bulgarian

By Aleko Konstantinov

1895

A comic classic about the encounter between East and West in nineteenth-century Europe, this collection of vignettes about a Balkan Everyman named Ganyo Balkanski ("Bai" is a traditional term of intimate respect) has had the distinction of being kept in print and assigned for reading in Bulgarian schools since its original publication, regardless of the regime in power. It has been translated into every national language of the Balkans and throughout most of Europe. Konstantinov, often known simply as Aleko, is a Bulgarian national hero whose portrait, along with a picture of the manuscript of the novel, has even appeared on Bulgarian banknotes.

At the time Aleko was writing, Bulgaria had only recently become an independent country, after five centuries as part of Ottoman Turkey, and the first half of the novel recounts Bai Ganyo's humorous encounters as he travels around "modern Europe" with his "old-fashioned Balkan" values, disrupting formality and always on the lookout for a free lunch. In the second half, Ganyo has returned to Bulgaria, and the tone of the humor becomes dark as he rigs elections, publishes a mudslinging newspaper, and bullies and bribes his way through Bulgarian society.

Bai Ganyo is a satire that is at times hilarious and at times bitter, and is always entertaining. While it is firmly grounded in a specific time and place, its critique of narrow-mindedness and corruption is universal enough to resonate strongly anywhere, anytime— whether ex-Communist Europe during its period of transition or the United States during its two contested elections. But, no matter when or where, Aleko's combination of ready wit, sharp perception, and deft technique makes for a very enjoyable read.

VICTOR A. FRIEDMAN

Victor A. Friedman is Andrew W. Mellon Professor in both the Slavic and linguistics departments at the University of Chicago. His research has been supported by Guggenheim, Fulbright-Hays,

NEH, and other fellowships, and has been recognized with academic awards and honors in Albania, Bulgaria, Kosovo, Macedonia, and Serbia.

Barney's Version

By Mordecai Richler

1997

The works of Bellow, Roth, and Malamud crowd the top twenty of Jewish-themed books of the twentieth century, and a novel like Roth's *American Pastoral* achieves a depth and resonance that Canadian writer Mordecai Richler's work never had. And yet Richler's *Barney's Version* is the novel I faithfully reread several times a year, not to mention whenever I feel my own writing starting to wilt. It's funny—oh, so damn funny—and its choice of targets is endless: the provincialism of Quebec separatists, the provincialism of Montreal Jews, of the left, of the right, of the supporters of Israel, of the supporters of the Palestinians. Come to think of it, provincialism is Richler's overall target, and the ache he feels for the world-class Montreal of his youth is genuinely touching. Whether you agree or disagree with him (and I tend to do both), this is the kind of courageous satire that is often missing from bookshelves these days. The Italians are already crazy for him (the term "Richleriano" is shorthand for "politically incorrect"). It's a shame he's not better known south of the Canadian border.

Gary Shteyngart

Gary Shteyngart is the author of the novels The Russian Debutante's Handbook, winner of the Stephen Crane Award for First Fiction and the National Jewish Book Award, and Absurdistan, which was selected as one of the ten best books of 2006 by The New York Times Book Review.

Baumgartner's Bombay

By Anita Desai

1987

Anita Desai is an author unlikely to be overlooked. She
is a recipient of several literary prizes; three of her
books have been shortlisted for the Booker Prize; her
novel *In Custody* was made into a film by Merchant
Ivory Productions; and her essays appear regularly in
The New York Review of Books. But it's possible that
Desai's readers, faced with such a sea of accomplishment, may have neglected some of her most powerful
work. The extraordinary novel *Baumgartner's Bombay*
offers a vision of Bombay in an unlikely context; it is
the place where Hugo Baumgartner, of Jewish heritage,
hopes to find refuge from Nazi Germany. Bombay does
not turn out to be the haven he imagined, and his
memories of Germany and his misadventures in India
slowly build to an uneasy and disturbing parallel. "In
both lands," we learn in the book's first pages, its hero
is little more than "the unacceptable."

The premise of the book—a Holocaust novel set in
India—intrigued me the first time I read it. But I've
returned to it for the clarity of Desai's prose, full of
insight about human nature and dazzling descriptions
of a city that I once believed might never be captured in
words. Walking down a crowded Bombay street,
Baumgartner finds himself "caught in the traffic like a
fish in a net teeming with a million other fish . . .
[facing] the piscine bulge and stare of so many eyes . . ."
The story itself is a lesson in boldness; Desai never
shrinks from what is unpleasant, disquieting, or
heartbreaking. But she creates such richly nuanced
portraits of Baumgartner and of Bombay that the

novel, unsparing though it is, has always struck me as a
work of great beauty and compassion.

NALINI JONES

*Nalini Jones is the author of a story collection, What You Call
Winter, and her work has appeared in Elle India, Creative
Nonfiction, Ontario Review, and other journals. She is a Stanford
Calderwood Fellow of the MacDowell Colony, and teaches at
Columbia University, Fairfield University, and the 92nd Street Y in
New York City.*

Bel-Ami

By Guy de Maupassant
Translated from the French by Margaret Mauldon
1885

It has always surprised me that Maupassant's novels
are so little known in America. His short stories are
read—"The Necklace," of course, and sometimes the
wonderful "Boule de Suif." Yet Maupassant was a
best-selling author, and it was his six novels, not his
three hundred short stories, that made him rich. He
spent his money on yachts (several called *Bel-Ami*),
women, and travel, as well as on his mother and
brother. *Bel-Ami*, his second novel, sold thirteen
thousand copies immediately, and within two years had
reached its fifty-fifth printing.

It is difficult to understand why the book is no longer
read. I had to remind myself that it was written in 1885.
It concerns the triangle, as irresistible today as then, of
money, sex, and power. Money is there from the first
word, as sex is in the last. These engines move the story
forward ineluctably. How will the young and handsome
Duroy survive on the change from a five-franc note that
he has in his pocket—an interesting, precise, and
believable problem? The text is peppered with the prices

of things: shirts, nights with a prostitute, a pair of pistols. People steal, lie, gamble, and buy for the pleasure of buying. We are in Winnicott's domain of the transitional object, mingling fantasy and reality. Duroy's financial gains in the newspaper world, his insatiable lust for power and women, and his avid longing for success are the backbone of the plot.

Duroy, a modern antihero, lacks all scruples and uses means both fair and foul to advance his aims. Yet we follow him with bated breath. Maupassant has the gift of perfect pacing; he is an ace at plotting. Any stalled writer in the middle of a novel should read this one. Maupassant alternates sudden surges of joy with the painful obsessions of his journalist's life. "He gave the driver a hundred *sous* and walked on, his step rapid and triumphant, filled with joy. At last he had one, a married woman, a society woman from real society. Parisian society! How easy it had been, how unexpected!"

The description of the minutes leading up to a duel is only one example of suspense, precisely told, moment by moment, and psychologically astute. I defy anyone who opens the book and reads a couple of pages to then put it down.

The story remains entirely believable, because we constantly catch glimpses of ourselves, as we must do when an author portrays the human mind with discernment and the appearance of sincerity without imposing authorial judgment. Maupassant looks at this world with wonderment and without illusions. Thus this book, inspired by Flaubert, is remarkably modern.

Though Maupassant used the precise details of his life to create verisimilitude, we see this fictive world through the lens of his characters, mostly through Bel-Ami himself. Maupassant seamlessly intercalates these imaginary toads in his real garden, with Duroy and his world viewed only in the necessary distance.

Paris, in all its beauty and eroticism, is often glimpsed from a carriage: "A vast river of lovers was flowing towards the Bois beneath a starry, burning sky. There wasn't a sound except the muffled rumbling of wheels on the ground. Again and again they drove by, two creatures in every carriage, lying back silently on cushions and clasping one another tightly, lost in the delusion of their desire, trembling in anticipation of the approaching embrace. The warm darkness seemed full of kisses."

Maupassant's attitude toward women here is particularly interesting. Though they are often portrayed as commodities, they bring power, money, and position. Duroy writes his articles in collaboration with his wife, who not only initiates the flow of ideas but also brings home the necessary political players and the essential information. She is the ghostwriter, though Duroy signs the articles, becoming du Roy de Cantal, the successful head of the paper and a recipient of the Legion d'Honneur. He now suffers from what the critic Harold Bloom might call the "anxiety of influence," since his world is colored by his obsession with the man who came before, his clever wife's previous husband.

Maupassant renders the details of our lives recognizable but places them skillfully within a design that transcends reality, thus creating a new one. Though Duroy's rise may testify to the decline of the society of his time, it is certainly a rise we follow with a frisson of recognition and delight.

SHEILA KOHLER

Sheila Kohler is the author of three collections of short stories and seven novels, including the most recent, Bluebird, or the Invention of Happiness. Kohler has twice been awarded the O. Henry Prize, as well as the Open Voice Award, the Smart Family Foundation Prize, the Willa Cather Prize, and the Antioch Review Prize. Her novel Cracks has been made into a film directed by Jordan and Ridley Scott and starring Eva Green. Kohler teaches at Princeton.

Belinda

By Maria Edgeworth

1801

Maria Edgeworth might be the most important nineteenth-century novelist to have gotten lost in the twentieth. Like Fanny Burney before her and Mary Shelley after her, Edgeworth was raised in the home of a famous father. Richard Lovell Edgeworth was an amateur scientist, a man of letters, and an "improving" landlord who returned from England to Ireland in 1782 with his thirteen-year-old prodigy of a daughter. Under his tutelage, she was already conversant at a tender age with the works of Adam Smith, but her literary education was also remarkable. She read widely and went on to write in many genres, sometimes in partnership with her father. In particular, she developed the new form of "national tale" in a series of novels about Ireland that inspired Walter Scott to try something similar for Scotland. The result was the Waverley novels. She was an innovator in domestic fiction as well, and her influence on Jane Austen is palpable.

Her first success, *Castle Rackrent*, was in the genre of the Irish tale, narrated by an illiterate servant whose master's Big House is gradually taken over by the machinations of the servant's son. The use of the servant narrator pioneers a strategy later used in *Wuthering Heights* and *The Remains of the Day*. *Belinda*, set in England, is Edgeworth's first triumph in the realm of domestic fiction. And though it helped shape the work of Austen a decade later, it reads like an experimental variation on Austen conducted before the fact. It is easiest to give the flavor of this remarkable book by pointing to three singular features about its plot and characters.

First, the titular heroine, an exemplary woman orphaned at a young age, is sent by her aunt in Bath to the house of an aristocrat in London with the hope (on the aunt's part) that she will find a fit husband. The aristocrat, Lady Delacour, flamboyant rouée estranged from her alcoholic husband, nurses a secret malady in her breast (literally), which, we later learn, resulted from the kickback of a rifle during a duel she had with another woman, both of them dressed in men's attire. The origin, meaning, and cure of this injury is crucial to the story.

Second, many of Jane Austen's novels turn on a contest between the marriageable young heroine's first and second affections, usually in the form of an irresponsible infatuation followed by a more sober and steady connection. In Austen, the result is predictable: not the flashy Churchill for Emma Woodhouse but rather her courtly senior, Mr. Knightly; not the dashing Willoughby for Marianne Dashwood but rather the avuncular Colonel Brandon. In *Belinda*, the marriage plot turns on a pairing of roughly this sort. In London, early on, Belinda meets the multitalented wit and man of society Clarence Hervey, friend of the problematic Lady Delacour. It is a connection that Lady Delacour seems to encourage. Later, at the home of Lady Anne Percival, the saner and more wholesome mentor to Belinda, the young heroine meets Mr. Vincent, a West Indian planter and a man far less flamboyant than

Hervey, and this apparently wiser match is encouraged
by Lady Anne. But remarkably, as though reversing a
formula that Austen herself had not yet perfected,
Edgeworth has her heroine make the match with the
flamboyant lover. And it is one that proves both good
and sound.

Third, in a scene that takes place at the Percivals'
home, some children, including a young daughter of
Lady Delacour who no longer lives with her mother,
are gathered around a fishbowl, tapping lightly on its
sides. They are interrupted by the jovial Dr. X, a
physician who will eventually diagnose and heal Lady
Delacour's breast injury, who asks what they're up to.
They explain that they are trying to determine whether
the goldfish can *hear* the tapping of their fingers or are
responding only to the vibration it creates in the water.
The doctor explains to them that they are debating a
vexed question in contemporary natural philosophy,
one explicated in some detail by the learned Abbé
Noilet. Later in the chapter, when Lady Delacour
comes to visit, someone makes a remark that causes
her young daughter to blush. We are left to wonder
how to connect the physiology of human blushing with
the puzzle of the goldfish bowl.

Belinda is a book that offers lively engagements with
late-Enlightenment writings in literature, philosophy,
and science. But it can engage the contemporary reader
as well. Like much of Edgeworth's other innovative
narrative writing, it presents fiction itself as a kind of
moral laboratory. As with many laboratories, it is a fun
place to be, and you can learn a lot there.

JAMES CHANDLER

*James Chandler is a professor of Cinema and Media Studies and
the Franke Professor of English at the University of Chicago,*

where he directs the Franke Institute for the Humanities. His books include Wordsworth's Second Nature, England in 1819, *and, as editor,* The Cambridge History of English Romantic Literature.

Betrayed by F. Scott Fitzgerald

By Ron Carlson

1977

Carlson, best known as a modern American master of the short-story form (in such collections as *At the Jim Bridger*, *Hotel Eden*, and others), is a novelist of equal nuance. His characters are full of longing, buffeted by the tiny heartbreaks of everyday life but determined to strive on. His most recent novel, *Five Skies*, has received much due attention, but for a hidden jewel, I recommend his very first work: *Betrayed by F. Scott Fitzgerald*. The title alone should be enough to compel, but the book, set in a world where time is measured by changes to the paperback cover of *The Great Gatsby*, more than lives up. In the great tradition of first novels about young men coming of age, it is far better than average: funnier, wiser, sadder, and, ultimately, more hopeful. It also reveals the nascent gifts of a writer who has continued to present us with characters who haunt both mind and heart.

TOM ROTHMAN

Tom Rothman is the chairman and C.E.O. of Fox Filmed Entertainment. He has received the Arthur B. Krim Award from Columbia University and is currently an emeritus member of the Board of Directors of the Sundance Institute.

The Big Love

By Mrs. Florence Aadland as told to Tedd Thomey
1961

"There's one thing I want to make clear right off: my baby was a virgin the day she met Errol Flynn." How can you resist a story that begins like that, especially when I tell you that this ludicrously odd, icky, riveting, sweet, hideous, and unintentionally comic account of the amour between the boozy swashbuckler (who had already been charged with statutory rape of minors) and Beverly Aadland, the so-called baby, is narrated by her mother, an unreliable raconteur if there ever was one? Mrs. Florence Aadland, as she calls herself on the book jacket, proudly tells us that her ingénue daughter, who'd started modeling at six months and taking singing and dancing lessons at age two, was noticed by forty-eight-year-old Flynn on the Universal lot when she was fifteen, and that they did it soon after, because their love was "preordained." As it happened, "He overwhelmed her. He tore her dress, the black one with the bolero ruffles in the back, and he was so eager she cried and she fought him." How does Mrs. Aadland know so much? "When the time came she told me everything she did with Errol Flynn. . . . Everything. And in detail, because she and I love details and get a kick out of sharing things like that." The public did not find out about the liaison, however, until Flynn died of a heart attack shortly after Beverly turned seventeen, and Mrs. Aadland was convicted for contributing to the delinquency of a minor and denied custody of her daughter. In retrospect, would she have been so supportive of her Beverly's carrying on with this middle-aged reprobate? "Of course I would. And I mean it from my heart. I would let Beverly have those two wonderful years again—even if I knew in advance what the ending would be!" Indeed, in one of the last scenes of the book, mother and daughter, visiting the grave of Errol Flynn, decide that, though his tombstone was graced with more flowers than any other in the cemetery, this extraordinary man deserved more still. And so they steal a larkspur from one dead person, a daisy from another, and a lily from another. What is it that separates this too-candid tale from trash? Is it Mrs. Florence Aadland's voice—somewhere between Anita Loos and Nathanael West? Or is it that the book is out of print and copies are fairly uncommon? Or is it, in fact, trash?

PATRICIA MARX

Patricia Marx is a staff writer for The New Yorker, a former writer for Saturday Night Live, and a party planner for the C.I.A. Her most recent novel, Him Her Him Again the End of Him, was a Thurber Prize finalist. She lives in New York City, and, as far as she knows, has never killed anyone. She once traded a puppy for a book.

Big Sugar

By Alec Wilkinson

1989

Alec Wilkinson is neither an unknown nor an underestimated writer. His work appears regularly in *The New Yorker* and appeals both to the sophisticated reader and to the young writer who studies his clean, elegant literary style, taking apart his sentences and stories in an attempt to discover how he does it. Yet such is the state of publishing and book-selling that most of Wilkinson's books are out of print. One of my favorites is *Big Sugar*, an account of the harvesting of Florida's sugar crop.

The book, written over several years, devotes a chapter to each aspect of the industry. This seemingly simple structural decision makes for a pleasingly designed book, allowing the reader to absorb and to keep straight a quantity of diverse information. These chapters at times contain no more than a paragraph, such as when Wilkinson recounts a brief conversation with one of the older cutters, to whom he is giving a ride. They can also describe in full detail the financial realities of the sugar industry, or give a summary of the evidence when U.S. Sugar was indicted in 1942 for conspiracy to commit slavery. Another short chapter, about lobbying, leaves one with no doubt as to why, after the indictment was dismissed on a technicality, the charges were never brought again.

Although the central theme of the book is the life and work of migrant cane cutters, *Big Sugar* is a good deal more than investigative reporting. There are poignant sentences—"With their eyes staring into the distance they look as if the landscape they see in their minds is not the one through which they are walking"—and poetic descriptions of the burning of the sugar fields, with egrets picking off grasshoppers above the flames and landing unscathed on the still-burning ground. Wilkinson is witty and at times funny, even with a subject as serious as this: there are a series of adventures with Caveman and Anthony, guides who have a modest agenda of their own (driving around in Wilkinson's rented car and being bought the occasional drink), who take him to meet men who are rarely at home. There is also a good story about a python in the trunk of a car.

Wilkinson himself is an egoless presence in many of the chapters: the event is never about him. Instead, his perception and his choice of words make immediate the fields of cane stretching green to the horizon with a "broad, uniform, slightly-swaying-in-the-wind look of a prairie," and the lives of the men who cut the cane and who, far from home, live in wretched and squalid conditions.

There is never a note of outrage; that is left to us. Wilkinson just presents the facts. Sometimes the order in which they are arranged can make them ironic or political. A chapter quoting an admiring article in the "fashion tabloid W" about a family called Fanjul, who have made an immense fortune from sugar, offers telling details: one member of the family and his wife live in a twenty-six-room house that had "belonged to a man whose family supplied arms to the Germans during World War II"; they have a library with "chintz-covered couches and drapes, and many objects as well as a few books." The next chapter describes the one-room home of a sugar cutter; it is built of cement, has a tin roof, and lacks running water.

Although Wilkinson's reportage is now twenty years old, this book will be timely as long as we live in a political climate in which the very phrase "immigration reform" brings a range of uninformed emotion. Wilkinson's prose, on the other hand, is timeless.

ANNABEL DAVIS-GOFF

Annabel Davis-Goff is the author of The Dower House, This Cold Country, *and* The Fox's Walk. *All three novels were selected by The New York Times as Notable Books. She is also the author of* Walled Gardens, *a family memoir, and editor of* The Literary Companion to Gambling. *She teaches literature at Bennington College.*

Birdflight as the Basis of Aviation

By Otto Lilienthal

1889

In 1884, a German inventor named Ottomar Anschütz (who developed the focal plane shutter, making chronophotography possible) published a series of photographs of storks taking off and landing at their nests. These photographs are largely unavailable today, but they are as dramatic in their sepia tones as any human dance figure, as miraculous as any glinting titanium behemoth floating into Newark or JFK. Anschütz deserves to be counted with Eadweard Muybridge and Étienne-Jules Marey among the great pioneers of photography.

Anschütz's photographs came to the attention of an engineer named Otto Lilienthal, who, from 1885 on, working with his brother Gustav, experimented with human glider flight. Lilienthal closely studied the flight of storks, from which he came to understand the design of a successful airfoil. His book *Der Vogelflug als Grundlage der Fliegekunst* was translated in 1911 as *Birdflight as the Basis of Aviation*. Lilienthal built a hill in Berlin from which to launch his glider flights; on August 9, 1896, he fell from a height of fifty feet and broke his back, and he died the next day. But the Wright brothers credited Lilienthal with the discoveries that were necessary to their own successful flight at Kitty Hawk, North Carolina, on December 17, 1903.

After the long separation of science and humanism that began in the eighteenth century and reached its climax in the bafflement and anguish of late-nineteenth-century writers like Henry Adams and Edmund Gosse, Lilienthal's book seems a weird kind of macaronic, combining as it does the language of mathematics and physics, the earnest labor of intuition and calculation with passages of lyrical and visionary prose. Having fled in fright years ago from math and science, I experience Lilienthal's formulae, to my shame, as dead spaces in his narrative. I slog through them with stupid incomprehension. But I am reminded that, as a boy, he was intrigued that the stork, a normally shy bird, would come toward him under certain circumstances when taking off, rather than veering in another direction. There was some imperative greater than fear for the stork, and that was the necessity of launching into the wind. And so I keep reading, in this quaint and antique text reprinted mainly for aviation buffs. It is as if I were walking through a museum of phrenology, as I admire the intricate figures, the densely inked wave patterns and Rube Goldberg devices by which the invisible habits of air were first understood.

Poor Otto Lilienthal! He was confident that the future lay with gliders, rather than with powered flight; he was confident that aircraft would be made not of metal but of willow. And yet, if I may say such a thing, he had a poet's soul. "What is it which causes the stork to seek the company of man?" Lilienthal asks. "Surely he is not in need of our protection, since he need not fear any enemy in the animal kingdom. . . . Is he likely to be attracted by the human voice or song, or does he appreciate other human activities?" He reports that, during his brief absence, those helping him have lost the storks he has bred to observe: "They informed me that [the birds] flew so beautifully, being able to rise higher and higher, and that their soft black eyes pleaded so eloquently for the free enjoyment of this ability, that they simply had not the heart to lock the birds up."

There is a ready heart in this engineer. I have learned a great deal from him. After all, so much of poetry is wrongheadedness and intuition; it is translating into words what belongs to the world of nature, to the empiricism that has allowed us to climb, not imaginatively but literally, into the sky.

KARL KIRCHWEY

Karl Kirchwey is the author of five books of poems, most recently The Happiness of This World: Poetry and Prose. *His essays and reviews have appeared in* Parnassus: Poetry in Review, *the* Philadelphia Inquirer, The New York Times Book Review, *and elsewhere. He is the former Director of the 92nd Street Y Unterberg Poetry Center, and is currently Associate Professor of the Arts and Director of the Creative Writing Program at Bryn Mawr College.*

Black Lamb and Grey Falcon: A Journey Through Yugoslavia

By Rebecca West

1941

Written in 1937 and published during the Second World War, Rebecca West's magnum opus is an idiosyncratic mix of travel, history, and memoir. First published in two stout volumes, *Black Lamb and Grey Falcon* is almost overwhelming in its scope, prolixity, and fanatical attention to detail. West sweeps through the Balkans, plunging deep into history—steering off into lengthy digressions about, among other things, the battles and dynastic struggles of fourteenth-century Serbian dynasties—while focusing intently on the complex ethnic and political struggles of the fragile civilization she saw before her. Travelling with West are her husband, Henry, a quiet, sardonic diplomat, and a guide named Constantine, a Serbian Jew, high-strung, charming, and temperamental. For much of the journey, the party is joined by Constantine's wife, Gerda, a mean-spirited German who, with her closed mind and nasty prejudices, serves as a foil to West's open spirit. After many grumblings and sideswipes at the Slav character, she eventually departs in disgust. The relief of the Wests is palpable; Constantine is embarrassed and sad, but plows on with the journey. Like us, he is by now utterly devoted to the author.

It is the eve of war, and Rebecca West can smell it in the air. She reflects back continually, almost obsessively, to the period she calls the Great War (it was not then known as the First, since the Second had not taken place). Her mind is ruminating at some deep level on the vicissitudes of nationalism, on the submission of one race to others, and on questions of sacrifice and defiance, qualities that are symbolized by the black lamb and grey falcon of the title. She retraces in hallucinatory clarity and detail the steps that led to the assassination of Archduke Franz Ferdinand in Sarajevo, an event that she sees as the zero hour of her age, the moment when history tipped forward into catastrophe. And she senses the profound and seductive pull of fascism as it gathers around her, while casting herself back to the early struggles of the Balkans against Turkish rule. Ultimately, and movingly, the book becomes a call to ethical arms, a vigorous argument for true courage and resistance. West measures her ambivalent Englishness against the fiery, virile Balkan myths and searches her soul for its inner strengths and weaknesses.

It is probably the intensity of the historical moment that gives the book much of its strange but undeniable power. But a large part of the book's appeal stems from the author herself. West stamps every line of this book with the imprint of her personality: she is wildly opinionated, funny, endlessly curious, occasionally maddening, always deeply informed. Her energy is prodigious: every battlefield, every minor church demands to be visited, and the layered history of every monument or sacred site is meticulously reconstructed. Landscape and architecture are described in language of great delicacy and tenderness.

For what West feels for the Balkans is a deep, romantic passion, and it is this passion that irradiates the book and gives it such magnetic appeal. Like all great travel books, *Black Lamb and Grey Falcon* is the story of an unrequited love affair, a love that is doomed to failure as history moves on and the traveler returns home. In this case, West knows that the ancient and modern trajectory of the Balkans is an essentially tragic one, and that there is nothing she can do to alter its course. It is West's exasperated, despairing, and sometimes ecstatic grappling with this paradox—as she writes, travels, argues, describes, meditates, condemns, celebrates—that makes this book such a moving read.

JONATHAN BURNHAM

Born in London, Jonathan Burnham has been publishing director of Chatto & Windus, and was the founding publisher of Miramax Books. He is presently publisher of HarperCollins in New York.

Black Milk: Poems

By Tory Dent

2005

How does a young writer who loves "time like a ship" bear witness to her own bodily decline and imminent death with invention, lyricism, intelligence, empathy, passion, and daring? As a poet and a person with AIDS, Tory Dent grasped that she must remember and forget in order to write and survive. Her singular work singes the peripheries of contemporary American poetry in unrivaled ways, so that "almost out of ash, [her] body reconfigures itself."

With her third and final book, *Black Milk*, Dent left a riveting legacy and anti-elegy, a document written "after faith for the lost." She died in 2005, at the age of forty-seven, a few weeks after the publication of *Black Milk*. With it, she adds a miraculous and necessary contribution to literature in English. She writes that:

> My death began on April 12, 1988,
> over a pay phone at an artist's colony in upstate
>   New York
> in a windowless, wainscoted phone closet, where
>   a single bare bulb
> suspended above me, the enucleated eye of some
>   god surveying its work,
> enshrouded me in newfound blindness.

She lived with her illness for seventeen years, "[waiting] like a soldier's wife for something," stating that "for seventeen years I've said 'I won't live another year.'" During this time, she wrote two other collections, *What Silence Equals* and *HIV, Mon Amour*, which, with *Black Milk*, form a trilogy chronicling in innovative ways the stages of her life from the time of her diagnosis through protracted hospitalizations, physical deterioration, adverse reactions to medications, the joy of marriage, and an energetic determination to write, up until the period just preceding her untimely death.

While *Black Milk* is a cri de coeur, it is also homage to and a dialogue with several of the poet's literary predecessors: Rainer Maria Rilke, Paul Celan, Sylvia Plath, John Donne, Gerard Manley Hopkins, and Stéphane Mallarmé, whom she translated. It is significant that Dent deploys words by the greatest of Holocaust poets and one of the major poetic innovators of the twentieth century, Celan, for her title, its source his poem "Death Fugue," which begins, in Michael Hamburger's translation, "Black milk of daybreak we drink it at sundown." The allusion operates as structure and form; although *Black Milk* bespeaks a different conflagration and death sentence, it presents the contrapuntal music of fugue as an interweaving of poetic voices with her own and as the poet's necessary paradoxical remembering and forgetfulness. The volume tellingly opens with an epigraph from Rilke's "First Duino Elegy": "Who, if I cried, would hear me among the angelic orders?" Dent responds with a query, for there are no clear answers, although her words are unclouded and unwavering:

> And how should we know, by what sign, by what
>   feeling,
> that they've heard us? We watch the sky darken,
> a cold heart at noon regardless of expectation,
>   regardless of desire
> and its intensity, not the rioting red of white cell-
>   producing hope,
> nor the leech-bled black purple of bottomlessness.
> No sentiment, no matter how exigently soulful,
>   proves exigent enough.

In *Black Milk*, an essential contribution to the literature of testimony as well as to the American poetic tradition of the twenty-first century, Dent shows us how to live under unimaginable circumstances, with a death sentence always looming. The human desire to persevere and the linguistic brilliance that the book exhibits, the poet's hope to "cling for more time with the people/things [she] love[s]," acts unforgettably upon the reader.

YERRA SUGARMAN

Yerra Sugarman is the author of two poetry collections, both published by Sheep Meadow Press: Forms of Gone and The Bag of Broken Glass. She is the recipient of many honors, including the 2005 PEN/Joyce Osterweil Poetry Prize. She teaches at Rutgers University.

The Burnt Orange Heresy

By Charles Willeford

1971

Raymond Chandler wrote that killing isn't about "hand-wrought dueling pistols, curare and tropical fish." His essay "The Simple Art of Murder" was a repudiation of the traditional post-Sherlock detective procedural. That crimes are solved by the subsequent discovery of incriminating or exculpatory clues isn't as interesting as the inherent brutality of the erect mammal. The mystery of crime isn't in the how of it but the why.

Once hard-boiled crime fiction became free of the constraints of professional detective work, it seemed that any profession was fair game. *Double Indemnity* is about an insurance investigator; *Strangers on a Train*, an architect. Anyone might find themselves involved in the solution (or, just as likely, the commission) of a crime. But this short novel stands as enduring proof that no profession is safely non-adjacent to murder.

James Figueras, an ambitious young art critic, is contacted by Joseph Cassidy, a wealthy collector, with the opportunity of a lifetime. Cassidy will give Figueras the whereabouts of Jacques Debierue, the reclusive "missing link between Dada and Surrealism." Figueras may ambush him for a career-making interview. In exchange for this lead, Figueras must steal a piece for Cassidy. You see, Debierue is a Salingeresque recluse whose creativity is allergic to public acclaim. His reputation endures, despite the fact that he hasn't shown any new work in decades. Cassidy and Figueras assume that he's still working, just not sharing. Figueras accepts, of course, and finds Debierue in Willeford's favorite setting, South Florida.

Debierue's exile is a repudiation of the artist-public symbiosis, and Figueras is more than willing to insert himself as a middleman, a bridge who can reap critical attention for himself by revealing Debierue's surreptitious art and concepts to the world.

The plot becomes a cat-and-mouse dance with unlikely participants, and the stakes get even more unusual. Willeford flatters his readership by presupposing its belief in the transcendent value of art. Maybe this is why he was drawn to the artist-critic axis. Intellectual property is a world where theft, if performed convincingly enough, can be synonymous with murder.

If the book sounds too brainy, don't worry. *The Burnt Orange Heresy* is a page-turner about jealousy, vanity, and situational ethics in their most brutal form.

Henry Griffin

Henry Griffin is a screenwriter and filmmaker in New Orleans. His films include Mutiny, Tortured by Joy, Flip Mavens, *and* The Flavor of Plaid. *He is currently artist-in-residence at the University of New Orleans.*

By Grand Central Station I Sat Down and Wept

By Elizabeth Smart

1945

Renowned as a drinker, thinker, and eminent wisecracker in the Soho scene of 1950s London, Elizabeth Smart mystified many. Lucian Freud tried to paint her, but only got down to her eyebrows. Few knew that this gorgeous blond advertising writer—who reportedly sniffed glue every morning, spat out dazzling copy, and left work by mid-afternoon to hit the Dean Street clubs—had written a novel; and not some wry comedy, either, but a profoundly tragic book that would be rediscovered in 1966 and become hailed as "one of the half-dozen masterpieces of poetic prose in the world."

Extensively referenced in the lyrics of the songwriter Morrissey, *By Grand Central Station I Sat Down and Wept* is best enjoyed by brilliantly intense people who can handle its intense brilliance. Simply put, it's an account of a love affair. But that's like saying that the woolly mammoth was quite furry. In inimitable, psalmlike language ("I weep for such a waste of life"), it captures the way a volcanic romance can boggle the mind and make all other matters—from money to adequately functioning lungs—seem irrelevant.

The book was inspired by a real-life drama: Smart's circa-1940 pursuit of the English poet George Barker, whose verse had slain the brainy beauty before she'd even seen his slightly rodentlike face. Though she soon discovered that Barker had, quite inconsiderately, already married another woman, she couldn't derail her passion. Barker, no slouch in the heedless-rapture department, was equally mesmerized, and, as he lied to both women, disaster ensued.

Smart reshapes these events into brief but grand art. At times, the writing has the richness and cadence of scripture. When I dip into the book again after a few years, I feel like I've returned to the High Mass after a stint of sensible agnosticism.

DALE HRABI

Dale Hrabi, a former editor at Details and Radar magazines, is the author of the satirical mock-manual The Perfect Baby Handbook: A Guide for Excessively Motivated Parents.

By the Lake

By John McGahern

2002

This beautiful and quiet novel tells the story of a couple who has moved from London to the Irish countryside to build a lakeside home and start a new life. As they integrate themselves into the lives of the townspeople, McGahern depicts the villagers' traditional way of life as it is governed by the seasons and rhythms of the countryside. His prose is lucid and polished and the pace of the novel is measured and slow, as if he were creating a painting by incrementally laying down brushstrokes. What tension there is in the novel results from this rural way of life coming under siege and being eroded, and by the subtle dance of rejection and acceptance encountered by the newcomers. This novel is McGahern's gentlest, least oppressive work, and it is probably no coincidence that it was written after the church had lost much of its influence in Ireland. The reader is quietly and expertly seduced by McGahern's fictional world.

CHRIS LENAHAN

Chris Lenahan has been the buyer and manager of New York City's Corner Bookstore since 1989.

C

The Cabala

By Thornton Wilder

1926

The two most important things in life—love and reading—are often accidental. You go to a new acquaintance's party because you're bored, and the attractive stranger across the room becomes, within the hour, your beloved for life. And for how many is a friend's casual recommendation the reason we pick up a book that comes to shape our emotional imagination? One day in the late 1970s, I was visiting the poet James Merrill at his home in Stonington, Connecticut. We were standing next to a bookcase filled with Fiction—as nearby cases were stacked with Art or Travel or French Literature. For some reason I can no longer recall, he pulled out a copy of Thornton Wilder's *The Cabala*. "I think you'll like this," he said.

I did. *The Cabala* was Wilder's first novel, published in 1926 and written between 1921 and 1925, mostly during his off-hours while serving as a French master and assistant dormitory master at Lawrenceville, the private boarding school for boys in New Jersey. It had begun as "Roman Memoirs," an account of a year spent in Rome at the American Academy, studying archaeology. The experience began to cross with his readings, especially *La Bruyère* and *Saint-Simon*. The novel's first sentence is the classic announcement of the innocent's arrival: "The train that first carried me into Rome was late, overcrowded and cold." But from there on, he takes neither Henry James's psychologizing elaborations nor Hemingway's erotic tensions as his model. Instead, our hero, Charles Mallison—malleable, to say the least—is taken up by an eccentric group of elderly Romans, who, it is hinted, may well be versions of the ancient Greek gods. Waugh may have written this sort of fable, but he hadn't started yet.

Mallison's friend Blair might suddenly announce, "Say, do you mind if I drop in and see a friend of mine for a minute? . . . He's a nice fellow, but he hasn't long to live. He's published some verse in England; one of the thousand, you know. It got an awful rap. Maybe he's quite a poet, but he can't get over that diction. He's awfully adjectival." And down the Spanish Steps they saunter to visit the dying Keats. Elsewhere Freud or Palestrina may be discussed. The novel has that kind of surprise everywhere.

When I first read *The Cabala*, I hadn't yet read Firbank, but I had read Wilde and Nabokov, Joyce and Stein, and at once I recognized—and thrilled to—a Stylist. That is to say, a writer for whom the paragraph is more important than the chapter, the sentence more crucial than the paragraph, the phrase more momentous than the sentence. A writer with an instinct for both epigram and architecture; for whom the heart is a Baroque court and the mind a classical academy. It is, I think, one reason Wilder's early novels are so elliptical and his later novels so leisurely—both effects are the result of his style. You might ask—at the time, *I* didn't have the wit to—how did Wilder *start* this way, and over the course of his career become broader, more precise but less exact? The truth is, of course, every natural stylist springs full-grown from the brow of Flaubert, and seems only to *unfold* as a writer, rather than to *develop*. And though today Wilder's stylization may seem retro, even quaint, in its day it was both enameled and spiky. Its polish was bright, its irony pointed. Waugh's *Decline and Fall*, say, was still two years in the future. What's clear to me is that its style is much closer to Hemingway's than to anything older, stuffier. Its modernism may not be apparent today, but when you consider its collage-like construction (rather than any overstuffed linear narration), its precise and lean phrasing, his interest in historical pastiche (even, dare I say, deconstructivist pastiche), his interest in (that is to say, dramatization of) repressed feelings, and much else that literary scholars will be exploring, it's a safe call to place Wilder's novel among the best of its time.

Wilder was aware at the very start—or seems to have been—that it is not a reputation for being precious that will hurt a writer but, rather, the fact of being semi-precious. For instance, while a schoolmaster in 1923, he writes to his mother that he is in the middle of volume thirteen of Saint-Simon's memoirs of court life during the reign of Louis XIV and that he is, as he puts it, "more adoring than ever." The terms of his enchantment are revealing. "This influence, believe me," he wrote, "arrived most à propos—henceforward whenever I am endangered of falling into silken felicities and jeweled or flute-like cadences I have only to remember this memoirist whose three great virtues are energy and energy and energy." I don't think Wilder is referring to Saint-Simon's astonishing, even dogged, prodigality as a writer so much as he is noticing the balance in the memoirs between the delicacies of word or phrase (I might note in passing that Saint-Simon is reputedly the first writer to use the word "intellectual" as a noun) and passages of vigorous narrative and character-drawing. Similarly, he could mock his own ambitions. Immediately after the publication of *The Cabala*, he wrote to his brother Amos, scoffing, "I am too young and too undedicated a person to achieve a restrained Grand Style (which I pretend after)—notes of burlesque, smartalecisms and purple-rhetoric creep in and are only discovered when it is too late."

If the rhetoric is at times purple, it is an iridescent purple. *The Cabala* is not just a brilliant example of a young writer finding his way, but it remains, too, a heady example of American cosmopolitan writing.

J. D. McClatchy

J. D. McClatchy is the author of six collections of poetry, most recently Mercury Dressing. He has also written three books of prose and edited dozens of editions and anthologies. Among his recent books is The Whole Difference: Selected Writings of Hugo von Hofmannsthal. His many opera libretti have been performed at the Metropolitan Opera, Covent Garden, La Scala, and elsewhere. McClatchy teaches at Yale University and is the editor of The Yale Review.

Cards of Identity

By Nigel Dennis

1955

Here's a remarkable novel you might not have come across, possibly because it's so peculiar as to elude categorization. It neither instructs nor consoles nor deeply moves, but the sheer profusion of its surprises and its glittering sentences, along with the tenor of its loopy inquiries into profound matters of "the self," are inebriating, and can send you soaring over all kinds of narrative and intellectual confines.

I was fortunate enough to have been given the book as a gift and to have known nothing at all about it when I opened it. That might be the best way to encounter it, so I'll provide only one more little clue about the content: the author was apparently a friend of the Viennese psychologist and theorist Alfred Adler, and he translated a certain amount of Adler's work. It's a very, very funny book, but so witty, too, that instead of laughing, one might find oneself just gaping and pointing at the pages. It's not for everybody—or, goodness knows, for every mood—but perhaps you will join those of us who discovered that we were waiting forlornly to come upon it.

DEBORAH EISENBERG

Deborah Eisenberg is the author of a play, Pastorale, some nonfiction, and four collections of short fiction, including, most recently, Twilight of the Superheroes.

Casanova in Bolzano

By Sándor Márai

Translated from the Hungarian by George Szirtes, 2004

1940

When Sándor Márai died in San Diego, California, in 1989, by his own hand, soon after his wife's death due to a long illness, he was as old as the century he had lived in, and his reputation as an author was so obscure, I've heard it said, that not even his granddaughter knew that in earlier years he had been the most renowned Hungarian novelist of his generation. He was an enemy of both the Fascist and Communist regimes, and having survived both, he left Hungary in 1948.

His novel *Embers*, published in 1942 under Nazi occupation, was translated into French in 1992, but it was not until the publication of a German version in 1999 that Márai's official rediscovery began. *Embers* was a sensation in Germany, the author was proclaimed one of the twentieth century's great masters, and in 2001 this enthusiasm was transmitted to the English-speaking world via Carol Brown Janeway's translation from the German. Two men of aristocratic and military background, now old, rehash the facts and melodrama attending the eternal triangle they had formed with the wife of the elder of the two; the book is also a powerful evocation of the vanished Austro-Hungarian Empire and its military and romantic ethos. It is all aftermath: embers indeed.

The next of his novels to appear in English was *Casanova in Bolzano*, in 2004, and it seems to me that only then, in George Szirtes's luxuriant translation from the original Hungarian, did we get the artistry of Sándor Márai more nearly in full. Szirtes, a prizewinning poet of Hungarian descent living in England, has delivered a masterpiece by means of a masterpiece of translation. I have read a lot of books, but I have never read anything quite like this one.

This much is historical fact: Giacomo Casanova escaped from a dread Venetian prison in 1756 with his accomplice, a priest named Balbi, and on his way north to safety in Switzerland stopped for a few days in the town of Bolzano. The rest is Márai's invention. The swashbuckling element of the opening is conveyed with great vigor and economy: "By the time they reached Treviso their money was gone; they sneaked through the gates dedicated to St. Thomas, into the fields, and by creeping along the backs of gardens and by skirting the woods, managed to reach the outskirts of Valdepiadene about dawn. Here he took out his dagger, thrust it under the nose of his disgusting companion, and told him they'd meet again in Bolzano; then they parted."

Once Casanova establishes himself at an inn in Bolzano, the narrative is enriched by a wealth of domestic detail: "The servants were busying themselves about the apartment: they brought huge gilt candlesticks, warm water in a silver jug, and canvas towels manufactured in Limburg." While word of the notorious man's arrival races through the town in a windstorm of rumor, people eager for a glimpse of him gather at the hotel, and maidservants peer through the keyhole in the hope of seeing the sacred monster. The rest of the novel takes place within this luxuriantly furnished enclosure.

A few things happen—Casanova makes a pass at a maidservant who feels, astonishingly, nothing beneath his expert embraces, etc.—and eventually we find out why he came to Bolzano. It turns out, that in a long life of multiple seductions, the only woman he ever truly loved, or thinks he did, lives in the neighborhood, currently married to the Duke of Parma. Eventually Casanova is visited by each of the pair in turn, and Márai employs the technique that would appear again two years later in *Embers*: that of the preposterously extended monologue. His beloved Francesca and her husband each has a go at him for seventy-five pages at a time, forbidding him to answer, telling him that they know what he would say anyway; and Casanova just sits there and takes it.

It is not a simple deflation of an erotic conqueror's persona. It is an extraordinary hyper-examination of romantic and erotic love in a dizzying succession of aspects—a pair of nearly endless arias in the eroto-comic opera that is life. The deliberate irrealism of the technique establishes the modernism of the book: this is not remotely historical fiction or a museum piece. Everything overspills its bounds, and Márai's combination of sheer brazenness and masterly control bowls one over for the duration. Conventional coordinates are flung awry and the clock and the compass sail out the window. This is a deeply complex and philosophical comedy.

Bravo, but to my mind this is not the most extraordinary thing about the book. Reading it was an unusual, unprecedented experience: I would read a few lines, or half a page, then find myself transported elsewhere, to return with a startled blink an hour or so later. This happened even when I read it on the hurtling, noisy New York City subway. Márai's power of evocation—of a place I've never been and a time I've never lived in—is so intense that it is like reading Proust, with this difference: the book is short, and you do all the lengthy Proustification yourself. Lost memories and atmospheres come to you, and you vanish into them, a character passing through the pages of your own mysteriously parallel book.

This experience is not unique to me. I have spoken to other readers who were sent spinning through similar journeys, lost in the novel's heady perfume.

As of this writing, five books of Márai's have been translated into English, four of them novels, one a memoir. I understand that this means there are still thirty-five to go. This is wonderful news.

RAFI ZABOR

Rafi Zabor's novel, The Bear Comes Home, won the PEN/ Faulkner Award for fiction in 1998. His second book, I, Wabenzi, was published in 2005. For a number of years he wrote about jazz for Musician magazine and other publications.

The Celebrity Circus

By Elsa Maxwell

1963

Ugliness seemed to be Elsa Maxwell's sword and shield, the quality that gave her liberty to puncture snobs while she tirelessly charged off in the direction of the beautiful people. A columnist and a party-giver who for decades lived in hotel suites (usually at a favorable price), Maxwell was candid about her looks. "In the annals of the press I have been variously referred to as a hippo, a rhinoceros, an Eskimo igloo during summer thaw, a charwoman at daybreak, and 'the fattest frump alive,'" she wrote. A German prince, seeing her swim off Eden Roc, mistook her for a rubber mattress, she claimed, while the *Tonight Show* host Jack Parr described her evening dress as an "unborn sofa."

I laugh each time I read this, and of course that's what Maxwell wanted. She wanted us on her side. Maxwell was not sufficiently sensitive to the trajectory of her own life—from birth in Keokuk, Iowa, in 1883, to an early vaudeville career, and finally, friendship with chic women like the Duchess of Windsor (referred to in her columns as "my darling Duchess")—to really produce a first-rate memoir of an age. Nor was she gifted like her pals Noël Coward and Cole Porter. Her ambition was to be known, to assert herself with important people and have an influence over them, and her writing style betrays a clever woman born to exaggeration. Her obsession with royals and playboys seems quaint by today's lower standards. By the late '50s, Maxwell was already huffing that the Côte d'Azur was washed up: "Even its celebrities look alike. They wear the same hats, they wear the same hairdos, they seem so *en masse*. They all come wrapped in the same package; tear off the wrapping, and they're all alike underneath." She doesn't say what that is, exactly. Perhaps she never knew what made any of these people interesting beyond magnetism and money. And doubtless she was too concerned about her own survival to bother finding out.

Maxwell died in 1963, apparently leaving only a few trunks of clothes and press clippings. When I first came across the *The Celebrity Circus*, maybe twenty years ago, the names in it still seemed glamorous. They are less so today. But I marvel at the energy of this small and quite round name-dropper who knew how to cultivate acquaintanceship with famous people and make the rest of us laugh at the audacity of her act.

CATHY HORYN

Cathy Horyn is the fashion critic of The New York Times and the co-author of Bare Blass.

Charlie: The Improbable Life and Times of Charles MacArthur

By Ben Hecht

1957

Charles MacArthur, the great American playwright and screenwriter, comes to life in the hands of his best friend and frequent collaborator, the brilliant Ben Hecht.

Told in stand-alone vignettes instead of chapters, the story begins in Chicago when Charlie was young; takes us through his experiences as a soldier in World War I; continues on to New York City, where MacArthur toiled and then got lucky as a playwright, found true love with Helen Hayes, married her, and had two wonderful children; and then moves on to

Hollywood, where Hecht and MacArthur made their mark as a screenwriting team.

The old Hollywood studio system comes alive on these pages, so much so that the words crackle. The reader is there as careers are built, as writers are wooed, overpaid, and honored, and then just as quickly destroyed, disregarded, and discarded like a lame bit of dialogue from an early draft of a B-movie script.

When Helen and Charlie's beloved daughter Mary dies at the age of nineteen, after a brief illness, MacArthur's grief is palpable, and his dazzling life is never the same. The portrait of Charlie's grief, a father carrying on in the wake of losing a child, is unlike anything else you will ever read on the subject. MacArthur's improbable but amazing life, well lived, filled with daring and romance, sprezzatura and hilarity, becomes a lesson in to how endure the worst.

There is a poignant scene at the end of the book when Charlie realizes that the end of his own life is near—and it comes through the eyes of a stranger, a beautiful young woman on a Manhattan street. She recognizes him not as the lusty, wry, and famous bon vivant he once was but as the frail old man he has become. Charlie's reaction to this moment is one you must read for yourself. I return to this book time and time again because it's a primer on how to live with abandon and risk while managing loss, which ultimately is what makes us human.

ADRIANA TRIGIANI

Adriana Trigiani is the author of nine best-selling novels, including Lucia, Lucia *and* Very Valentine. *She has also written for the theater, television, and film, including the screen adaptation of her novel* Big Stone Gap.

Close to Jedenew

By Kevin Vennemann

Translated from the German by Ross Benjamin

2005

Kevin Vennemann is a very young writer whose novella, *Close to Jedenew*, was a phenomenal success in its original German. His theme may be that, in the natural action of time and by the atrocities people commit upon one another, "everything changes, nothing remains."

The narrative mode of *Close to Jedenew* is incremental in revealing its place, time, and characters. It is the critic's business to make clear without making straightforward what in fact moves in circles. Vennemann's sentences revolve, expand, recur, and turn in upon themselves. (Vennemann has said in conversation that he has not read Gertrude Stein.) It is the choreography of words on the page that impels the writer, and the modernist possibility, once rid of the dreary convention of the flashback, to render thought in action: thought remembers in the present tense while it experiences what is happening and tries to deny what's coming.

From the second sentence on we hear the locals in nearby Jedenew, "singing, bawling, playing the . . . accordion." They are nineteen in number. (In the German they are *Bauern*, whom the translator has no choice but to simply call "farmers," since American English does not have a word for *peasant* farmers.)

The place is where Germany borders Poland (a breeding ground, Vennemann has observed, although not inside the story, for evil mythologies). Time is never specified, but these farmers, who used to be partisans, are now singing, bawling patriotic songs; the garrison is dismantling; and on the dock in the pond behind the house, the radio brings the latest news of invasion.

The consciousness that is remembering, experiencing, and narrating turns out to belong to one of two young girls—the one who isn't Anna. (Are they twins?) They braid each other's and their doll's hair: "In the evening we sit nine in number," eight if you don't count the unborn Julia in Antonina's belly; seven because nobody knows, or will ever find out, what's happening to Kacia the cook's little Zygmunt. The count is downward.

Marek, the eldest boy, the one who can do everything, is tender and bossy: he "holds Anna on his arms and adjusts Anna's little dress and brushes the sand out of Anna's hair, and gives Anna a pat when she fights with Antonina." Children quarrel: "You're not my father, [Anna] screams at least once a day." Time is the betrayer: Marek is changing into a man, right on the page; he smokes, and works in his father's and Antonina's father's shared veterinary practice. He does duty at the Jedenew garrison. When he marries Antonina, he "is all red in the face with pure happiness."

It is art's superb cruelty to make the reader part of the family—the two families—slated for imminent destruction. We come to know their myths and their landscape: the adjacent houses, the lay of the fields and woods, the clearing the children cut into the corn, where it is summer bliss to lay or to hide. The dock from where you jump, laughing, from where you throw each other into the pond or sit and listen to the radio. There is the never-to-be-finished tree house in the woods, childhood's castle, the eventual hiding place from where you watch Antonina's house burning,

watch the soldiers ransacking the neighborhood—
bringing out the furniture from upstairs, from Kacia's
pantry (where it was too small for everyone to hide),
where you baked the yearly Chanukah cookies and the
Christmas cookies that father never had the conviction
to finally forbid, which is how we learn that one of the
families is Jewish, the kind of Jewish that never gets the
Christmas-cookie business right.

We learn the nineteen names of the singing,
bawling, accordion-playing Jedenew farmers. Soft-
spoken Antonina "can be heard calling something to
Krystowczyk"—that first syllable can't be an accident—"across the yard, a cry of greeting or simply his
name whenever Krystowczyk walks along the dirt
road to our house or rides his old bike to our house. . . .
Because he's bringing by an installment of the money,"
money lent to him by his father for the purchase of
his farm. Krystowczyk comes over in the evening and
helps Antonina with the homework she will good-
naturedly do over correctly after he leaves. Or he'll
come by "because he wants to bring us a new soda
or . . . chocolate or just ordinary candied apples."
Krystowczyk is one of those men who, having failed
to create a family of his own, needs to make himself
indispensable so as to get himself adopted into a
ready-made one.

Vennemann is taking on that inexplicable phenomenon: what has turned our old neighbor and friend
of decades into our sudden murderer? *Close to Jedenew*
is set in the days before the atrocity, before the
victims know what is going to happen to them and
the perpetrators don't know what they are going to
do—before they know of what they are capable.
Can it be only to avoid repaying the debt for which

Father hasn't dunned Krystowczyk—knowing well
enough that he hasn't the money? "Who invents,
who spreads—who believes the outright calumny that
the Jew is working for the Russians?" What is the
mythology in drunken Krystowczyk's head that makes
him beat up Marek on the village square, rub sand
into his face, and worse, much worse? Everything
is changed. On the dock, at the pond behind the
house, Antonina says, "They are coming." Nothing
will remain.

LORE SEGAL

*Lore Segal is a novelist, essayist, and translator. Her children's
books include Tell Me a Mitzi and The Juniper Tree and Other
Tales from Grimm, with illustrations by Maurice Sendak. Among
Segal's fictions are Other People's Houses, Her First American,
and Shakespeare's Kitchen, a finalist for the 2008 Pulitzer Prize.
Segal is a fellow of the Cullman Center for Scholars and Writers.*

Closely Watched Trains

By Bohumil Hrabal
Translated from the Czech by Edith Pargeter
1965

Bohumil Hrabal (1914-1997) was a spectacular old
soak, but, unlike many great writing drinkers, he
managed to complete a substantial body of fiction that
includes at least two masterpieces, the epic comedy *I
Served the King of England* (1971) and this ninety-page
novella, which I believe is one of the greatest books
about World War II. It has everything: love, sex,
disaster; disobedience, exuberance, class. Surrealistically
funny, it is as tense as a sprung trap. I can never
understand why everybody hasn't taken a couple of
undisturbed hours out of their lives to read it. It is
superbly translated into witty and resonant English

by the novelist Edith Pargeter, probably now better known as Ellis Peters, author of the Brother Cadfael crime novels.

The storytelling is so compulsive and so apparently simple that it is easy to miss its subtlety. The narrative moves seamlessly between horizontal and vertical planes: horizontally, in a straight sequence of events over a few hours during the bitter winter of 1945, and vertically, through a subtext that intimates both earlier events in the lives of the characters and the lingering death throes of war in the Europe that surrounds them. This is territory immanent with both banality and violence. No living creature is safe.

From the very first page, Hrabal never loses sight of the big picture beyond the microscopically well-observed local scene. A German fighter is shot down outside a village, and the villagers run through the fields to strip it of sheet metal to cover their rabbit huts, something they will talk about for the rest of their lives. They will remember less well the real historical significance of the crash—that the Luftwaffe has, finally, lost control of the skies. The plane's clock is still ticking, but time is running out: the war will be over by May.

The setting is as near the heart of the ruined continent as you could get: a provincial railway junction in northern Czechoslovakia, not far from the German border. Lines go in every direction. Trains pass through carrying cattle, local passengers, and Nazi ammunition; healthy German soldiers to the Eastern front, dying German soldiers in the opposite direction. No train carries Jews, but such is the tension Hrabal sustains that with every train passing through you think it might. Toward the end, stunned citizens of

Dresden arrive from the firestorm wearing little but their striped pajamas.

The twenty-two-year-old Milos, a trainee dispatcher who tells the story and makes sure that the right trains go on the right lines, will remember the destruction of Dresden because this is the night he finally loses his virginity. Failure to do so earlier led to a botched suicide and five weeks off work. The torments of adolescence take precedence over total war. So does the stationmaster's passion for his pigeons, which land softly on his outstretched arms like feathered stars of the music hall. So does the sexual appetite of the head dispatcher, Hubicka, the fervor of whose earlier coupling with the telegraph operator Virginia had ripped the station-master's couch, following some inventive foreplay in which he printed all the station's destination stamps on her buttocks.

Since the joyful Virginia refuses to press charges and all Czech destinations are now translated into German, it turns out that Hubicka's greatest offense is to have insulted the German language. This could involve the Gestapo. The greatest irony of all, however, is that the fabled lover is working for the Czech resistance and is in charge of the plot to blow up a Nazi ammunition train. He engages the help of the newly enfranchised Milos.

I'm not going to give away any more of the plot. Read the book, a herald of the Prague Spring later filmed by Jiri Menzel, and savor Hrabal's irresistible mixture of earthiness and refinement. He was the master who stayed in Prague after 1968, to whom all exiled Czech writers have deferred. Proscribed, forgiven, published in samizdat and abroad, he found a way to drink, write, remain subversive, and survive.

MICHAEL RATCLIFFE

Michael Ratcliffe is a freelance cultural writer in London, formerly literary editor and chief book reviewer of The Times and theatre critic of The Observer. He contributes to the travel section of The New York Times, where he has written on several destinations in Central Europe.

Collecting the Animals

By Peter Everwine

1972

This collection of poems by the poet Peter Everwine was the Lamont Poetry Selection for 1972. The poems are delicate lyrical meditations that—for me, at least—stick in the back of the brain and refuse to leave. I once told a class that the day I could fully understand and explain the poem "Learning to Speak" would be the day I felt I'd finally grasped the essence of lyric poetry. That poem, a sort of reverse alba (or dawn song) takes you to the edge of light and dark, field and wood, word and name. It expands the notion of "bird" into a plethora of species—blackbird, oriole, flicker, gold finch—causing the reader to think about these names in visual terms as they exist at once as words and things. This poem in particular offers a verbal bouquet that expresses, without dispelling the best of lyric poetry, the complex evolution of thoughts and feeling.

SARAH SPENCE

Sarah Spence is Distinguished Research Professor of Classics at the University of Georgia. She has published widely on the literature of antiquity and the Middle Ages. Her most recent book is Figuratively Speaking: Rhetoric and Culture from Quintilian to the Twin Towers.

Colomba

By Prosper Mérimée
Translated from the French by Nicholas Joutcham
1840

"You are rather too civilized a savage," complains
Miss Nevil, the Anglo-Irish beauty who encounters
Orso della Rebbia on his homeward journey to
Corsica. The year is 1810. Orso, a lieutenant in the
French army, belongs to an ancient family that has
embraced the Napoleonic cause. Cashiered after his
hero's fall, he is ostensibly returning to marry off
his only sister, Colomba; in fact, he is back to solve
the mystery of their father's murder.

Orso's native village of Pietranera tensely awaits the
young officer's return. It has been the seat of an age-old
blood feud between two rival dynasties, the della
Rebbia and the Barricini. All Pietranera believes that
the Barricini clan is responsible for Orso's father's
assassination; all Pietranera—and above all, Orso's
sister—expects the young man to do his duty and blow
away the Barricini boys. But Orso, educated in
Enlightenment France and sworn to restraint by the
super-refined Miss Nevil, is determined first to discover
"the facts."

What ensues is an adventure tale recounted with dry
wit and a satisfying narrative intricacy. Mérimée is not
afraid to broach all the complexities of colonialism—
the educated "savage" who finds himself at home
neither in his native land nor at the center of the
empire; the British heiress who falls in love with this
intensely civilized man for his supposed primitivism.

The star of the novella, however, is Colomba.
Ferociously beautiful, strong as a lumberjack, and

utterly worldly-wise, it is she who manipulates her brother into avenging their father's murder and makes sure he gets out of it alive, she who manipulates Miss Nevil into so compromising a propinquity with Orso that there is no choice but marriage, she who, having already realized that Miss Nevil's fortune will do very nicely to restore the della Rebbias' ruined towers and picked which of their neighbor's lands Orso should acquire with his wife's dowry, will devote herself to ensuring that her future nephews do not grow up effete Anglos but can speak broad Corsican, use a dagger, and compose a funeral dirge as needed.

In his lifetime, Prosper Mérimée (who also wrote *Carmen*, on which Bizet's opera was based) was a much admired man of letters. Tutor to the future Empress Eugénie, friend of Delacroix and Stendhal, he was the first translator into French of Pushkin and Turgenev. In today's France, Mérimée's novellas have the sorry distinction of being the first works of real literature that adolescents are assigned at school, meaning that it may be up to us non-Francophones to rediscover with any genuine relish this disarmingly wry and subtle storyteller.

FERNANDA EBERSTADT

Fernanda Eberstadt is the author of five novels, including RAT and of Little Money Street, a nonfiction book about Gypsy musicians in the South of France.

The Colony of Unrequited Dreams

By Wayne Johnston

1999

I don't think of myself as having much interest in historical novels, but two of my favorite pieces of fiction could be included in that category: *The Colony of Unrequited Dreams*, by Wayne Johnston, and *The Siege of Krishnapur*, by J. G. Farrell. (The winner of the Booker Prize in 1973, *The Siege of Krishnapur* takes place almost entirely within a British fort under siege during the Sepoy Rebellion against the British Raj in 1857. New York Review Books reissued it in a handsome paperback edition in 2004.) The improbable hero of *The Colony of Unrequited Dreams* is an actual historical figure, though one most Americans are unaware of—Joey Smallwood, who led Newfoundland into the Canadian federation. The major events Johnston describes in the novel actually happened: as a labor organizer in 1925, Smallwood actually did walk across the entire colony to unionize railroad section men, for instance, and Newfoundlanders did actually vote to join Canada in 1949. But the most vivid character in the book, the St. John's newspaper columnist Sheilagh Fielding, is fictional. The novel has the sweep of a grand Hollywood movie, complete with seal hunt, and it manages to make a fully rounded character out of a place—the strange and fascinating colony of unrequited dreams. I once described it as "the great American novel, except it happens to be about Newfoundland."

CALVIN TRILLIN

Calvin Trillin, a longtime staff writer for The New Yorker, is also The Nation's "deadline poet." His books include the novel Tepper Isn't Going Out, the memoir About Alice, and Deciding the Next Decider: The 2008 Presidential Race in Rhyme.

Coming through Slaughter

By Michael Ondaatje

1976

Once, as a gift, I gave this book to a friend of mine, also a writer. Upon next seeing him, I eagerly asked how he liked it.

"Well . . ." He poked at the coleslaw he was eating with his barbeque. "It's one of those books."

"Oh, yes, yes, yes, it is," I agreed, thinking I knew what he meant. It is *one of those books*. Books that give you a new lease on writing, on thinking about writing, on reading, and on enjoying the sheer possibilities only fiction can provide. In a slim volume, Ondaatje manages to capture the life and sudden madness of legendary jazz cornet player Buddy Bolden. Accessing narrative from every possible angle—interviews, lists, playbills, conversations, song lyrics, headlines, medical records—the book is an exercise in scattershot storytelling, ultimately revealing more about Bolden and his demise than any standard first-, second-, or third-person narrative could. There are pages with only one line on them and pages with images and pages filled with long sentences and unindented paragraphs. What I am left with at the end of each page is Ondaatje's careful intention to slip out of his skin—with few precise words, relations, or dramatic episodes—and into that of the old Louisiana world where Bolden lived and was ultimately driven to a madness as devastating as it is beautiful. High emotion is difficult to write, and in this miasma of place and violence, temperature and sound, we, the readers, are ensconced in the textures of the life of America's first "great" (according to Louis Armstrong) cornet player and pulled through Bolden's heavenly and powerful struggle of grappling with the new jazz sound.

Just to make sure my writer friend and I were on the same page, I asked him what *kind* of book he thought it is, expecting him to tell me the things I already knew—things about its innovative structure and impeccable word choice, its use of multiple voices and perspectives, etc., etc. He put down his fork and looked at me with a distant exasperation.

"The craziest kind," he said. "You know; the kind of book where you read the first page and then have to stop immediately because you're forced to go and write."

I smiled, knowing well that lovely urge.

"I'm still on page two," he smiled back.

Laleh Khadivi

Laleh Khadivi is the recipient of a Whiting Award, the Carl Djerassi Fiction Fellowship, and an Emory Fiction Fellowship. Her debut novel, The Age of Orphans, is the first in a trilogy about the Kurds of Southwestern Iran.

The Complete Poems

By Edwin Denby
1986

One of the first champions of Balanchine, Edwin Denby was a prominent dance critic for much of the twentieth century. Denby's poetry, however, has not often been anthologized, and he is not usually included when mention is made of the New York School of poets. Yet he was an archetypal poets' poet and a favorite of painters, dancers, and composers. His contribution was a revivification of the sonnet form, considered, along with much else, to be dead at mid-century. His sliding, eliding approach to the

form—maintaining rhyme and meter but not rigidly—
represents an important advance, as was recognized by
the poets Frank O'Hara and Ted Berrigan.

Denby's early sonnets take New York City as their
topic and setting: not New York as a glamorized
exemplar of The Modern—that moment had passed—
but rather as a friendly, if glamorous, site for ordinary
encounters. "The Subway" is one of Denby's best early
sonnets, comparing a ride to a fantastic drug experience, with sexual enticement included. As the trip
progresses, words begin to take on multiple signifi-
cances: "O how the immense investment soothes
distress, / Credit laps you like a huge religious myth."
The investment is both the money paid for the fare and
an emotional investment; credit is money owed one
and a moral value.

Denby's great love was for the crowds in New York
City's streets. When he hits it just right, as in the longer
poem "Elegy—The Streets," no one creates better odes
to the city. It is a New York whose details have changed
but whose essential elements we can still recognize:

> They pass in droves, detouring packing cases
> They press up close at crossings, dart at cars,
> Some stop, some change direction, and their faces
> Display unconsciousness, like movie stars.
> The rage that kicked me howling in my room,
> The anguish in the news-sheet, is here a dream.

Denby trained this city-eye, honed in New York, on
Greece and Rome in *Mediterranean Cities*, a book
made in collaboration with his longtime friend,
photographer Rudy Burckhardt. Each poem takes a
place for its title and subject. Here is "Villa d'Este."
Surrounded by Italians, "single" as the park itself, the
American poet finds sexual metaphors in abundance in

the shapes and actions of fountains and trees, which
contrast with the city's governmental remorse. Italians
are "childish," which would be pejorative were the
modifier "as love" not added:

> Beneath me this dark garden plunges, buoyant
> Drops through the trees to basins furtive below
> Under me wobbles the tip of a mast-thick fountain
> I laugh and run down; the fat trunks heavily grow;
> Then cypress, ilex rise reflected immense
> Melancholy, and the great fount thrusts forceful
> Tiny, their seclusion perches over the plains
> For plains billow far below toward Rome
>   remorseful;
> But riling streams draw me back in, up above
> To the spurt, dribble, gush, sheath of secret water
> Plash, and droves of Italians childish as love
> Laughing, taking pictures of laughter, of water
> Discovering new fountlets; so dense, so dark
> Single on a desert mountain drips the locked park

Similar to characters from Forster's novels, the
narrator here finds release in being anonymous in Italy;
unlike them, this person seems actually freed by the
experience. These Mediterranean sonnets are striking
for the way they paint pictures without being descriptions; a surprising modernism lurks within the form.
Details are specific, but actions are not narrated; rather
the poem allows the reader to experience through
fragments what has happened.

Denby is able to turn on a dime from the epic
to the intimate. Sometimes, this intimacy seems like
a personal revelation:

> Harbor, lost is the Greece when I was ten that
> Seduced me, god-like it shone; in a dark town,
>   trembling
> Like a runaway boy on his first homeless night

Ahead I rush in the fearful sweep of longing
A dead longing that all day blurred here the lone
Clear shapes which light was defining for a
   grown man

Other times, the intimacy is more generalized, as in the concluding poem of the series, in which the poet sees himself in the long frame of generations passing. Finally, he stopped writing poetry; then, at eighty, his health failing, he took his own life. It would be interesting to examine where Denby fits in the history of writers like Hart Crane and Gertrude Stein, whom he admired, and John Ashbery and James Schuyler, who admired him. In the meantime, we have the distinctive pleasures of his verse.

VINCENT KATZ

Vincent Katz is a poet, translator, and critic. He is the author of ten books of poetry, including Alcuni Telefonini, a collaboration with Francesco Clemente, written in Europe while Katz was the 2001-2002 John Guare Rome Prize Fellow in Literature at the American Academy in Rome. Katz won ALTA's 2005 National Translation Award for The Complete Elegies of Sextus Propertius.

Cronopios & Famas

By Julio Cortazar
Translated from the Spanish by Paul Blackburn, 1999
1978

Most books lead you to other books. Faulkner and Nabokov and Melville entice you into the library; pick up an Elmore Leonard novel and you'll be onto another one almost before you've finished; same with P. G. Wodehouse or Patrick O'Brian. Not Cortazar. At least not *Cronopios & Famas.*

This is a book that forces you off the page, outside the book. You start by looking over your shoulder, and then you begin to notice a peculiar smell in the air, like peaches left out in the sun or very wet dogs on a screened-in porch. You put the book down. You'll find it later. Possibly where you left it. Though not necessarily.

Less revered than Borges, less read than García Márquez, Cortazar is the odd man out of Latin-American letters: he is the patron saint of impossible jazz, unreadable traffic signs, the vengeance of children, and the whisper of women's legs as they walk to and fro in the cool of the evening.

If Cortazar is known at all in the States, it's for the short story "Blow-Up" (upon which the Antonioni movie was based) and for *Hopscotch*, a novel that forces the reader to give up any sense of the linear, but to skip madly around the book, back to front and back again, like a crazed shopper racing floor to floor in a soon-to-be-abandoned department store, stocking up on mints, garden implements, and sheets of Egyptian cotton. The playfulness, the gamesmanship, is not a distraction from the text—it *is* the text. And here, in *Cronopios & Famas*, which does away with plot and narrative altogether, he indulges in the mad desire to make sense of the world by offering short and painfully elegant instructions on how to wind a watch, how to climb a staircase, how to kill ants in Rome, how to comb your hair when no one is watching.

Think of it as a cookbook that conveniently leaves out the recipes. You pick it up now and then to remind yourself of what hunger is.

BRIAN CULLMAN

Brian Cullman is a writer and musician living in New York City. His first album, All Fires the Fire, was released on Sunnyside Records in 2008.

D

A Dance to the Music of Time

By Anthony Powell

1951–1975

Anthony Powell's masterpiece is now sold in four volumes, but *A Dance to the Music of Time* originally appeared as twelve separate novels, published to rising acclaim between 1951 and 1975. That's the way I first encountered them, and I can't help feeling that a dozen wry, somewhat slender books is a better correlative to Powell's special narrative approach than four heavy tomes. Likewise, if the Poussin reproduced on the omnibus set does literally illustrate the title, the original Mark Boxer cover drawings do a better job of capturing the books' view of culture as a dark, often farcical social contract.

Powell's subject is the London art scene between the end of World War I and the beginning of flower power, and his work is populated with dozens of writers, editors, composers, painters, gallerists, spiritualists, theater types, patrons, spouses, lovers, and hangers-on, as well as — in the three volumes covering World War II — the occasional philistine colonel or quartermaster. Amazingly, you never get lost, a fact that's related both to the precision and briskness of Powell's narrative voice and to his skill in handling the very large scene. For the large scene is the primary building block here, and gatherings of all kinds abound, including book launches, garden parties, dances, banquets, funerals, gallery openings, receptions, and so on. In fact, each of the twelve volumes is composed primarily of two or three such big scenes, from which other, more intimate ones open in the form of recollections, flashbacks, conversations, and ruminations. It's a nifty strategy, one I've not seen employed to quite this effect elsewhere, and it suits Powell's comic instincts by emphasizing story, swift pacing, and sharp, revealing social dialogue.

If the heart of *Dance* is its portrait of a generation of variously gifted creative types, the book is dominated by a singular outsider figure: Kenneth Widmerpool, personification of the mediocre and striver extraordinaire, whose inevitable rise to cultural power gives the series its through-line. Widmerpool, of course, is not merely a villain but a gloriously comic narrative force, a boor battering at the ivory tower and a man whose self-preservation instincts remain eerily infallible—until they suddenly are not. *A Dance to the Music of Time* is a delight for many reasons, but if nothing else, the intersection of this complicated toady with the looser attitudes of the swinging sixties makes the final volume, *Hearing Secret Harmonies*, a well-earned payoff.

DAVE KING

Dave King is the author of The Ha-Ha, named one of the best books of 2005 by The Washington Post, The Christian Science Monitor, the Pittsburgh Tribune-Review, and other publications. He is the winner of the 2006 John Guare Writer's Fund Rome Prize Fellowship from the American Academy of Arts and Letters.

Dancing Lessons for the Advanced in Age

By Bohumil Hrabal

1964

Josef Skvorecky, writing pseudonymously as Daniel S. Miritz in an introduction to *Closely Watched Trains*— Bohumil Hrabal's best-known work because of Jiri Menzel's 1966 Oscar-winning film of the novel—maintained that Hrabal's writing inimitably combined surrealist outrage and the well-oiled talk of Prague's bars and taverns.

No work of Hrabal's better exemplifies this than his novel *Dancing Lessons for the Advanced in Age*, a short book in one run-on sentence that is one of the comic masterpieces of the last century. The sentence is the monologue of a pleasantly drunk retired soldier and shoemaker, among many other occupations, ogling six young girls sunbathing in a garden; it is his flirtation with them, his oblique and inconsequential love song and, above all, his excuse for keeping himself in their company. The ladies' response is left to our imagination. All we get is his almost infinite sentence, casually punctuated by commas and veering from the erotic to the workaday to the military-calamitous. It is at once completely believable and utterly out of this world: a wild ride, 117 small, nearly square pages, and over all too soon.

The book's atmosphere can be conjured only by itself, so here are two quotes, chosen nearly at random, to give you the general idea:

> . . . the crown prince had syphilis and that Vetsera woman shot him, but then she got shot by the coachman, though any young lady will tell you you might as well be buried alive if the man in your life has a faulty fandangle, when I was serving in the most elegant army in the world I told our medical officer, Doctor, I said, I've got a weak heart, but all he said was, So have I, boy, and if we had a hundred thousand like you we could conquer the world, and he put me in the highest category, so I was a hero, I walked out of there on cloud nine, but he called me back and said, You've got time on your hands, take my wife to the station, she was a beauty, his wife,

the spitting image of Marenka Zieglerová and a
giant like Maria Theresa and dressed like a queen
too, and the first words out of her mouth were,
Are you a bachelor? and when it was over she
tried to give me a tip, six kreuzers, but I wouldn't
take it, that's called chivalry, Havlicek and Christ
wouldn't have taken one either . . .

. . . once when I was helping a baker deliver his
wares in Moravian Slovakia I saw a drunken
wedding party trying to pour slivovitz down the
saints' throats, and when the priest got wind of
it he tore in like a fighter plane and called them a
band of Tartars, Is that how you behave in God's
temple, out, the lot of you, and don't come back
until you're sober, or at least less drunk! from
there I went to Hradisko, where I worked in a
brewery, and then I made a triumphant return
in a striped suit, white knobbed cane, and the
last word in Parisian boaters, some people are
dragged home by the police looking like something the cat's dragged in, while I came home with
a hundred gulden in my pocket, enough to pay off
all my debts and buy a cow from Ponivke . . .

Hrabal lived from 1914 to 1997. Many of his works
were unpublishable during the Communist regime, and
others were bowdlerized by it. He was particularly
beloved by a younger generation of Czech writers
including Milan Kundera and Josef Skvorecky. All his
books are worth reading, but *Dancing Lessons for the
Advanced in Age* is a howler and may be the best place
to start. He died a Hrabalian death, passing out while
feeding pigeons on a hospital windowsill and then
falling out of the window.

Rafi Zabor

Bio on p. 63

Darkmans

By Nicola Barker

2007

Perhaps it is the length (838 pages) or the backwater English locale. Or maybe it is the disorienting opening scene. Whatever the cause, this superb novel has been largely overlooked by the American reading public (despite being shortlisted for the Man Booker Prize), and it deserves a much wider audience.

Darkmans is set in contemporary Ashford, England, on the south coast of Kent, near the U.K. entrance to the Chunnel. But at the same time, this sublime book takes place in the medieval past of Ashford. And it is Barker's ability to conjure interrelated historical worlds, identical in place but multitudinous in time, that gives the novel both its off-kilter laugh-out-loud humor and its breathtaking dramatic immediacy.

The novel is populated by a Dickensian array of memorable characters—from Gaffar Celek, the Kurdish boxer who suffers from a pathological fear of lettuce, to Fleet, a precocious five-year-old boy, who is building a scale model of Albi Cathedral out of matchsticks and knows more about medieval England than is healthy for a boy of his tender years. Towering above them all is Daniel Beede, hospital laundry supervisor and "vengeful tsunami of history," whose obsession with an ancient mill and with his late wife's chiropodist drives this phenomenal book to its many unexpected ends, including (sad to say) the strangulation of Chairman Miaow, Beede's unfortunate blue Siamese cat. But by whom? Perhaps John Scogin, the murderous jester to the court of King Edward IV, who occupies the dark corners of this unpredictable novel like spectral Bob lurking behind the shady doings of David Lynch's "Twin Peaks."

And then there is Kelly Broad, the teenage ex-girl-friend of Beede's son Kane and one of Barker's most original creations, who spends most of the novel laid up in a local hospital. There she finds both history (discovering herself, she thinks, to be descended from a king's physician) and God, though her brand of religion is strictly nondenominational. "I mean think about it, Rev: God pushed me off a wall to get me here, yeah? You said so yourself. Then he gave me my allergy to prove to Kane how I was innocent. Then he sent Paul over at eight, on the dot, to snap my bra strap. Those was my signs. An' he gave you a special vision about the whole thing—which was yours, see? So I don't rightly care what kind of a Church it is, yeah? . . . That's just blah, that's just details . . ."

Idiosyncratic to its core, *Darkmans* is preoccupied with the power of language and the persistent presence of the past within the stuff of everyday conversation. The novel is also curiously faux bilingual. Beede understands some Kurdish, and when he is speaking with Gaffar in that language, their dialogue, which remains English, appears in bold type, and this device is remarkably successful in conveying the notion that we are reading English subtitles, while actually hearing the words spoken in Kurdish. Bilingual and yet not. Like so much else in this delightfully complex novel, it is one thing, and it isn't.

More than anything else, this is a tale about the countless ways in which Beede, Gaffar, and the rest of Barker's crew are bedeviled by history on every level—cultural, familial, and linguistic. Novelists invariably devote a fair amount of their craft to the relationship between past and present; it's part of the job description. However, I recall no instance in which the temporal structure of a work of fiction makes such a strong case (as it does here) for the existence of parallel universes.

As I mentioned at the outset, *Darkmans* clocks in at 838 pages, which in itself is hardly noteworthy. However, while reading this mischievous book, I happened to be rereading the Penguin edition of George Eliot's *Middlemarch*, which is also (I was surprised to discover) 838 pages in length. Coincidence? Perhaps. Or maybe just another prank from our old friend John Scogin. I do feel compelled to offer one word of warning. Be careful with this one. It has dark powers, and it might just get behind your eyes and refuse to give up its perch.

George Sheanshang

George Sheanshang is an entertainment attorney in private practice in New York City.

The Daughter of Time

By Josephine Tey

1951

I can trace my love of reading in a straight line back to the Stratemeyer Syndicate, starting with the maniacally cheerful antics of Bert, Nan, Freddie, and Flossie—*The Bobbsey Twins*. I was even more excited by Nancy Drew, fantasizing about a life of consequential intrigue with a bit of Ned Nickerson on the side. And after reading *Harriet the Spy*, I actually went so far as to buy a little journal and start furtively stalking my neighbors, hoping to ferret out some quirk in their habits that would point to a mysterious double life. This was the high Cold War era, and since there were nuclear missile silos in Kansas, why couldn't there be Soviet spies in my Kansas City suburb?

But it was a dozen years later, in 1978, that my future father-in-law introduced me to *The Daughter of Time*. Those kiddie mysteries that I'd devoured as a girl had, it turned out, whetted my appetite for the real thing, the graceful and lyrical Josephine Tey (a nom de plume of the Scottish writer Elizabeth Mackintosh). The novel begins by introducing Tey's hero, Scotland Yard Superintendent Alan Grant, bored senseless and bed-bound in the hospital as he recovers from a leg broken in the line of duty. He asks his actress friend Marta to relieve his tedium. Believing that a police-man's stock-in-trade is assessing people's faces, Marta brings him photographs of portraits from the National Gallery. Grant becomes obsessed with one image, a picture, he guesses, of a judge. Told that the painting is of the infamous Richard III, he's troubled that his professional eye failed him—that he'd mistaken a beast for a good man.

Tey seamlessly weaves together fifteenth- and twentieth-century England, provocatively probes the nature of truth (the epigraph at the beginning of the book is "Truth is the daughter of time"), and posits a compelling argument vindicating Richard III, conven-tional history and Shakespeare notwithstanding. Each book in Tey's entirely too small canon, just six novels in all, is as beautifully crafted as *The Daughter of Time* and deserves to be savored.

ANNE KREAMER

Anne Kreamer, author of Going Gray, is a former executive vice president and worldwide creative director of Nickelodeon/Nick at Nite, and was part of the founding team of Spy magazine.

Day

By A. L. Kennedy

2007

How can there be any more brilliant novels about World War II, especially one by a writer who was born twenty years after it ended? A salutary answer is provided in the questing, tortured, blackly humorous, stream-of-memory *Day*, by the Scottish novelist A. L. Kennedy. The novel employs time as a controlling force, a powerful character enacting its will in the narrative. Deftly, sinuously, Kennedy portrays the adventurous, misadventurous wartime and postwar experiences of one Alfred Day—the name itself, of course, a unit of time—a working-class British tail gunner on a Lancashire bomber.

Like Alan Lightman in *Einstein's Dreams* ("suppose time is a circle, bending back on itself"), or even Stephen Hawking ("if one can go forward in imaginary time, one ought to be able to turn around and go backward"), Kennedy plays creatively with time. Now we're four years after the war, when Alfie ditches his job in London to become an extra in a movie being shot in Germany at a fake POW camp like the real one he himself endured during the war. Now we're back in the war, ready to soar through the night sky on a bombing mission. Listen for a moment to Kennedy's prose as Alfie waits for his Lancashire bomber, which could be his weapon or his coffin, to arrive at the RAF airfield: "Circling in from the north-west came a single Lanc, big-chinned, blunt as a whale and open-armed and singing. When you heard them like that, far off, you could think they were trying to speak, words hidden underneath the roar, and if you could only

work them out, you would understand everything, you
would be saved."

Then we're caught in a German air raid over
London when Alfie, on leave, meets a woman who is
named—a tribute to the twentieth century's master of
associative prose—Joyce. Later in the war, when his
other beloved, his Lanc, has been shot down, Alfie
yearns shyly for Joyce from the real POW camp after
his capture by the Germans: "*Letters to Joyce*. Real
letters, and a fight to make them carry what they
should, not to scare her, but to keep her, not to love her
too plainly, but to touch her enough." Alfie is far less
educated than Joyce, and he aches not only for her but
for greater literacy as he plans his letter: "Apologise for
the terrible handwriting and check the spelling of
everything and the commas, apostrophes, all the
punctuation, practically each fucking chicken scratch
that made it to the paper. . . . She wouldn't say so, but
she'd know he wasn't right for her."

Joyce knows, of course, nothing of the sort. Yet
there is a complication—she's not only married,
unhappily, but married to another soldier so damaged
by the war that she can't leave him. But now, before we
dwell too long on what will come of that predicament,
we're back in Alfie's wretched Dickensian childhood
with his abused mother and brutal father. Alfie himself,
physically small and fearful, is bullied by his father until,
in a solution that would please Sophocles, he's not.

Now we're flying another bombing mission
described so meticulously it's hard to believe the author
hasn't squirreled herself into the tail gunner's turret
along with Alfie. The other crew members—joking,
swearing, killing, dying—become the happy family
Alfie never had. And now once more we're in the fake

POW camp four years after the war where Alfie, by returning to the scene not of his crime but his trauma, may possibly purge his demons. As Kennedy circles her time-bursts like the Lanc Alfie watched circling the English airfield, as she twirls time sequences that fade into and out of one another in the literary equivalent of dissolves, we wait to see what this original, poetic prose magician will pull out of her hat.

War is generally regarded as a male sport belonging to male writers, yet Kennedy portrays aerial combat with the same certainty and specificity that Pat Barker achieved with trench warfare in *Regeneration*. In *Day*, as in any novel written with excursions into a sensibility that is by turns agonized, highly disturbed, depressed, and passionate, it is prudent to be patient and allow Kennedy to drop things illuminatingly, deliciously into place. Meanwhile, let the prose carry you.

Never famous for his modesty, Thomas Mann described *Death in Venice* as a little work of inexhaustible allusiveness. Kennedy's work is not little, but its allusiveness *is* inexhaustible. Her pages are stalked by guilt, vengeance, death, and, finally, love, tunneling Alfie through to the place where he'd lost himself. For Alfie, it's about time.

Peter Davis

Peter Davis's documentary film on the Vietnam War, Hearts and Minds, received an Academy Award; his film on Defense Department propaganda, The Selling of the Pentagon, received an Emmy and a Peabody Award; and his Middletown film series received ten Emmy nominations and two Emmys. He is the author of three books of nonfiction, Hometown, Where Is Nicaragua?, and If You Came This Way. Davis is a former contributing editor for Esquire, and he covered the war in Iraq for The Nation.

Decameron

The Decameron
By Giovanni Boccaccio
1353

The Heptameron
By Marguerite de Navarre
1558

The Women's Decameron
By Julia Voznesenskaya
1986

Ten Days in the Hills
By Jane Smiley
2007

Boccaccio wrote the first *Decameron* a few years after the Black Death decimated Europe in 1348. Its characters, seven women and three men, leave Florence to look for relief from anguish and loss in a countryside miraculously untouched by tragedy. During their days of rest and relaxation, they amuse one another by telling stories — one each every day over the course of ten days. The first story sets the tone, describing how priestly gullibility and peasant greed transformed a character as wicked as Judas Iscariot into a miracle-working local saint. In a parallel story at the beginning of the second day of narration, three Florentines fake a miraculous cure to gain front-row seats at a crowded funeral. On the fourth day comes the story of a royal father who punishes his daughter's infidelity with the gift of her lover's heart. The murderers, three Sicilian brothers, then steal the heart — her only consolation — which has been buried in a flourishing pot of basil. In the hundredth story, a psychopathic duke takes pains to make life miserable for his saintly wife. *The Decameron*, which some have described as an encyclopedia of plots, is the kind of book that makes us rethink the Middle Ages.

Over the centuries, its qualities have made *The Decameron* a literary Mother Ginger. In Tchaikovsky's *Nutcracker Suite*, Mother Ginger — usually danced by a man — releases from beneath her massive hooped skirts a host of little children who pour onto the stage. In the centuries after Boccaccio's death, his book spawned troupes of Italian imitators. The thousands of stories they wrote in their turn ghosted Shakespeare's *Romeo and Juliet*, Cocteau's *Beauty and the Beast*, and Prokofiev's *Love for Three Oranges*, among a host of others.

Boccaccio's greatest and most enduring influence, however, has been among women. The Renaissance Queen of southwestern France, Marguerite de Navarre, wrote an appreciative imitation of *The Decameron* in the sixteenth century. Her *Heptameron* featured seven days of storytelling by Protestant noblemen and women stranded by floodwaters in a Pyrenees monastery. While the secular narrators tell their tales, the monks hide behind a hedge and eavesdrop. Marguerite's setting and many of her stories contrast the engaged piety of her worldly-wise narrators with the self-righteousness of cloistered men. Her second story is one of the first accounts of rape to present the crime as an act of gratuitous male violence against an innocent woman, who nonetheless suffers for what is done to her.

In the turbulent years just before the collapse of the Soviet Union, a Russian novelist named Julia Voznesenskaya wrote her *Women's Decameron*. Confined to the maternity ward of a Leningrad hospital after an outbreak of puerperal fever, ten quarantined women while away the days of their confinement by telling stories. The narrators run the gamut from Zina, the Dostoyevskian prostitute, to Albina, the mercenary stewardess, to Valentina, the censorious wife of a party hard-liner. Their stories span an equally broad spectrum from rape, betrayal, and abandonment to lost love and politically incorrect sex. The stories chronicle the bad old days of the Soviet era, with its exiled dissidents and pampered party bosses, its public pieties and rampant exploitation of the weak and disadvantaged.

Boccaccio wrote in reaction to Dante's *Divine Comedy*. Voznesenskaya never mentions Aleksandr Solzhenitsyn, the leading dissident Soviet writer and author of books such as *Cancer Ward* and *The Gulag Archipelago*, but

Solzhenitsyn's take on Soviet corruption is always in the air. In targeting Solzhenitsyn, Voznesenskaya did not defend the Soviet system but responded to the older writer's overwhelming tragic sensibility. The maternity ward is a place of hope and renewal, the direct opposite of the cancer ward, where mere survival is an unexpected triumph.

Voznesenskaya may have been the last dissident, rebelling against a system that has had its day. The fall of the Soviet Union, however, has not made her book irrelevant. Though one repressive, self-serving form of government has fallen, justice and democracy have yet to prevail. A group of fictional women speaking out with common sense and compassion for those who share their oppression still deserve a hearing.

The most recent *Decameron* homage, by the novelist Jane Smiley, came out in 2007. Called *Ten Days in the Hills*, the novel features a group of Angelenos holed up in a glamorous refuge in the Hollywood Hills. They have fled the multiple disappointments of Tinseltown and the domination of the news cycle by the 2003 invasion of Iraq. Rather than tell stories, they recite monologues in one another's presence. Their self-absorption and their constant references to films both real and imagined echo Boccaccio's concern with clerical, political, and artistic manipulations of appearance.

JAMES H. S. MCGREGOR

James H. S. McGregor is the author of Rome from the Ground Up, Venice from the Ground Up, Washington from the Ground Up, and Paris from the Ground Up. He is Professor and Co-Head of the Department of Comparative Literature at the University of Georgia.

Dersu Uzala, by Vladimir Arsenyev

see p. 124

The Desert of Love: Selected Poems

By János Pilinszky

Translated from the Hungarian by János Csokits and Ted Hughes

1989

In 1977, when asked by a BBC reporter about his favorite new writers in English, János Pilinszky (1921-1981) answered earnestly: "Dostoyevsky." This may sound like an arrogant comment, yet Pilinszky was a most gentle and generous man with a single-mindedness in his spiritual and intellectual interests. His vision was formed by World War II and his concentration camp internment, and by his Roman Catholic existentialism. He was forcibly enrolled in the retreating Hungarian army in the fall of 1944, and transported with his battalion into Germany. I remember him telling how, determined not to get involved yet with an instinct for survival, he began to shoot in the front line lest the man opposite shoot him—much like Céline's description of the experience of war in his famous novel.

At some point in the confusion of the retreat Pilinszky managed to desert, only to end up in a concentration camp and soon transferred to another. With only weeks until Liberation, he survived. But these months of war, the camps, and the inmates left an indelible mark on him. He called it the Scandal of the Century. In attempting to capture his experiences he became one of the major masters of metaphor and economy in modern writing—like Paul Celan, a genius of the intense, naked gesture. As Ted Hughes writes in his introductory essay about his close friend Pilinszky's poetry, "The result is not comforting. But it is healing. Ghastliness and bliss are weirdly married."

Pilinszky wrote a handful of extremely powerful poems until 1948, when for ten years he was forbidden to publish while Stalinism and its "esthetics" ruled in Hungary. He lived an apparently marginal life, and continued to do so after 1970, when he became widely known outside his native country. Yet he was always counted as a major presence in the hidden intellectual life of those dark years under Soviet rule. For a living he wrote short essays for Hungary's Roman Catholic press, a major body of work which, still not completely collected, makes up an elegant and incisive contribution to our ideas on faith and doubt, on modern art, on the absurd, on totalitarian thinking.

Pilinszky found inspiration in the writings of Simone Weil and later in the theater of Robert Wilson in Paris, "But most beautiful of all—the lovers! / Their manes glowing out of the shadows / the last beautiful tent of their modesty," as he writes in "Improptu." A new generation of readers deserves to meet the harsh and tender beauty of the poems in *The Desert of Love.*

GYULA KODOLÁNYI

Hungarian poet and essayist Gyula Kodolányi originally taught American Studies in Budapest, and visited the U.S. on ACLS and Fulbright Fellowships in 1972-73 and 1984-85. He became involved in the unofficial opposition movements in Hungary of the late 1970s, and was appointed Senior Adviser to Prime Minister Antall in the democratic government of 1990-1994. Since 1992, he has been editor of Magyar Szemle (Hungarian Review), a general-issues journal in Budapest. He is a member of the European Academy of the Arts and Sciences, Salzburg.

The Devil to Pay in the Backlands, by João Guimarães Rosa

see p. 124

Diary of a Provincial Lady

By E. M. Delafield

1931

To grasp the appeal of this comic gem, try imagining *Bridget Jones's Diary* as rewritten by Jane Austen, even if the exercise makes your head explode, leaving you with some steep dry-cleaning bills.

Combining Bridget's self-mockery with Austen's bone-dry wit, *Diary of a Provincial Lady* is a book I've recommended to umpteen people, all of whom have thanked me, in most cases convincingly. This lightly fictionalized "journal" of a middle-class wife and mother trapped in a British village in the period between the two world wars seems trifling at first. Little happens. The Provincial Lady endures the hilariously tactless local aristocrat. She placates her children's melodramatic Gallic nanny (whose brief outbursts in French are funny, even when inscrutable). She tries, and fails, to coerce her Dutch bulbs to bloom.

This subtle book's larger theme, however, is the Lady's struggle to resolve her ego's cravings—for literary fame and passably chic style—with familial duty and a nagging overdraft. She strives simultaneously to amuse and nurture, to impress and economize, to distinguish herself and efface herself. If only she had any sincere desire to see the Italian Pictures Exhibition about which her chic London friends so fatuously rave! But she just doesn't.

The Lady's compulsive, wretched honesty is one reason why she touches me so deeply and why she has, I suspect, become such an insider pleasure, recently inspiring a four-thousand-word essay in *The New Yorker*.

As stupendously deadpan as the book's wit can be, it's
the truths behind the social satire that really crackle.

DALE HRABI

Bio on p. 54

The Diary of "Helena Morley"

Translated from the Portugese by Elizabeth Bishop

1957

While living in Brazil with her lover Lota, the poet
Elizabeth Bishop translated the diary of a girl from
Diamantina, a diamond-mining town in the highlands
of Minas Gerais, written near the end of the nineteenth
century. Helena Morley—a pseudonym (the real diarist
was named Alice and had an English father) was a
high-spirited, witty girl whose main failing seems to
have been too much hilarity. In our family we don't
have to fight, she says; we invent a new nickname and
that's revenge enough.

Every entry is a vignette: an anecdote about the
members of her vast, funny family, about neighbors
and visitors, priests, dogs, and monkeys—set in the
streets, in parlors, diamond mines, classrooms, kitch-
ens, and kitchen gardens. Helena had a special eye for
what was strange, surprising, and moving, and seems
to have taken great pleasure in getting it all down.

This joyous book also offers insight into Elizabeth
Bishop's way of seeing and describing. Helena's style is
close enough to be hers: brisk, bright, and naïve, with a
touch of irony. The sense of humor is bold and prim—a
mixture of iconoclasm and girlish moralizing. The
diary, I've often thought, represents a childhood Bishop
that might have longed for. Her father died when she
was five; her mother was confined in a mental hospital

for perpetuity. As a young girl she shuffled alone from relative to relative in the cold north, all her life suffering from bouts of sadness. In the translation, we hear the poet's precise, pointed voice: she has made young Helena into an extension and expression of an imagined self, a kind of soul mate in wisdom and glee.

"He said that he and his wife had had only one child, Jose. When he grew up they were unhappy, the two of them, and they wanted a little boy or girl and so God remembered them, and sent them Maria in a very strange way. They had gone to bed and the house was all shut up, when his wife said she heard a baby crying under the floor. He told her it was just her imagination. Then she said, 'put your ear here and see if it's my imagination.' He put his ear down and heard a little baby crying. He rushed to the kitchen, got the axe, and took up the floor-boards. Then he took a mattock, pulled away the stones and opened the gutter that ran under the house, and there was the poor little thing, who had rolled all the way from Carmo Street as far as Bomfim Street. She was all cut with splinters of glass and filthy dirty. He picked her up and his wife gave her a bath in water with salt and arnica in it. The little girl didn't die because she was a present from heaven, sent to them by God."

SARAH ARVIO

Sarah Arvio's two books of poems, Visits from the Seventh *and* Sono: Cantos, *were published in England in a combined edition, with an audio CD. She has won the Rome Prize of the American Academy of Arts and Letters and a Guggenheim Fellowship, and she was for many years a translator for the United Nations in New York and Switzerland. Arvio teaches poetry at Princeton University.*

The Disenchanted

By Budd Schulberg

1950

Budd Schulberg's old man was a big-shot movie producer in Hollywood. David Smolensky's father sold secondhand shoes from a barrow in London's East End. Despite giving it his best, the youthful David Smolensky—later to change his name to Sinclair, later still to marry my mother and father me—failed to find work in the equally youthful movie industry. Instead he joined his brothers in founding a furniture business—Simbros—which generated sufficient income in its good years for him to take his family to the French Riviera in the summer. It was on the private beach of the Hotel Martinez that he sat reading Budd Schulberg's *The Disenchanted*. There was no need to inquire if the book was any good. The orange livery of a Penguin paperback proclaimed its quality. Holding the same book now—some forty-five years later—I cannot help but wonder if my father recognized himself reflected in Len Deighton's cover illustration of a bald man looking forlornly through a length of 35 mm film, saw in that image an emblem of his half-remembered dreams. Did he think: I could have been a contender? And what did he make of the book itself? That I cannot recall. I do not think he handed it to me with the words, "I think you'll enjoy this." Most likely I picked it up from the beach towel where he had left it and began to read. At the time that's exactly what I was, a reader: not yet a writer, barely even a liver, but already an omnivorous devourer of books.

The narrator of Schulberg's novel is Shep Stearns. Barely a decade older than I, he was already a

Hollywood script writer working on a movie called *Love on Ice*, a little hard-boiled, but far from being disenchanted. No, that role belonged to Manley Halliday, prose wizard of the Jazz Age, whose matinee-idol looks and prodigious talent had been corroded by the demon drink. Youth and Experience were betrothed by Victor Milgrim—"Czar of all the Rushes"—and ordered to turn *Love on Ice* into a money-spinner. It wasn't so much the story of Shep's desperate attempts to keep Halliday at his typewriter and away from the booze that so captivated me but the limitless zing of Schulberg's prose. It made Manley Halliday as real to me as any middle-aged man on the beach, including my father. How I wanted him to overcome his dipsomania, to pen triumphant prose again, to begin his life's second act, and—on the book's last page—to survive the inevitable heart attack. It wasn't fair, either on me or Manley Halliday. I wanted more of him. Then I noticed a note on the book's flyleaf: "Many people have seen in this the story of the final years of one of America's finest novelists, F. Scott Fitzgerald." I had never heard of him, but found in Mill Hill Public Library the lovely Bodley Head edition of his works, and read all six volumes. Now I know that Schulberg's father—capo of Paramount pictures—had hired Fitzgerald to work on a picture called *Winter Carnival* with his son, and that Manley Halliday's *grande bouffe* was based on a research trip young Budd and Fitzgerald had taken to New Hampshire. "I liked Scott a lot," Schulberg (still sharp at ninety-four) recently told a reporter. "He'd quit drinking for a year at that time. Unfortunately my father sent two bottles of champagne for our flight. By the time we arrived at the hotel the first thing Scott did was order a drink and he carried on drinking from then on."

Schulberg made one or two bad decisions himself, most particularly appearing as a friendly witness before the House Un-American Activities Committee. But what the hell, nobody's perfect, and besides I owe him. I am in his debt for introducing me to a peerless writer, and for producing the kind of prose that cried out to be imitated, that flipped me from reader to writer. "Hey, Dad," says my own son (an actor). "What's the book?" I hold up the old Penguin. "My god," says my boy, "that could be you on the cover."

"It could be, but it isn't," I say, "because I'm still in thrall to the enchantment of books like this one."

CLIVE SINCLAIR

Clive Sinclair is the author of thirteen books, a few of which have won prizes. His latest is True Tales of the Wild West, *a mixture of travel, history, and fiction. He has a doctorate from the University of East Anglia and is a Fellow of the Royal Society of Literature.*

Doing Battle

By Paul Fussell

1996

For over four decades, Paul Fussell has been one of our country's shrewdest literary and cultural critics. In work that is scholarly yet readily accessible, Fussell has written brilliantly on eighteenth-century English literature (*The Rhetorical World of Augustan Humanism*), travel writing between the two world wars (*Abroad*), and a funny and trenchant study of the American class system (*Class*).

But it is in his writings on both world wars that Fussell is at his best and most impassioned. *The Great War and Modern Memory*, his widely praised study of the literature of the First World War, illuminates the rhetoric, metaphors, and euphemistic inventions the English culture devised in order to make sense of the unfathomable carnage of the Great War.

In *Wartime*, his bitter and relentlessly ironic view of the stupidity, waste, and boredom of a foot soldier's life, Fussell writes with the firsthand knowledge of, as he describes it, the viewpoint of "the pissed-off infantryman."

But it is in the merciless self-examination in his autobiography, *Doing Battle*, that Fussell tells his own tale of innocence and experience. Here the Second World War is the transforming event that turns "Boy Fussell"—fat, self-satisfied, privileged, and naïve—into the skeptical, observant, authority-hating adult who will narrowly escape death and go on to study literature, teach, write, and claim for himself a degree of humanity and what one might term melancholy happiness.

Of course we have heard this story before—as novel (*Catch-22*, *The Naked and the Dead*) or as memoir (*Goodbye to All That*, *Undertones of War*). But Fussell's memoir, with its mordant humor focused on scenes by turns terrifying and poignant, is also a journey toward wisdom. Self-deprecating yet sure of his own intelligence, Fussell reveals his acceptance of man's tragic condition. It is fitting that one of his favorite terms of contempt is "credulous" and that one of his heroes is Samuel Johnson, the great-souled writer who transformed the fallen nature of man into a virtual life force.

Doing Battle shows us life during wartime and peacetime, but lived always on the front line, where our humanity is under attack and the battle is more often lost than won.

RICHARD LAVENSTEIN

Richard Lavenstein is a principal at Bond Street Architecture & Design.

Peculiarities of 19th-Century America

Domestic Manners of the Americans

By Fanny Trollope

1832

Inventor of the Disposable Culture: King Camp Gillette, 1855–1932

By Tim Dowling

2001

As someone who often likes to organize her reading by theme, I am recommending a pair of books—one classic memoir and one relatively recent biography—that both capture the complex strengths and weaknesses of American society through telling nineteenth-century details.

Fanny Trollope's book is available as a Penguin Classic and was a controversial best-seller on both sides of the Atlantic when published, yet it is seldom read today. Best known as the mother of the novelist Anthony Trollope, Fanny lived with her young children in Cincinnati, Ohio, for two years in the late 1820s and afterward recorded her fairly scathing, often witty observations on Midwestern society. For a while after the book was published, the (useful) verb "to trollopise"—meaning "to insult Americans"—even gained currency. While her British snobberies and personal biases are frequently apparent, many of her comments remain amusingly valid today. (I write as someone whose much-loved family comes from Minnesota.) She is baffled by the utilitarian speed with which Midwestern meals are consumed, without pause for conversation, and the tedious lives of Ohioan housewives, a result of the prudish separation of the sexes. Fanny

Trollope grasps the centrality of religion in American life, in contrast to British, puts her finger casually on various profound American hypocrisies ("You will see them with one hand hoisting the cap of liberty and with the other flogging their slaves"), and yet gives equality of opportunity its due as a radical idea put miraculously into practice. Her book reminds us, lest we forget, just how new a nation the United States is, and how it was built against the odds on the muddy banks of the Mississippi.

Tim Dowling's biography of King Camp Gillette, the man who invented the disposable razor and hence the very notion of mass-market disposability, is a model of modern biographical style, contained concisely in ninety-five pages. Gillette wrote his own autobiography in hundreds of pages of convoluted prose, from which Dowling has extracted a short story encapsulating the quintessential, eternal contradictions of the American national character. Gillette was an inventor-philosopher who naïvely wanted to remake the whole world according to a corporate utopian model. He designed a futuristic metropolis powered by Niagara Falls, and, without any sense of irony or hypocrisy, described individualism as capitalist society's "disease." Formed during one of the United States' infrequent bouts of enthusiasm for radical self-reform (one of which may be coming again soon), Gillette's grandiose political ideas were overshadowed by one little, inspired idea that he had in front of his shaving mirror in 1895. Dowling's dry British wit describes both the bathos and heroism of this archetypal American life, defined in every aspect by untrammeled imagination. This is a book that you can read in an hour and then find yourself remembering, for one odd reason or another, for the rest of your life.

OPHELIA FIELD

Ophelia Field is the author of two British historical biographies, The Favourite: Sarah, Duchess of Marlborough and The Kit-Cat Club: Friends Who Imagined a Nation. She has also worked for many years as a consultant on human rights, particularly those of refugees, most recently for Human Rights Watch and PEN, the international writers' association.

A Dream Like Mine

By M. T. Kelly

1987

A fever dream. A stab to the carotid. A cry from the very center of the Earth.

The hulking Native American who kidnaps a mill executive and a reporter (our narrator) is perhaps one of the most frightening characters ever committed to paper. Is he human or demon? Did the bleeding-heart reporter somehow conjure up his own nightmare? Or is this all simple madness? Revenge in the cold Canadian wilderness is not pretty, but of course it can't be. The politics of pollution, of First Nation rights, and of human dignity aren't children's games. This is strong medicine, bad medicine. And though a brief, wicked poem of a book, it weighs more than many longer volumes. I've thought about *A Dream Like Mine* at least once a month since I first read it; the book haunts.

This novella won the 1987 Governor General's Award and was made into a fine movie, *Clear Cut*, yet it never found much of a readership outside of Canada. One can only ponder how people sympathetic to the environment and human rights don't cotton to ostensibly politically incorrect displays of naked rage. But Kelly's vision is too complex to be reduced to a polemical reading.

A Dream Like Mine is a crystal. Beautiful and hard.

RANDALL KENAN

Randall Kenan is the author of five books, including Let the Dead Bury Their Dead *and* The Fire This Time. *He has been the recipient of a Whiting Writers' Award, a Guggenheim Fellowship, and the Rome Prize. He is a professor of English and Comparative Literature at the University of North Carolina at Chapel Hill.*

E

Earthly Powers

By Anthony Burgess
1980

It should not be a mystery why Anthony Burgess is best
and often solely known for his 1962 tour de force, *A
Clockwork Orange*. The inventive linguistic play, the
attempt to exorcize anxiety about youthful anarchy
and Cold War doom, came together like lightening
between hard covers. Stanley Kubrick's indelible movie
version starring the cherubically demonic young
Malcolm McDowell didn't hurt the short novel's fame.

Yet Burgess—who started publishing novels in his
mid-forties—was a true original. His oeuvre is vast and
intimidating. A composer, a poet, a book reviewer of
prodigious breadth and depth, and a linguist, he is
difficult to get your arms around. Many of his great
works have fallen into neglect: *Nothing Like the Sun:
A Story of Shakespeare's Love Life*, a masterful and
convincing romance as much about language as love;
Napoleon Symphony, not only an engaging novel
about the Emperor but a brilliant realization of
Beethoven's "Eroica" Symphony; *Man of Nazareth*, a
novel that grew out of writing the teleplay for Franco
Zeffirelli's gorgeous 1977 miniseries, is a dazzling
display of erudition, theological rigor, and humanity;
the *Enderby* quartet, four books that redefined the
comic novel and raised the bar very high indeed.

Yet Burgess's Mount Everest must remain *Earthly
Powers*. The plot is simple and simply riveting: an old
English novelist happens to be related, by marriage, to
the recently deceased Pope. The Pope in question is on

the fast track to sainthood. At least three miracles need to have been witnessed for him to be named a saint. Our hero, who has the bad habit of always being in the right place at the right time, just happens to have witnessed all three. The Vatican enlists this decadent, famously homosexual, globe-trotting British novelist in-law of the late Pope to formally document these events. Therefore the novelist embarks on a mission to revisit all the scenes of the "crimes" in order to refresh his memory; hence a journey and a six-hundred-page epic.

Kenneth Toomey is a little bit Somerset Maugham, a little bit Graham Greene, a little bit P. G. Wodehouse, and a little bit James Joyce. He has been everywhere; he has known everyone. These traits make him sometimes annoying, but always fascinating. The book becomes an improbable but convincing history of the mid-twentieth century, from England before and during the Battle of Britain to the danger-filled jungles of Malaya in the late 1950s to the atrocities of Jonestown, Guyana. The famous names who parade across these pages feel like cameos of the gods and goddesses in *The Metamorphosis*, golden threads in an enormous tapestry.

Earthly Powers is powerfully audacious, a rare sort of performance little attempted these days. Burgess clearly wanted to create a financial locomotive, and he came close. Meant in many ways to be a parody of the long, best-selling tomes of Leon Uris and James Michener, this massive book—with its death-defying prose, sweeping intelligence, sophisticated architecture, and sheer genius with character and place—reaches a level occupied by a rarified few. I suspect that *Earthly Powers* was the *Name of the Rose* of its day: a book that many bought but few finished. Not because the book is bad but because it is a twenty-course meal, including several rich desserts.

In the mix—like fine wine and spirits—is another of Burgess's obsessions: philosophy and theology. I have encountered few entertaining works that are so serious about the nature of good and evil, the fundamental questions of God's relationship to man, and the ancient Christian preoccupations over whether a human being can be good. Some long books deserve to be shorter; one is amazed that Burgess got so much into a book shorter than the Bible.

One final note: Burgess/Toomey has a fascination with sesquipedalian words, which will either madden or captivate you. I still have a notebook in which I scribbled the great big or unfamiliar words I encountered when first reading the book (sidereal, micturate, etc.). I see Burgess grinning every time he sends his reader scurrying for a dictionary.

RANDALL KENAN

Bio on p. 108

Edith's Diary

By Patricia Highsmith

1977

Highsmith is most famous for her Ripley series, but it's the nonseries books, such as *Those Who Walk Away, Tremor of Forgery, Suspension of Mercy, The Glass Cell,* and *The Blunderer,* that grip me. But of all the thrillers written under her name, *Edith's Diary* is the only one with a female protagonist. Edith is a perfectly ordinary desperate housewife in Pennsylvania, tending to her senile uncle and her crooked son, Cliffie, who masturbates into his socks. She wants the perfect

American Dream of a life, but instead she has got hell.
So she starts writing a diary and, slowly but surely in
the privacy of those pages, begins to invent the perfect
life she craves. Patricia Highsmith was the world's best
purveyor of eerie and uncomfortable worlds, and she
never failed to wriggle right inside the minds of her
characters, so that, however mad they might appear to
others, everything they do seems utterly reasonable. In
this book, she manages to spin horror from self-delu-
sion. After all, lying to your own diary is surely a long
way down the road to madness.

FIDELIS MORGAN

Bio on p. 29

The Elected Member

By Bernice Rubens

1970

Admittedly, the synopsis of *The Elected Member*
sounds grim. Norman Zweck, the forty-one-year-old
son of a London rabbi, is addicted to amphetamines. A
child prodigy, then a renowned barrister, Norman
becomes a paranoid shut-in, tormented by his delusions
and furious at the family's plan to have him committed.
Bella, his virginal sister who still lives at home, must
find a way to align the competing realities of her
drug-addled sibling and their rage-blinded father.

Bernice Rubens's analytical sympathy telegraphs
what each character has to gain from the crisis, without
ever resorting to diagnosis. Jargon and catchphrases
have nearly obliterated the paradoxes of addiction, as
if to label is to cure. Rubens mines the situation as
much for its absurdity as its anguish. Norman instigates
the troubles, yet he is also the fall guy. "Perhaps it was

all a hallucination. 'No' he screamed into the sheets. Not that word. Not that filthy rotten family word that his father and sister had picked up from his psychiatrist. They were blind, all of them, and they tossed the word at each other knowingly yet shamefully, comforted by its overtones of impermanence. 'He's hallucinating,' they would nod at each other, and he could have killed them for their coziness."

Wry and ruthless, Bernice Rubens deserves a much wider reputation, especially in the United States, where she is known, if at all, for *Madame Sousatzka*. She was particularly fascinated by scapegoats, and never to greater effect than in this Booker Prize–winner. Dire and unsparing, *The Elected Member* also happens to be mordantly funny.

MEGAN RATNER

Megan Ratner has contributed to Film Comment, Film Quarterly, Cineaste, Filmmaker, and Bright Lights Film Journal, where she is an associate editor. She also reviews books for Art on Paper and writes about art for Frieze. Her essays have appeared in BlackBook and The New York Times.

The Engineer of Human Souls
By Josef Skvorecky
Translated from the Czech by Paul Wilson
1977

On first encounter, the volume seems a forbidding object: a door-stopping 571 pages of rather crowded print, an unpleasantly mechanical title—actually *The Engineer of Human Souls* refers ironically to Stalin's prescription for what a writer should be in the socialist paradise—its seven chapters named after American authors (Poe, Hawthorne, Twain, and so on), the first of them beginning with a middle-aged Czech emigré professor lecturing his Canadian class idiosyncratically about "The Raven"; and the author's unpronounceable name is not that of Milan Kundera. To perfect the presentational disaster, the cover of the American edition is dominated by an old manual typewriter on whose keys the title of the book is spelled out. One quickly decides that it is bookish, fusty, antiquated, and abstract. In fact, it is not only one of the greatest but one of the most purely enjoyable novels of the twentieth century—caviar for a knowing reader, delight from beginning to end.

Skvorecky has written a variety of books, but his creative mother lode lies in his adolescent years, when Hitler's army occupied his native town—called Kostelec in his books—and his fictional stand-in Danny Smiricky spent his energies trying to stay alive, play jazz on tenor saxophone, and chase a number of usually unattainable girls (unlike Kundera, Skvorecky does not present himself as a winner in the world's erotic steeplechase). He began working this material in his first novel, *The Cowards*; written shortly after the war, the book detailed the Russian "liberation" of Kostelec. Published in 1958, it was banned by the Czech government (and the title tells you why). He continued through a number of volumes, including his acknowledged classic, *The Bass Saxophone*, a short masterpiece that badly needs a new translation: I suspect that the current unaccredited English version of the book, rhythmically inadequate to the complex, Faulknerian sentences that twine their way through its narrative sense of time, was done by the author at a time when his Canadian was not as fluent as it is today.

The Smiricky saga reaches its apotheosis in the volume in hand, which was published in English in

1984. The Germans are in Kostelec. Danny Smiricky has been requisitioned as a worker in a Messerschmitt factory, where he is attempting to sabotage machine-gun mounts. Molly Dreslerova and Irena remain tantalizingly out of reach. Everything is in peril. The tone is that of humane and rueful comedy, and a continuous smile graces your features as you read, though on a few occasions this smile gives way to laughter over virtuoso comic scenes involving, for example, an attempt to smuggle a five-legged pig on a train, or how to follow a trail of drunks in Russia. Contrariwise, the unvarnished reality of war and occupation periodically break through, as they must.

In alternating passages, the mature Professor Smiricky recounts his life in Toronto, among his students and amid the emigré community, and corresponds with the Czech diaspora around the world. He is courting a beautiful student of his whose name, inevitably, is Irene. These passages are of lower expressive voltage, necessarily, than the Kostelec story, but they broaden and deepen the book's perspective and its rendering of human life in the long view and close up. *Engineer* is one of those rare novels, like those of Tolstoy, that improve by getting longer, because by some magic its narrative view is not sequential but cumulative: the world it is telling us about deepens and grows richer, and the human beings in it become more resonant and fully rendered as it goes along. In the end, the expressive and contemplative sum of the book is simply staggering.

In Paul Wilson, formerly the sole American member of the famous Czech rock band the Plastic People of the Universe, Skvorecky found his ideal translator. The book's idiom is effortlessly intelligent and conveys

Skvorecky's essential warmth and friendliness as a writer, along with an appropriate hardness of detail when required.

And a great deal happens in the book: the war goes on, quite seriously; the town is liberated and reoccupied; people are imprisoned and killed; Irena remains beyond reach, but Danny finally loses his virginity to a tubercular factory girl in a sub story whose tender exactitude banishes sentimentality from it; and an older professor achieves his Irene. It is the sort of book one wants to go on forever, but 571 pages will have to do. It is concentrated, various, beautifully organized, and seems to read itself. I believe that it, like Tolstoy's great novels, is one that alters and enlarges our contemplation of human nature, and that one leaves the book as a different and slightly better, wiser person than the one who went in.

Engineer is best read with a lighter prelude: Skvorecky's previous volume, *The Swell Season*, a set of linked short stories set during the occupation of Kostelec that concern themselves almost exclusively with the serious matter of playing music and chasing girls. It is the perfect appetizer for the extraordinary feast of Skvorecky's magnum opus.

RAFI ZABOR

Bio on p. 63

"Erika Imports" (from *How to Be Alone*)

By Jonathan Franzen

2002

Maybe every writer strives for truth and beauty in their writing, though I know from experience that they don't come when called, and they don't work on the barter system. If they did, I'd happily trade pages of dialogue, description, plotting, and weaving for just a few lines of those elusive qualities.

"Erika Imports" is the shortest essay in Jonathan Franzen's nonfiction collection *How to Be Alone*, a waif squashed between longer, better-known heavy hitters like the National Magazine Award–winning "My Father's Brain"; a piece related to Franzen's infamous stint as an "Oprah" author; and what may be the most extensive piece of writing in any genre on the shortcomings of the U.S. Postal Service. I'd encourage you to read every essay in *How to Be Alone*, and though I'm a person who reads magazines backwards and usually skips around in anthologies, here I'd suggest following the order of the table of contents. Hidden in the middle is where "Erika" shines brightest.

But maybe that's not exactly the right way to put it. (So much for truth.) The essay does shine, but Erika — with her snoring and body odor and housecoats that peep open "to reveal an Old World bra or girdle" — certainly does not, and neither does her husband, Armin the finger-licker. Erika and Armin Geyer are a German couple for whom Franzen worked during high school. They ran a home business importing tchotchkes from East Germany to sell to gift shops across America's heartland. Franzen was their packing boy, an experience that he describes with the sort of bitterness and exactitude familiar to anyone who ever had one of those nonstandard, immensely character-building jobs where one feels less like an employee than a sitcom character.

Franzen urges you into the Geyers' dank, stinky house, plops you on the sofa with the fat schnauzer by your side, and presents the pathos of this most excruciating after-school job. You see the heart-sinking piles of tacky Christmas baubles; you feel Franzen's guilty longing for a predictable job at a fast-food joint; you smell the precise odor of sweet wine, old food, and Erika's heavy perfumes that is distinct to the Geyers' home. But all of that description is just icing on the stollen. Because at the end Franzen yanks you out with this:

> Poor Erika and Armin, with their blood clots, their broken bones, their abrupt hospitalizations! Each step of their downward progress was faithfully reported by my mother in her letters to me. Now everyone is dead, and I wonder: Is there no escaping the personal? In twenty-five years I have yet to find a work situation that isn't somehow about family, or loyalty, or sex, or guilt, or all four. I'm beginning to think I never will.

As much as I enjoy the story of how young Franzen bristled against the peculiar confinements of his after-school job, I would trade all of the delightful, evocative details for that little bit of truth and beauty at the end. Fortunately, though, Franzen has given me both.

CAITLIN LEFFEL

Caitlin Leffel is a writer and editor. She is the co-author of The Best Things to Do in New York: 1001 Ideas and NYC: An Owner's Manual.

The Escape Artist

By Matt Seaton

2002

That good books about the sport of cycling are few and far between shouldn't come as a surprise; as with most sports writing, all but the best tend to be about as compelling as instructions for fixing a flat. A game, a race, a match—all exist in heightened moments almost always set against a clock, and writing about this sort of "time out of time" is faced with the problem of needing to offer a new insight or angle that is often beside the point when removed from the context of when and how it happened in the first place and the fact that if you're reading about it, it's already a done deal.

Luckily, great sports writing can transcend its genre, as does Matt Seaton's *The Escape Artist*. Like Lance Armstrong's *It's Not About the Bike*, Seaton's memoir is only ostensibly about cycling. True, the machine is present on every page, with a silent omnipotence that propels both reader and story forward from beginning to end, perfectly illustrating Seaton's mandate that one "must always obey the bike's mechanical imperative, its instinctual quest for perpetual motion." The bicycle remains the only constant in Seaton's life as his world changes around him, and he along with it, from an idealistic teenager subconsciously searching for a passionate vocation to a father and a husband facing the loss of his wife to breast cancer.

Seaton, a journalist and editor, has deep emotional and psychological ties to the bicycle. Embroiled in the intricacies of training, maintenance, and the accompanying culture, Seaton's descriptions are clear and detailed (he perceptively calls his stationary trainer a "reverse time machine"). Seaton's own obsession with cycling cuts to the heart of the seductive draw that attracts thousands of men and women to the sport: the controlled environment where cyclists become "engineers of themselves."

Seaton spends six pages describing the practical benefits of shaving one's legs: "It made me proud," he writes, "like earning the badge of membership to a select fraternity." But, as his cycling narrative rolls along without so much as a pause, telling details begin to emerge in the story of his life off the bike, and in particular his decade-long relationship with his wife. Seaton recounts their struggle to conceive and his subsequent anxieties that too much time in the saddle may have resulted in a low sperm count. In the same passage, he tells of having to give his wife a hormone injection as part of a course of IVF therapy, brilliantly using the episode not only as a bridge to a discussion of the scourge of doping in cycling but as a telling example of his ability to use the bicycle to divert the pressures and problems of his daily life. Throughout the book, Seaton documents his marriage with little emotion and even less sentimentality. Milestones from his relationship—including his wedding day, his wife's misdiagnosis for breast cancer, and her final days—are significant simply for having been almost entirely omitted. What is astonishing is how this memoir's profundity lies in its silences.

Elegant and perceptive, *The Escape Artist* is more than a description of a life spent on two wheels. It is a skillfully rendered portrait of maturation and loss—of life as an athlete, a husband, and a father—by a supremely gifted writer evaluating the sum of his experiences and emerging with a moving work of unflinching clarity and grace, as perfectly crafted as a bicycle itself.

Robert Grover

Robert Grover is a freelance editor whose recent clients include Archipelago Books, a not-for-profit press publishing international literature in translation. He is also a senior editor at the John Richardson Fund for Picasso Research.

Essays in Idleness

By Yoshida Kenko

Translated from the Japanese by Donald Keene, 1967

1330–1332

I like to compare the *zuihitsu* with fungus: neither flora nor fauna, it is a species unto itself. In the West, little is known about this classic Japanese genre. Scholars have referred to this term, literally "follow the brush," as "poetic miscellany" and "pillow book." Unknowingly, Westerners may have seen this quintessential Japanese writing in *The Pillow Book* by Sei Shonagon, a cult classic among the Beat poets. To this day, poets emulate the author's utterly subjective "random thoughts" with appropriately distilled paragraphs, faux journal entries, and lists. But *zuihitsu*? In choosing an unappreciated volume, I also wish to draw attention to a peculiar species.

Kenko's *Tsurezuregusa*, or *Essays in Idleness*, is less known than Sei Shonagon's earlier work. Donald Keene, one of the masters of translation, notes in the introduction that this "collection of essays ranging in length from a line or two to several pages [has] exercised an influence out of all proportion to its [size], and would surely be included in any list of the ten most important works of Japanese literature." This statement places Kenko in exalted company. It also places the *zuihitsu* itself among other genres such as the minuscule haiku form made popular by Basho, as well as the first psychological novel ever written, *The Tale of Genji*, by Murasaki Shikibu. Keene's translation, the result of a United Nations Committee to "transmit to Western readers representative works of the major Asian traditions," was published in 1967 by Columbia University Press. Unless you study Japanese literature, you are not likely to come across this masterpiece.

Kenko (circa 1283–1350) was a court poet when he took Buddhist orders after the death of the retired emperor whom he served. However, rather than becoming a hermit or focusing on doctrine, he remained in the world of the capital. Kyoto during this feudal period was filled with tumultuous political intrigue and shifting alliances among emperors, exiled emperors, and the shogun. Kenko did not concern his writing with such mundane events. Instead, he made observations on such themes as beauty, honesty, and propriety, as they are imbued with the feeling of impermanence, a hallmark of Japanese aesthetics.

For centuries, his entries have been models of style for students and writers alike. These fragmentary works are spontaneous and incomplete in feeling, full of contradiction and restraint in sensibility, opinionated in tone, and completely whole in composition. Here is my favorite:

> You should never put the new antlers of a deer to your nose and smell them. They have little insects that crawl into the nose and devour the brain.

I love the scrap of self-portrait here. I love the sense that what one might consider a fragment is actually a whole. In fact, I love the sheer, straight-faced wackiness in a number of his entries. Still others are random odd anecdotes.

To this day, Japanese writers continue to craft and publish such miscellanies. And it is surprising that Westerners have not caught on to them as a genre. With the boundaries between poetry and prose constantly continuing to blur, the *zuihitsu* strikes me as very contemporary. It is akin to, but not the same as, the prose poem or creative nonfiction. Perhaps it is closest to a new subgenre, the lyric essay, which I suggest already exists in Melville's *Moby-Dick*, William Carlos Williams's *Paterson*, Charles Wright's *Quarter Notes*, or Michelle Cliff's *The Land of Look Behind*. All of these American texts remind me of the *zuihitsu*, this "formless form," to use a contemporary scholar's description of Kenko's work.

Whether or not one is fascinated by new genres, there is extraordinary delight in *Essays in Idleness*. In fact, we are fortunate to have this work, which the public probably did not see in Kenko's time. Legend has it that a disciple assembled this collection after tenderly removing scraps pasted on the walls of the Buddhist priest's cottage. Now is a good time to find an idle moment to follow Kenko's simultaneously alien and familiar brush.

KIMIKO HAHN

Kimiko Hahn's seven collections of poetry include most recently, The Narrow Road to the Interior. Her latest writing for film, Everywhere at Once, was narrated by Jeanne Moreau and presented at Cannes. Recent honors include the Shelley Memorial Prize and the PEN/Voelcker Award. Hahn is a Distinguished Professor in the M.F.A. program at Queens College, City University of New York.

In Praise of the Obscure

Eternal Fire
By Calder Willingham
1963

Dersu Uzala
By Vladimir Arsenyev
1923

The Devil to Pay in the Backlands
By João Guimarães Rosa
1956

Ever since I was old enough to choose books for myself, I've been seeking out those that were, if not obscure, not particularly well-known. Whether this was an esoteric passion for reading at a time when there was no such thing as "young adult" books or whether it was blatant one-upmanship I'm not sure. Probably the latter. My smarter, better-read, one-grade-ahead cousin turned me on to Mazo de la Roche's Jalna books and we became obsessed with them. They were dark and exotic—set in Ontario!—things were windswept, and there were secrets, family dysfunction, an ancestral manor house, and what for us in the fifties passed for sex. My cousin was always a book or two ahead and kept me scrounging for fresh material at the bookmobile or on the shelves of homes where I babysat. This often led me to books that were totally inappropriate, like Calder Willingham's *Eternal Fire*, a best-seller in 1963 but now long out of print. A southern gothic classic, its pulpy pages were shockingly engorged with miscegenation, suicide, corruption, incest, courtroom drama, graphic sex, and, of course, a dwarf voyeur. Coming on the heels of *To Kill a Mockingbird*, it had all the same pat southern gothic ingredients, but it's as if Willingham were saying, "O.K., then, let me show y'all the kind of thing that was going on with Bob Ewell and his daughter, Mayella, and then I want to tell you what small-town lawyers are really like . . ." But there was also some great, kick-ass writing—Willingham is one of our most underrated novelists and a fine screenwriter (*The Graduate* (with Buck Henry), *Thieves Like Us*,

One-Eyed Jacks)—and I still treasure my yellowed Dell paperback edition of *Eternal Fire* with the pages folded down on the dirty parts.

As with the Jalna books and *Eternal Fire*, what usually makes a book obscure is geography and the passage of time. One country's or one generation's best-seller or classic is another's obscurity. I've long loved the Russians, all of them, whatever century, genre, religion, or political persuasion, and any list of my favorites would have to include *Dersu Uzala*, the remarkable account of an army surveying expedition in Siberia from 1902 to 1907 that came to rely on the native intelligence and mysticism of a Mongolian trapper encountered along the way. A used paperback edition with an oddly sci-fi cover was given to me by a Russian friend in 1991 as her country was crumbling. I felt that she wanted me to think of the book as emblematic of her homeland, with one foot in an ancient world and one in the new, but always trudging onward, no matter what, and since then I've enjoyed hand-selling it and giving it as a gift, thanks to a reissue (*Dersu the Trapper*).

If you held the Pistol of Cruel Choices to my head and made me pick only *one* all-time, cham-peen favorite obscure book, it would have to be *The Devil to Pay in the Backlands*, by João Guimarães Rosa. Published in Portuguese in 1956 and in an English translation in 1963, it is a story told by an old *jagunço* about his outlaw days fighting government forces and rival rebel factions in the *sertão*, the backlands of northern Brazil; a spectacular, variegated landscape of jungle, mountains, rivers, and desert. The colorful, conversational narrative is full of humorous asides and arcane maxims, the descriptions are rich with flora and fauna, and the action is realistic and engaging. But the real power of the novel is in the *jagunço*'s deep perception and understanding of human nature, warfare, and the *sertão*, which he experiences practically as a being—or a god. *The Devil to Pay in the Backlands* is as lyrical and captivating a book as I've read, and recalling it makes me think that it's high time for a reissue. The author photo of Guimarães Rosa, who was also a diplomat and a physician, was taken by Alfred A. Knopf himself, and it deepens the intrigue for me. It shows a natty, mid-century gent with a bow tie and a cigarette: a Brazilian incarnation of William Faulkner or Cormac McCarthy. Guimarães Rosa looks to be at home in the modern world, but writes of rare, rough landscapes, the impellent, sui generis characters who inhabit them, and the old verities.

LISA HOWORTH

Lisa Howorth has been a librarian, bookseller, and an editor; she is also a writer who has published two books, and she recently completed a novel. She lives in Oxford, Mississippi, where her husband, Richard, established Square Books in 1979.

Ethics

By Baruch Spinoza

1677

Among the wisest lines in Western literature are those ending Baruch Spinoza's masterpiece, *Ethics*. Spinoza (1632–77) attempted to understand basically everything (reality) in terms of a system of thought not unlike a spider's web, using definitions and axioms and proofs (the form of geometry). He then asks why, if it's clear to him how one should live one's life, others don't ask the same questions and use his methods to achieve understanding—i.e., to choose intelligently and freely, to acquire the habit of thinking, to live better lives. His answer: "For all things excellent are as difficult as they are rare."

In so much of Western philosophy—from Plato to Descartes, from Rousseau to Hegel—there is the need to convince. Its texts often exude elusive anxiety, even in translation. The authors seem to want so badly to be believed, all the while looking anxiously over their shoulders at their predecessors. But these boys are clever. They make the beds they want to lie in, but convince us that they were made while they were already lying in them. Yet "all truths reside in all things." They can't hide behind their systems, these human hearts in their system-craving selves.

Spinoza seems to be one of the few Western philosophers without this need to convince. He might have looked back at Descartes, but only to ground himself, only to say, I see you; having done so, he unfolded his umbrella and walked away. It's said that one doesn't read Spinoza's great work but, rather, studies it; it's true, not because the book is "difficult" but because there is, even in translation, a calm knowingness rare in such works.

This knowingness, this calmness, pervades his vision. The reason to read *Ethics* isn't so much for the systematic philosophy—although it is a life manual, if there ever was one—but for the poetry of his vision, the vision of his poetic self, and the calm acceptance of his wayward brethren. This radical rationalist was a poet-philosopher with that rarest of human qualities: empathy. "I have striven not to laugh at human actions, not to weep at them, nor to hate them, but to understand them," he wrote.

Bertrand Russell said that others have surpassed Spinoza intellectually but that he is the supreme ethicist. Being a supreme ethicist, his life was defined by choice, most notably when much was at stake—the only time when choice is defining and therefore interesting. Rejecting a prestigious teaching position, the "enchanted one," as Borges called him, lived his life alone, earning a living by grinding and polishing lenses so that all could see the truths in all things, including themselves.

ROBERT DREESEN

Robert Dreesen has been an editor in New York for almost twenty years, and is currently at Cambridge University Press.

F

The Field of Mustard

By A. E. Coppard

1926

One day while teaching a poetry workshop in Crete, I was handed a stack of photocopies by my co-tutor, the English poet David Swann, and asked to report back. There were five or six short stories by different authors. As I began one called "The Field of Mustard," by an author I'd never heard of, I felt something change in the air. At once I was captivated. The duende was in these pages, or perhaps a wood sprite, a wodwo from the English forests. It was a work that transcended the hand of its author, the kind we're always looking for.

A. E. Coppard is mostly forgotten now, but he had his time in the sunshine. In the '20s, '30s and '40s, he published short stories on both sides of the Atlantic, with Cape and Knopf, and was praised by the likes of L. P. Hartley, Elizabeth Bowen, Rebecca West, and Ford Madox Ford. He only wrote short stories, apart from some poetry and an autobiography, and of those perhaps only a handful are absolutely successful, transcending, like all great works of art, their own terms, kicking away the ladder of their parts to live as entities unto themselves. One of the best is "Field of Mustard"—also the title of a 1926 collection. It's about two poor rural women collecting firewood in the English countryside. The story—or tale, as he preferred to call his works—is a study of passion, love, disappointment and disillusion; of loss, mortality, and the place of human beings in the cosmic scheme, all accomplished in fewer than a dozen pages. The landscape in it seems to come alive; the woods and fields where it's set are as animated and vital a force as the small cast of characters.

Coppard led a checkered, unusual life. One partner said of him that the tragedy of his life was that he put freedom over love. After a childhood in poverty, when he worked variously as a messenger for Reuters and a tailor's errand boy, at the age of seventeen he happened to take shelter from a rainstorm under the awning of a secondhand bookseller, and while there read Keats's "La Belle Dame Sans Merci." It changed his life, engendering a lifelong fascination with words and with women. Many of his stories are about mysterious women, part femme fatale, part angel. He read voraciously, and became a marathon runner, a swimmer, and a boxer while working in clerical positions; he settled finally as a clerk-cost accountant in the Eagle Ironworks, in Oxford. But at the age of forty-one, in 1919, he abruptly left his wife and children and went to live in a primitive hut in the woods. There, supporting himself on £50 worth of savings, he devoted himself wholly to his writing. Two years later, his first volume of stories came out, *Adam and Eve and Pinch Me.*

Many of his stories are about random couplings: man and woman meet in a wood or remote tavern. Eros possesses them; they become elevated into figures out of mythology or fairy tale, and then go their separate ways, sadder, deeper, wiser, and somehow emptier. He continuously treads a liminal no-man's-land between this known world and some other realm that isn't exactly unreal or fabulous but disturbingly mythological. It's as if some psychoscape from an uneasy dream had risen to the surface; you never quite know if you're standing on solid ground or in some quagmire of the unconscious.

In Coppard's best work this uncertainty works triumphantly to unsettle our complacencies, to reawaken our love for humanity and for this (as we now know) fragile planet, not to mention for the art of the short story. He thought of himself as a folktale-teller, and his tales do seem to reach back through the centuries into a collective ancestry of the story. The ephemeral and the everlasting are both somehow evoked. I hope his ephemeral reputation will become, if not eternal, then at least longer-lasting than it has been so far.

HENRY SHUKMAN

Henry Shukman won the 2006 U.K. Author's Club First Novel Award and an Arts Council England Writer's Award. His second novel, The Lost City, was a Guardian Book of the Year. He won the Jerwood Aldeburgh Poetry Prize in 2003 for In Doctor No's Garden, a Book of the Year in both the Times and the Guardian. His poems have appeared in many publications, including The New Republic, The Hudson Review, The Independent on Sunday, and the London Review of Books.

The Flowers of Unceasing Coincidence

By Robert Kelly

1988

1. Here is a book of poems—or one long poem sequence made up of 672 numbered chunks—that you can enter anywhere. The coincidence turns out to be unceasing enjoyment, the movement—nomadic—that belies the linearity of number; this book is multidirectional at all points. Which makes for strange flowers: neither head nor tail, this is not a stem-root-flower flower, the old botanical tree image as mimetic

paradigm/alibi of human shape and act (hubris of Leonardo's renaissance male centrally inscribed in a circular cosmos).

2. And thus the book also proposes a disruption of our reading habits. No way to pull the petals one by one and murmur, "Oh muse she understands me, she understands me not, or a little, or very much." Can't eat this daisy by the roots. That old conundrum, meaning, or at least any singular truth, always lies just beyond the horizon, a line of sight, a line of flight. But Kelly says as much clearly, leading us on and in: "don't make sense make difference."

3. Beyond the horizon, or on it: tangential line of our laborious, straight minds touching the curved earth. Meaning as the spark of the meeting of what we imagine we think and what is. Meaning never more than this: sparks, shards of light, a breath held. You set out to find and what you find is:

> world of soft grammaticals, fractals of typography
> cheating any horizon — geology of pure punctuation
> all you can hear is the gap singing

4. The book is full of flowers — "speed-well sweet-william saxifrage / little-sword chrysanthemum / I have said them before I will say them again / blue chicory New York aster lupine vetch" — which come to feel like the most solid entities when we encounter them at the turn of a verse — "me too little flower / as of roadside chicory." A solidity undermined by a Gertrude Stein-like sense of play or play of sense playing between the thing and its name — "to know the name / of any flower is / to live in it."

5. The shape of the whole thing — if a botanical image has to be used — is that of the rhizome, i.e. a non-hierarchical space, a burrow where you, the

reader, can go to earth for as long or as little as you like. You can think of it as gnomic wisdom-shards ("language is the litmus of law / by it alone judge / the honor of thy State") or an epic bouquet of unheard-of flowers. But "flower" is a trope that names the trope of poetry, which brings to mind Jean Paulhan's *The Flowers of Tarbes; or, Terror in Literature*—but I will save that book for another time. Today, as the snow begins to fall, I'll keep the company of *The Flowers of Unceasing Coincidence.*

PIERRE JORIS

Pierre Joris is a poet, translator, essayist, and anthologist. He has published more than forty books, including Aljibar II (a bilingual edition of poems, with French translations by Eric Sarner), Justifying the Margins: Essays 1990-2006, Aljibar I, and Meditations on the Stations of Mansour Al-Hallaj 1-21. His translations include Paul Celan's Lightduress, which received the 2005 PEN Award for Poetry in Translation. He is Professor of Poetry and Poetics at the State University of New York, Albany.

For the Time Being

By Annie Dillard

1999

When people think of Annie Dillard, they think of *Pilgrim at Tinker Creek*, her Pulitzer Prize–winning first book of essays, or *An American Childhood*, her memoir about growing up in Pittsburgh in the 1940s and '50s. Unfortunately, her greatest book, *For the Time Being*, is her least known. It received virtually no attention, won no awards, and sold modestly. I suppose this is not surprising; for all its greatness, *For the Time Being* is not for the faint of heart. It is, in fact, one of the most terrifying books I've ever read. It weaves together a dazzling array of stories about heart-wrenching birth defects; natural disasters; the depredations of history; what Christian and Jewish mysticism has to tell us about the nature of God, the universe, and human suffering; the formation of sand; and Dillard's own travels in Israel and China. But its principal subject—the story behind the stories Dillard masterfully tells—is the impenetrable mystery of undeserved and unredeemable pain. The questions Dillard can neither answer nor stop asking are: why are we here? What place do our loves and attachments have in an impersonal, indifferent, and ever-changing universe, a universe that permits joy and love but isn't joyful or loving? Her method is to juxtapose long views of history that dwarf any sense of the importance of any one individual existence with short views of particular lives and startling instances of personal attachment: life seen from the hawk's impersonal perspective and the day-to-day, year-to-year life as we each personally experience it. Dillard can neither do without God nor quite believe in Him. "Maybe," she says, "'all your actions show your wisdom and love' means that the precious few things we know that God did, and does, are in fact unambiguous in wisdom and love, and all other events derive not from God but only from blind chance, just as they seem to." But no sooner does she reach this tentative conclusion than she adds, "What then of the bird-headed dwarfs?" The ultimate value that the book promotes isn't faith, or skepticism, but sheer wonderment at the dazzling, overdetermined, evanescent, unlikely spectacle of our being here at all. *For the Time Being* enacts the kind of attention it promotes. It shows us how to live in the presence of mystery without the terror of existence blinding us to

the beauty of the world, and without the beauty
blinding us to the terror.

ALAN SHAPIRO

Alan Shapiro is the author of ten books of poetry, most recently
Old War. He is the William R. Kenan, Jr., Distinguished Professor
of English and Creative Writing at the University of North
Carolina, Chapel Hill.

The Fox of Peapack and Other Poems

By E. B. White

1938

E. B. White is deservedly well known for *Charlotte's
Web* and *Stuart Little* and his updating of William
Strunk's *The Elements of Style*. People know that for
years he wrote for *The New Yorker*, and he is one of
the heroes of James Thurber's *The Years with Ross*,
about that magazine's early years. What a pity, then,
that most of the people I ask have never heard of
White's *The Fox of Peapack and Other Poems*. White is
arguably the greatest writer of light verse in twentieth-
century America. (His wife, Katharine, was poetry
editor for *The New Yorker* in its palmy days of
Dorothy Parker, Ogden Nash, and the rest.) Among
my favorites in *The Fox of Peapack*: "I Paint What I
See," a delicious imaginary dialogue between Diego
Rivera and an irritated Nelson Rockefeller over the
Marxist murals that Rivera has had the effrontery to
paint for the Rockefellers' RCA Building in New York.
"I paint what I see," declares Rivera imperturbably. "I
paint what I paint. I paint what I think." When
Rockefeller protests that, with such a mural in a public
space, he won't be able to rent offices to capitalists—
and complains that "after all, / It's *my* wall"—comes

the answer of the unrepentant artist: " 'We'll see if it is,' said Rivera."

And then we have "Lines Long After Santayana," a meditation on Santayana's observation that "animal love is a marvelous force," concluding its tour of Eros in the natural world from Gila monsters and starfish and snails with the following:

> Animal love is the marvelous force
> Marsupials take as a matter of course;
> You find it in Aryan, Mongol, Norse,
> In beetle, tarantula, ostrich, horse;
> It creeps in the grasses and blows in the gorse,
> It's something all sponges are bound to indorse—
> And only in humans it causes remorse.

DAVID BEVINGTON

David Bevington is the Phyllis Fay Horton Distinguished Service Professor Emeritus in the Humanities at the University of Chicago. He is editor of The Complete Works of Shakespeare, Sixth Edition, and a senior editor of The Norton Anthology of Renaissance Drama and the Cambridge edition of the works of Ben Jonson. His books include Shakespeare, This Wide and Universal Theater, and Shakespeare's Ideas.

The Franchiser

By Stanley Elkin

1976

Every sentence that Stanley Elkin wrote deserves our attention. Unlike anyone else since Kafka, Elkin wrote sentences so beautiful and with such emotional depth and comic bite that upon reading you don't know whether to laugh or cry, ending up doing a little of both. So often his subject was America itself, and *The Franchiser*, about a man named Ben Flesh who drives around the country buying franchises, is the book that describes this country best. Ben is a man who loves nothing better than to wake up in a city somewhere in the United States, drive around for a little while, and still have no idea where he is, because where he is now looks identical to where he was yesterday and the day before. Elkin knew what we had become before we became it, and he brings us the news without judgment or didacticism, but with humor and real life, in the fictional flesh of a man named Ben.

DANIEL WALLACE

Daniel Wallace is the author of Mr. Sebastian and the Negro Magician and Big Fish, which was made into a movie directed by Tim Burton. He lives in Chapel Hill, where he teaches at the University of North Carolina.

The Futurological Congress

By Stanislaw Lem
Translated from the Polish by Michael Kandel
1971

Before he can deliver his paper to the meeting of the Eighth Futurological Congress in the 164-story Costa Rican Hilton, Ijon Tichy, famous scientist, ultimate loner, and Stanislaw Lem's frequent hero/antihero/victim, flees a government bombing attack into the city sewer system, where the rats walk on their hind legs; is evacuated by a helicopter that subsequently crashes; and upon waking in the hospital discovers that his brain has been transplanted into the body of a pretty black girl.

Then things get weird.

And really funny.

Lem wrote huge amounts of fiction, poetry, essays, and philosophical and social tracts. He grew up (a Jew) under the Nazis and outfoxed the Communists by writing with a humor and scientific complexity that was beyond the scope of the apparatchik. He finally quit his native Poland and moved to Germany, where he died in 2007.

In *The Futurological Congress*, Lem takes us on a whirlwind ride through micro and macro cosmos, solar systems, pasts, and futures. The tone, as usual with Lem, is mordant and playful, deeply skeptical, and frighteningly learned. Allow me to drop some names (you can't stop me)—if Jonathan Swift and Franz Kafka had a son (this surely will be possible someday), and he fathered a child with the daughter of François Rabelais and Jorge-Louis Borges—that person might sound like Lem. And maybe even write like him.

Unlike the relatively quiet ambiance of *Solaris*, probably Lem's most famous work thanks to the two high-profile films adapted from it, the sound of *The Futurological Congress* is loud, sometimes frantic and wildly deceptive; each twist of the plot is mirrored by an event suggesting that what just happened wasn't necessarily true. The theme of illusion is a constant in Lem's work—the illusions of religion, society, and self—what we think we know, and why most of it is nonsense. If the robots can't tell whether or not they're human, why should the humans be able to tell whether or not they're robots? And in the end, does it matter?

Mention must be made of the extraordinary translation by Michael Kandel, who had to deal with the book's very complex wordplay. Just the names of drugs invented for the story—in Lem's future world everyone is controlled and organized by chemicals— might give pause to the most resolute translator. Here's a short list of what parents give their children:

uncompromil, rebellium, opinionates, sordidan, and practicol. As for adults—here's my personal favorite: a drug specially devised to counter the layers of illusion imposed by all the official drugs. It's called up'n'at'm.

Are you listening, Eli Lilly?

BUCK HENRY

Buck Henry began his career as an actor in the 1940s; since the '60s he has written screenplays for television and film, many of which have won major awards but even more of which haven't. His writing credits include some big hits and some real dogs. Mr. Henry looks back on all (or most, or some) of them with modest pleasure.

G

Geological Ancestors of the Brook Trout

By John D. Quackenbos

1916

Dr. John D. Quackenbos is the high Romantic of brook-trout literature. His book *Geological Ancestors of the Brook Trout*, fifty sparse pages "read at a regular meeting of the Anglers' Club of New York, Hotel Navarre, March 9th, 1915," is elegy, pastoral fantasy, and amateur natural history all wrapped into one. Three hundred and fifty copies were published by the Anglers' Club of New York (it was their first publication) with a quotation from Tennyson's poem "The Brook" printed in gilt on the green leather cover:

> I wind about and in and out
> With here a blossom sailing
> And here and there a lusty trout
> And here and there a grayling

Before I owned my own copy of the book, I visited one in Yale's Mudd Library, as an undergraduate. It was in poor condition, but I was allowed to make a photocopy (maybe I didn't ask permission, I can't remember), which I bound and kept for my own use for about three years until I found and bought an original from an antiquarian bookseller specializing in sporting literature. It had been re-bound in forest green cloth, and I cherish it to this day. Besides Quackenbos's signature, there is an inscription in the author's billowy cursive: "Yours for the joy of living under the forest boughs, April 25, 1916."

The prose is poetic, flowery even, but I want to believe in the fantasy realm in which this little trout

dwells, as well as the world of the fisherman who
pursues it. Speaking of him, Quackenbos says:

> He naturally informs himself also regarding the
> plant life associated with his sport, the pink and
> snowy chequer of the spring; the mosses, and
> fungi and ferns; the rose purple fire weeds, blue
> gentians, cardinal clusters, and silvery clematis
> tangles of the summer; the waxy stems of Indian
> pipe nodding their corpse-white flowers over the
> roots on which they feed, and orchid beauties that
> tessellate the forest floor or hide their blooming
> wonders in the wannish-gray light of the fens.

But I get it, because I too have been obsessed with
the small char with light spots and red bellies,
commonly known as the brook trout. Quackenbos
summered on Lake Sunapee, in New Hampshire, and
besides catching brook trout in nearby streams he
caught and admired the lake's native char, the Sunapee
trout. His description of its spawning habits, for me,
is one of the most absurdly beautiful passages in
angling literature:

> As the pairing-time approaches, the Sunapee fish
> becomes resplendent with the flushes of maturing
> passion. The steel green mantle of the back and
> shoulders now seems to dissolve into a dreamy
> bloom of amethyst through which the daffodil
> spots of midsummer blaze out in points of flame,
> while below the lateral line all is dazzling orange.
> The fins catch the tones of the adjacent parts,
> and pectoral, ventral, anal, and lower lobe of the
> caudal are striped with a snowy white band. There
> are conspicuous differences in intensity of general
> coloration, and the gaudy dyes of the milter are
> tempered in the spawner to a creamy white or
> olive chrome, with spots of orient opal. The

> wedding garment nature has given to this char is
> indeed agleam with heavenly alchemy.

Did the brook trout and its ancestors somehow reflect
Quackenbos's own wish to be beautiful, to live in cold,
clear lakes and streams, to spawn over gravel and stone,
to swim and eat? Judging by the author's photo in the
book—holding his pocket watch and wearing black tie
and with a big white mustache like a frozen waterfall—
the man was as concerned with his own appearance as
anything, but for some reason he loved the brook trout.

"Can we wonder," he asks, "that the brook trout is
the one perfect fish in all the world? God be praised
that he had the good taste to abandon in the course of
his evolution the lacustrine depths where we never
should have known him, and give his life to the riffles
that chatter through the enameled Champaign and to
the stately flow of the silent river under the demitints of
the soundless forest."

Since there are no circulated reprints of the book
(except for my photocopy), and only three hundred
and fifty copies floating around, I will leave you with
Quackenbos's conclusion:

> And last is our transcendent beauty, the Angel of
> the Brooks, among all the fishes the Lord Para-
> mount of our affection, the brook trout. It has
> taken millions of years at the hands of the Divine
> Artificer to bring to its present perfection the fin-
> ished product. In our comprehending admiration
> of it, we are indeed carried into the very presence
> of the God who fashioned it in the aeonic march
> of events—the God who kindles and extinguishes
> suns and constellations.

> When I was a lad of eleven, good old Dominie
> Fowler of Monticello introduced this fish to me. I

was captivated. I lost my heart then and there, and never, in the long years of my life, have I felt impelled to ask the object of my passion to return it.

JAMES PROSEK

James Prosek is a regular contributor to The New York Times and won a Peabody Award in 2003 for his documentary about traveling in the footsteps of Izaak Walton, the seventeenth-century author of The Compleat Angler. He is the co-founder of World Trout, an initiative that raises money for cold-water-habitat conservation.

A Giacometti Portrait

By James Lord

1965

A Giacometti Portrait, by James Lord, is an account of Lord's sitting for Giacometti, over the course of nearly three weeks, in a year that isn't specified but which one guesses is during the early 1960s. It is a straightforward description of the days—how Giacometti behaved, what he said, how the portrait progressed—and it is interesting, of course, because Giacometti was a superb artist and so every decision and every gesture he made is singular. It is also interesting because, as the friend who gave it to me said, it reads like a brief comic novel with two characters, the great artist and the American from New Jersey who is fortunate enough to be his friend. One of them cares deeply that the painting be completed, and the other is convinced that to portray anything as it really appears is impossible.

The painting, in black and white, is planned to take a few hours, "an afternoon at most." Lord is visiting Paris, where Giacometti, although rich and famous the world over, lives and works in four rooms down a passageway off a street in an overlooked part of the city. Lord arrives around three. For a time he sits in a chair while Giacometti works on a bust of his brother, Diego, and occasionally looks over at Lord. Giacometti's mood is gloomy. Several times he remarks that nothing he does is any good and that he will never be any better. He moves to another sculpture. Nearly an hour passes. Giacometti seems to be doing anything he can to avoid starting something new. Finally, he positions an easel according to red marks on the floor and chooses a canvas. He does not suggest a pose, but he insists that Lord face him directly. He looks at him for a minute or so and then says, "You have the face of a brute," which amuses Lord. As Giacometti paints, starting with black, he talks and smokes and sometimes leans back and squints through his glasses. When Diego calls him to the phone in another room, Lord jumps up to examine the painting and sees that it is a sketch of the room behind him and his figure. Except for the details of the background it strikes Lord as complete. He assumes they are done. Giacometti returns and paints for half an hour without speaking and finally says, "Now it's beginning to look like something, only now."

From the paints and brushes Giacometti is using, Lord tries to determine what part of the painting Giacometti is working on. Having gone on for nearly another two hours, Giacometti says he is tired. The background appears to be finished, but the face and neck are done only in black and gray. "The head isn't too bad," Giacometti says. "It has volume. This is a beginning, at least."

Lord says that he had thought they were going to work only once.

"It's too late for that now," Giacometti says. "It's gone too far and at the same time not far enough. We can't stop now."

At a café afterward, where Giacometti, who is nocturnal, has his customary lunch—two hard-boiled eggs, two slices of cold ham, two glasses of Beaujolais, and two cups of coffee—he says that he admires Cézanne, who, having gone as far as he could with any painting, abandoned rather than completed it. "That's the terrible thing: the more one works on a picture, the more impossible it becomes to finish it," he says.

The record of the days that follow presents a version of an artist whose standards are absolute, a genius who wrestles with the tormenting attempt to accurately paint what he sees. The more, by his lights, he fails, the more intensely he perseveres. The comic elements follow from his good nature, and from the sitter's and the painter's unreconciled ends. Giacometti paints, then erases what he painted. "I'm destroying everything with great bravery," he says one day. Often he announces that matters could not be worse. The body has no substance. He can't manage the nose. The head is at an angle. "If only I could paint a head, a single head," he says more than once. Nevertheless, "There is always some progress, even when things are at their worst, because then you don't have to do all over again all the negative things you have already done."

Giacometti's habit is to work into the evening. Meanwhile, the room becomes too dark to see. Then they switch on the lights and look at the painting. Lord, anxious to return to New York and having put off departing several times, wonders if the portrait will ever be finished, or if Giacometti will give it up in an imperfect state, leaving Lord permanently illegible. He mentions to Giacometti's wife his concern that it might go on for months, and she says, "Sometimes it does." After innumerable erasings, Giacometti says, "It's possible for me now to undo the whole thing very quickly. That's good." Lord asks why. "Because I'm beginning to know what it's all about."

"What?"

"A head," Giacometti says.

The madder ranges of talent are difficult to describe, because so much of what is compressed and excluded in the delivering of a vision remains unseen, but this is a sturdy and unmysterious attempt to depict the company of a great mind and eye possessed with a near-desperate hunger to record and create. Giacometti throughout seems the embodiment of Rilke's remark about having gone up in flames as he wrote *The Duino Elegies*.

Alec Wilkinson

Alec Wilkinson has been on the staff of The New Yorker since 1980. He is the author of nine books, including The Protest Singer: An Intimate Portrait of Pete Seeger; My Mentor: A Young Writer's Friendship with William Maxwell; and The Happiest Man in the World, about Poppa Neutrino, the only man to cross the Atlantic in a raft made of trash.

The Glory and the Dream: A Narrative History of America, 1932–1972

By William Manchester

1974

If you really want to understand modern America—who we are, and how we got here—this is the book you should read. It's a brilliant thirteen-hundred-page epic that charts our rise from a largely rural, isolationist nation to a continent-striding superpower, taking into account everything from politics to pop culture, and putting it all into a unique historical context. Worried about the power and influence of Rush Limbaugh? You may decide that there's less there than meets the eye (or ear) when you learn about his precursor, Father Coughlin, a Minnesota-born preacher who dominated radio airwaves during the 1930s, railing against Roosevelt's New Deal.

The book begins with a description of Washington D.C. in a time not dissimilar from our own. We were in the depths of the Depression. America was out of work and frightened. And in the first chapter alone you get a taste of Manchester's genius as he finds the city under siege, occupied by twenty-five thousand penniless World War I veterans dubbed the Bonus Expeditionary Force.

> Foggy Bottom, the site of the present State Department Building, was a Negro slum. The land now occupied by the Pentagon was an agricultural experimental station. . . . The government employed fewer than two thousand foreign service workers. . . . It is an astonishing fact that the Secretaries of State, War, and Navy were all under one mansard roof, across the street from the White House. If you called on the Secretary of State, he sometimes met you at the door. Army Chief of Staff Douglas MacArthur, on the same floor of the Executive Office Building, was separated from his sole aide by a single slatted door. When the general wanted help he called "Major Eisenhower," and Ike came running.

And with this as a launching point, Manchester adds the one truly astounding detail: When MacArthur sent Ike to testify about the Bonus Army in front of Congress—by trolley, as the army had only one car—Ike had to "walk down a hall and fill out a form, in exchange for which he received two streetcar tokens. Then he would stand outside on Pennsylvania Avenue and wait for a Mt. Pleasant trolley car."

From here, Manchester takes us through the New Deal, World War II, the atom bomb, Korea, Sputnik, the Cold War, McCarthyism, the Kennedy assassination, Elvis, the Beatles, Vietnam, the rise of the Silent Majority, and 1968, the Year Everything Went Wrong, with the murders of Robert Kennedy and Martin Luther King Jr. There are thumbnail biographies along the way of people like Ralph Nader, Eleanor Roosevelt, Benjamin Spock, and Marilyn Monroe. Manchester ends at what some might argue was either the pinnacle of our power or the precipice of what we were to become: a section titled "Nixon, After All," whose last chapter, "Pride Goeth," details the disgraced president's final days in the White House and his resignation.

William Manchester's true genius lay in pulling together the disparate strands of culture, politics, art, and society, which resulted in books that enlighten and delight his readers by putting it all into a larger context. He more or less invented the "narrative history," a technique ably used by the current masters of the form: Robert Caro, Doris Kearns Goodwin, Walter Isaacson, and A. Scott Berg.

If you turn to the bibliography pages of most contemporary histories of America, I'm willing to bet that nine times out of ten you'll find a reference to *The Glory and the Dream*. It represents Manchester at the height of his powers, with his uncanny ability to find the one telling and sometimes heartbreaking detail. Read the book, and savor these few sentences on the announcement of Franklin Roosevelt's death:

Obscure mourners offered special eulogies . . .
The alarm system of the New York Fire Department sounded "four fives" to all fire stations—
the signal that a fireman had died on duty. A
little boy in Chicago picked a bouquet in his
backyard and sent it with a note, saying he was
sorry he couldn't come to the funeral. Other boys
at Groton were told just before supper that the
President, a member of the class of 1900, had just
died. . . . And the *New York Post*, in a gesture
which would have moved the President, simply
headed its daily casualty list:

ARMY-NAVY DEAD

Roosevelt, Franklin D., Commander-in-Chief,
wife, Mrs. Anna Eleanor Roosevelt, the White
House.

BRUCE FEIRSTEIN

*Bruce Feirstein is a longtime columnist at The New York Observer,
a contributing editor at Vanity Fair, and the best-selling author of
Real Men Don't Eat Quiche. His screenwriting credits include the
James Bond films GoldenEye, Tomorrow Never Dies, and The World
Is Not Enough.*

Gogol's Wife and Other Stories

By Tommaso Landolfi

1963

Why Tommaso Landolfi isn't a household name like
Gogol or Poe, Kafka or Borges—all authors he is fairly
compared to—is anyone's guess. I can easily imagine
the parallel universe in which it is a cliché to say of an
alarming juxtaposition or when your skin suddenly
begins to crawl, "Oh how Landolfian!" Instead, even
in his native Italy, where his exquisite stories languish
unread, his reputation is rarefied. Landolfi,

a passionate gambler obsessed with the eternal entanglement of chance and fate, would probably find the state of his literary legacy affirming.

Landolfi insisted that he had nothing particular to say, and once he finished a piece of writing he was almost entirely uninterested in the publication process. His stories are darkly weird, always discomforting, and often bitingly funny; above all, they're masterful manipulations of language, experiments in the vicissitudes of vocabulary. The rigor of his thought and composition is entirely dedicated to making his reader terrifyingly aware that it's all a senseless waste. As Italo Calvino said of his work, Landolfi is continuously placing the meaninglessness, the nothingness of life up against the richness, precision, and coherence of language.

Each story in this collection, representing only a minor sampling of his oeuvre, reveals Landolfi's maniacal mind. In the title story, which Harold Bloom calls the funniest and most irritating he's ever read, we are introduced to the renowned Russian author's wife, a life-size inflatable plastic doll, initially the perfect partner but one who gradually exerts a wicked influence on her devoted husband. Susan Sontag called the story an "incredibly pure potion of the grotesque and the ludicrous," and claimed it was impossible to praise the story too highly. "Pastoral," written in epistolary form, reveals the increasing terror of a woman who has moved from Paris to a remote provincial town where the inhabitants all slowly disappear into a kind of hibernation by crawling into foul-smelling fur bags hung from the ceiling, leaving her utterly alone. "Dialogue on the Greater Harmonies" centers on the question, If poetry is written in a language no one understands, possibly not even the poet himself, is it still poetry? Certainly to be counted among great first lines is the sentence that launches "Wedding Night": "At the end of the wedding banquet the chimney sweep was announced." "The Death of the King of France," originally entitled "W.C.," accompanies the protagonist So-and-So on his impressionistic meanderings across five sections or movements, beginning and ending with him straining on the toilet. "Giovanni and His Wife" describes a pair of tone-deaf lovers who nevertheless pursue their passion for music to the death and, as the narrator suggests with a reference to Poe's "Annabel Lee," perhaps beyond.

My favorite story in the collection, a perfect example of what Gabriel Annan calls Landolfi's "freakish philosophical invention," is here entitled "The Two Old Maids." Landolfi considered it his best story, and Eugenio Montale called it one of the great psychological and moral nightmares of modern European literature. If a nightmare can also be hilarious, then I very much agree. The story centers upon two unmarried middle-aged sisters who live with their old mother, a servant, and their pet monkey, next to a monastery in a drab provincial town. When Tomba, their spoiled and doted-upon pet, a gift from the sisters' dead brother, sneaks into the monastery chapel at night and performs seriously sacrilegious acts, the ensuing scandal leads to dire theological debate regarding the crime and its punishment among the sisters and two priests.

Landolfi's greatness as a writer lies in a paradox: his magnificent prose is at once a view into as well as a defense against the beguiling horror of existence. "Might I ever truly write randomly and without design," he asks in another of his stories, "so that through the mayhem, the disorder, I might at least catch a glimpse of my deepest self?"

JENNY MCPHEE

Jenny McPhee is the author of the novels A Man of No Moon, No Ordinary Matter, and The Center of Things. Her translations include Paolo Maurensig's Canone Inverso and Crossing the Threshold of Hope, by Pope John Paul II.

Green Thoughts: A Writer in the Garden

By Eleanor Perényi

1981

I begin with a confession: I hate gardening. I have been known to accept, grudgingly, a command to weed a bed or two, but I do not like dirtying my hands or bending my back to the point of injury. I do not mind tending to things in pots on the back deck, or watering and clipping and dead-heading, all of which take about fifteen minutes of my time on a summer morning before the sun gets too high in the sky.

Reading Eleanor Perényi, I can at least share, vicariously, the thrills, frustrations, and successes of a person who has devoted decades of her life to a never-ending activity. Vigilance is mandatory. One severe drought, flood, or other natural disaster, an invasion of unwanted varmints, or a week of human inattention, and all is lost. In the garden, nothing is ever finished. A gardener can never rest on her laurels, metaphorical or actual, because it is the process, the doing, not the product, that matters. Writing involves process, too, but once done it can be returned to and savored. The words on the page do not change; they resist nature and meteorology; they can continue to delight even when they are designed to instruct.

Pick up this book of information—hardly an encyclopedia or a manual, but rather a series of stately and whimsical essays arranged alphabetically from "Annuals" to "Woman's Place"—and even the most horticulturally challenged reader knows that he is in the presence of a master stylist. The foreword begins: "I have had only two gardens in my life. The first was a large rather mournful park in the style called a *jardin anglais* on the Continent, attached to my husband's castle in Hungary." Who would not want to know more about this woman? (She wrote a touching memoir, *More Was Lost*, published in 1946 and republished in 2001, about her marriage to a Hungarian count.)

The second garden—and the subject of *Green Thoughts*—is the garden in Stonington, on the southeast Connecticut shore, where she lived for more than a half century, first as a weekender, then full-time until her death, in 2009.

Gardeners cannot work by theory. Practice and practicality, diligence and attention are all. But results are not guaranteed. Trial and error is the name of the game; what works for one person will not work for her next-door neighbor, although conditions may be identical. A gardener must be willing to suffer defeat, to see effort go unrewarded. Gardeners must be optimistic and hardheaded at the same time. So must writers.

Green Thoughts appeals at all levels, starting at the most basic: the level of word and sentence. For example, from "Failures": "It takes a while to grasp that a garden isn't a testing ground for character and to stop asking, What did I do wrong? Maybe nothing." Or, from "Help": "When I look back on the long procession of incompetents, dumbbells and eccentrics, young and old, foreign and domestic, who have worked for me, I wonder how I and the garden have survived their ministrations." Perényi's eagle eye extends equally to her own foolishness and bad decisions; she does not spare herself in order to blame others. For a writer with such a strong sense of self and style, she comes across, paradoxically, as utterly devoid of ego.

Her book contains anecdotes; practical advice of the "I do it this way, but don't necessarily trust me" sort; astute observation ("Nature's favorite color is a washed-out magenta"); historical information (where certain plants came from to America, and when); literary criticism (what Alexander Pope thought about gardens; how other gardening writers both garden and write); horticultural common sense ("I read about chopping and freezing herbs into ice cubes and can't imagine a messier business"); and philosophical equilibrium ("No doubt about it, for all the marvels they have produced, it is the hybridists and their accomplices, who, however unwittingly, have introduced previously unheard-of vulgarisms to the garden world").

Like most great books, it transcends its nominal subject: *Green Thoughts* teaches you about more than gardens. Most of all, it teaches the lesson of patience, which any gardener or writer would be well advised to heed.

WILLARD SPIEGELMAN

Willard Spiegelman is the Hughes Professor of English at Southern Methodist University and is editor-in-chief of the Southwest Review. He is the author of five books of literary criticism and of the recent collection Seven Pleasures: Essays on Ordinary Happiness.

Growing Up with Impressionists: The Diary of Julie Manet

By Julie Manet
Translated and edited by Rosalind de Boland Roberts
and Jane Roberts
1987

Julie Manet was the daughter of Berthe Morisot and Eugène Manet (the younger brother of Edouard). She began her diary in 1893, when she was fourteen years old, and continued writing it for the next six years, recording not simply the details of her own life but providing a private and somewhat dazzling view of the lives of her family's intimate friends and fellow artists: Renoir, Degas, Monet, Sisley, Valéry, and Stéphane Mallarmé, among others. Her father is already dead at the time she begins her diary, and Julie, after the death of her mother, in 1895, becomes the ward of Mallarmé, the father of her best friend, Geneviève. The diary closes with Julie's engagement to the painter Ernest Rouart, son of Henri, and their double wedding with Jeanne Gobillard, Julie's cousin, and Paul Valéry. The daily, delicious details of the many intersecting and interlocking lives sketched here are simply irresistible.

DAVID ST. JOHN

David St. John is the author of nine collections of poetry, most recently The Face, for which he's written a libretto for a chamber opera by Donald Crockett. His honors include a Rome Fellowship and an Award in Literature, both from the American Academy of Arts and Letters, and the O. B. Hardison, Jr., Poetry Prize from the Folger Shakespeare Library.

H

Hank Williams: The Complete Lyrics

Edited by Don Cusic

1993

I'm not one of those people who think it pays a songwriter a compliment to say, "The lyrics are like poetry." I have found that all those volumes that lay out Bob Dylan or John Lennon lyrics as fpoetry only serve to remind me why they were great songwriters, and why Robert Lowell and Carl Sandburg were great poets.

Poems turned into songs have (with rare exceptions) a grim history. The only power on earth that restrains me from making a Rod McKuen joke is that today, not many people would get it.

But I do enjoy reading lyrics by people I consider masters of the form: Gilbert, Coward, Sondheim—and Hank Williams.

I keep *The Complete Lyrics of Hank Williams* by my desk, and I find that when I reach a stale spot in my prose, I sometimes try to stoke the fires of imagery by immersing myself in a little Hank. He reminds me that the thoughts that drive our lives are direct and real; that's what made his writing unforgettable, as opposed to merely clever. I don't think I have to stretch very far to make the case that the words to "I'm So Lonesome I Could Cry" stand alone as a clear, compelling portrait of heartbreak:

> Hear the lonesome whippoorwill
> He sounds too blue to fly
> The midnight train is whining low
> I'm so lonesome I could cry

I've never seen a night so long
When time goes crawling by
The moon just went behind a cloud
To hide its face and cry

The silence of a falling star
Lights up a purple sky
And as I wonder where you are
I'm so lonesome I could cry

Scott Simon

Scott Simon, the host of NPR's Weekend Edition Saturday, is the author of two novels, Pretty Birds and Windy City, and of the forthcoming book Baby, We Were Meant for Each Other.

The Heptameron, by Marguerite de Navarre

see p. 94

Hind Swaraj

M. K. Gandhi

1910

Between November 13 and November 22, 1909, on a return voyage from England to South Africa aboard the ship *Kildonan Castle*, the forty-year-old, Indian-born, London-educated, Natal-based lawyer-activist Mohandas Karamchand Gandhi surrendered to the frenzied composition of a Gujarati manuscript first published as *Hind Swaraj*. Destined to become a key manifesto for the Indian anticolonial movement and the gospel, thereto, of Gandhian nonviolent non-cooperation, this book has a history almost as compelling as its content. Legend has it that Gandhi, writing as though possessed, worked on *Hind Swaraj* without pause for some ten days, venting his newfound prolixity upon the ship's stationary, and using his left hand when his right was tired, such that at least forty of the 275 pages of the original text may be attributed to the right-handed author's left hand. A rare modern instance of the heroics of inscription, this first occurrence of ambidexterity in Gandhi's writerly practice is often invoked, poetically, as confirmation of his place in the mythic genealogy of the *savyasachi*: a type perfected in the figure of Arjuna, epic hero of the Mahabharata, who can wield a bow and shoot fatal arrows equally with both hands. Yet, if anything, it is hardly a fluency in violence that the preparation of *Hind Swaraj* achieves or advocates so much as its opposite, namely, a fluency in the complex technologies of *ahimsa*, or nonviolence. To this end, in Gandhi's hands ambidexterity prefigures a bisexual or gender dexterity crucial for counterbalancing the hypermasculinity that he held culpable for all modern injuriousness. If by a long shot, then, the very material and scribal aspects of this text's composition mark an early, perhaps originary, instance of Gandhi's developing conviction that the nonviolent revolutionary must first consent to becoming equitably male and female, in his words, "God's eunuch." It is worth noting in this regard that an (albeit heterodox) reading of the Mahabharata likewise finds Arjuna to be a true *savyasachi* not so much in his guise as indefatigable archer as through his lesser-known training in gender ambiguation, achieved in the single year he is compelled to spend exiled as *kliba*, or transgendered, in fulfillment of an ultimately beneficial curse from a spurned and vengeful nymph.

Fully cognisant of *Hind Swaraj* as an epochal spiritual event in his own formation as demi-yogi and part-political leader, Gandhi consistently claimed its advent as conclusive clarification of his spiritual vocation in the iniquitous world of twentieth-century imperialism. "The thing," he wrote to his close Jewish collaborator Henry Polak, "was . . . the progressive step I have taken mentally." Gandhi's unabashed enthusiasm about his own book notwithstanding, he would be bitterly disappointed by its subsequent reception. On March 10, 1910, copies of the newly minted Gujarati edition were intercepted at Bombay upon order of the Madras High Court, and fifteen days later, further to a hostile state-interpreter's report, the book was banned by the Home Department on grounds of sedition. This ban, which would remain in place until December 1938, fuelled among the general English reading public the rumor that M. K. Gandhi had penned a poisonous invective against the English race, no less, thus eschewing all former loyalties to the numerous individuals who and organizations that had offered him generous ongoing hospitality from the time of his first arrival in London in 1888 as a somewhat gormless law student. Clearly piqued by the proscription and the negative press, in his preface to the English translation of *Hind Swaraj*, Gandhi is at pains to distinguish his condemnation of English civilization from his love for English people. Indeed, he argues, believing the latter simply to be misguided by the pernicious values of the former, his book is meant as an act of love or a reverse civilizing mission, enabling Europe to finally liberate itself from the backward condition and lamentable habits of colonialism.

Caught in the harsh polemic of colonial contestation, Gandhi's projected reformation of Europe in this early work proceeds upon the assumption of civilizational priority, the questionable belief "that . . . the ancient civilisation of India . . . represents the best that the world has ever seen" and that, given time, the English would "become Indianised or find their occupation in India gone." Further to these designs, he catalogs various deleterious aspects and emissaries of "modern civilisation," among them machinery, doctors, lawyers, railways, Parliament, politicians, the discipline of "history," formal education, and so on. Shorn of its theoretical underpinnings, this aspect of *Hind Swaraj* is regrettably and all too readily available for culturalist misuse. Simplistically reduced to the twinned mottos "the West is evil" and "East is best," Gandhi's manifesto supplies unintended shorthand for the repressive anti-Westernization programs by which non-Western social and religious conservatives rationalize a range of strictures against alleged deviancies of gender and sexuality. In such cases what is often forgotten is the fact that Gandhi's critique of the West and his corrective paean to the East are profoundly nourished by rich late-nineteenth- and early-twentieth-century Western critiques of Western civilization, especially in its ongoing territorial and capitalist voracity. We are directed to these self-critical subcultural traditions as to the collaborative aspects of *Hind Swaraj*'s anti-imperial polemic in the eclectic bibliography appended to the text by Gandhi himself. Included here in dense intertextual nexus are works such as these: *Civilisation: Its Cause and Cure* by the fin-de-siècle homosexual socialist Edward Carpenter, recommending as remedial therapy for the West "a fresh influx of savagery"; Belle Epoque thinker Thomas Taylor's *The Fallacy of Speed*, condemning the nervous pace of consumer culture; Thoreau's famous pamphlet "On the Duty of Civil Disobedience"; and Tolstoy's

"Letter to a Hindoo," urging Indians to perfect a new global ethic of nonviolence, also translated into Gujarati by Gandhi during his busy and productive journey on the Kildonan Castle.

Whatever Gandhi's sources, the genius and originality of *Hind Swaraj* lie in its thick and exacting definition of nonviolence as the prophylactic against modernity/imperialism. Conceiving modernity, much in the spirit of the philosopher mystic Simone Weil, as a "brute force" that turns people into things, Gandhi finds the source of such violation in our collective turn to mediating agencies (governments, lawyers, doctors, teachers), which progressively atrophy our affective and ethical sensibilities. In these terms, Gandhian nonviolence does not consist, as is commonly assumed, in pacifism so much as in militant refusal to be transformed into insensate, nonrelational things. The *swaraj*, or "self-rule," of the title especially presents the radical resensitization of personality and deregulation of self as the conditions of possibility for nonviolent collectivities to come. The *Hind* prefixing this condition refers, of course, to Gandhi's beloved India, crucible of nonviolent methodologies and thence "best" in the world primarily for the gift of sensitivity and recoil from the brutalization of others that comes, or ought to come, with the historical experience of suffering. Would it were the case, as Gandhi so devoutly proposes, that nations and peoples who had suffered atrocity at the hands of others believed themselves uniquely equipped also "to deliver the so-called weaker races of the earth."

LEELA GANDHI

Leela Gandhi is Professor of English at the University of Chicago. She is author of Postcolonial Theory, Measures of Home: Selected

Poems, Affective Communities, and co-author of England through
Colonial Eyes. She is also a founding co-editor of the journal
Postcolonial Studies.

History

By Elsa Morante

Translated from the Italian by William Weaver

1974

There are many mothers in fiction but, in my view, not
nearly enough serious explorations of the complicated
state of motherhood. One of the things I most admire
about Elsa Morante's epic novel *History* is that it is just
such an exploration—and a masterly one. Set in Rome
during World War II, the novel begins when Ida
Mancuso, a poor widow and schoolteacher, is raped by
a drunken German soldier. From this brutal act a child
is born. The child, called Useppe, becomes the great
passion of Ida's life. Through Mussolini's Fascist reign,
the Nazi occupation, the brutal clashes of Germans
and Partisans, and the chaotic postwar period, Ida
devotes herself single-mindedly to keeping her child
alive. All her efforts, however, cannot save Useppe
from malnourishment, or from the epileptic seizures
that worsen as he grows.

But dark as it often is, *History* also has its share of
fairy-tale magic. Against all odds, Useppe blooms into
an otherworldly creature of sweetness and joy. And as
good as she is at depicting motherhood, Morante is
even better at depicting childhood, particularly the way
children perceive and interpret experiences that they
are still too young to understand. She is also a genius at
imagining how animals might think and feel, and a
certain sheepdog, Bella, whose maternal instincts

toward Useppe rival Ida's own, is one of the story's most memorable and delightful — if minor — characters.

Morante wants above all to show the effects of war and fascism on the powerless, particularly impoverished women and children. But she is a warmhearted and enchanting storyteller; again and again we are reminded that human beings, undeniably capable of every sort of cruelty and depravity, are also capable — even in the worst of times — of poetry, and of selfless love.

SIGRID NUNEZ

Sigrid Nunez is the author of five novels, including A Feather on the Breath of God, For Rouenna, and The Last of Her Kind. She has received fellowships in fiction from both the American Academy in Rome and the American Academy in Berlin.

Hollywood Director

By David Chierichetti

1973

My appreciation for David Chierichetti's *Hollywood Director* as a great but little-known book is twofold, because not only is it underappreciated but so is its subject, Mitchell Leisen. Though he first established himself as an art director and costume designer, Leisen went on to direct some exquisite films during Hollywood's Golden Age, such as the screwball gem *Midnight* and the period bonbon *Kitty*, plus some extraordinary performances, notably Barbara Stanwyck in *Remember the Night* and Charles Boyer in *Hold Back the Dawn*. This richly detailed film-by-film analysis operates as a fascinating look at the inner workings of the studio system, as well as a passionate critical study of Leisen's output. Not only that, but Chierichetti includes his own interviews with Leisen and many of the films' stars. The book is further distinguished by many rare behind-the-scenes photographs of people like Lombard and Dietrich that are absolute treasures. Leisen designed for Cecil B. DeMille, directed scripts by Billy Wilder and Preston Sturges, and guided Olivia de Havilland to her first Oscar, for *To Each His Own*. It's a career and an oeuvre that merit a book as celebratory as this one. Chierichetti's unmistakable love of Leisen's work—and overall admiration for the man—is infectious, making for an inspiring reading experience and an invaluable look at the creation of some genuine movie magic. Leisen—and Chierichetti's book about him—deserves any film lover's attention.

JOHN DILEO

John DiLeo is the author of And You Thought You Knew Classic Movies, 100 Great Film Performances You Should Remember But Probably Don't, and Screen Savers: 40 Remarkable Movies Awaiting Rediscovery.

The Vicarious Chef

Home Cooking
By Laurie Colwin
1988

More Home Cooking
By Laurie Colwin
1993

It's not primarily professionals, or ordinary cooks, or even people who like to eat who relish the late Laurie Colwin's collected food columns, done originally for *Gourmet*. It is people who like to read, and to feel the human contact that's possible between writer and reader.

Colwin died unexpectedly in 1992, at the age of 48. Most of her readers considered her their personal friend.

Although they didn't really know her, they found her voice—in all of her publications—comforting, encouraging, and friendly, tough but easygoing. She was everyone's ideal sister, chum, and Dutch aunt, all rolled into one.

Colwin makes cooking seem like the easiest thing in the world. While often her recipes are somewhat imprecise, the stories attached to them help one realize that all cooks make mistakes and that the best of them improvise and experiment, that they are just human beings like the rest of us. A really bad meal gives you fodder for writing, or at least for storytelling. Cooking, she insists, is like falling in love: you do not have to be rich or famous or smart do it. You just need the desire. She reminds us that having bad equipment, and working in what amounts to no kitchen at all (see "Alone in the Kitchen with an Eggplant," about her first studio apartment in Greenwich Village), should not deter you from feeding yourself or others. And her common sense tells us something we already knew: when you are invited to someone's house for dinner, you must reciprocate. Perfect one or two dishes, and invite people back. Then, learn one or two more things, and, voilà! You have a social life. Colwin's writing offers lessons in good manners and civility, as well as practical advice and reassurance.

Even a non-cook can cozy up with these wonderful essays, as with a warm cup of tea on a cold winter afternoon, because their style is so delicious and comforting. As you read (about Boston brown bread, lemon rice pudding, or shepherd's pie for 150 people), you say to yourself, "Oh, I could do this," even though you know you probably won't. The reason for her appeal is that Colwin writes engagingly. Good writing is something that makes us interested in a subject that we normally have no interest in. Reading *Home Cooking*, I become, if just for a moment, a foodie.

Two signs of Colwin's literary worth are, first, that her books are still in print, and, second, that many of her readers still think of her in the present tense. When I get around to discussing recipes, I always say, "Well, Laurie says to do it this way." I can hear her voice coming from the pages of her books.

The last entry in the posthumously published *More Home Cooking* reprints a talk Laurie gave to the Radcliffe

Culinary Friends, on May 17, 1992, five months before her death. She adapts Dr. Spock's sage advice at the beginning of *Baby and Child Care* ("Trust yourself") to the art of cooking: "You just have to relax. I assure you that if you keep it simple, everything will turn out just fine." This is excellent advice for life outside the kitchen as well. Not for nothing was Colwin's most successful novel titled *Happy All the Time.*

WILLARD SPIEGELMAN

Bio on p. 153

The Hooligan's Return

By Norman Manea

2003

Norman Manea is a Jewish Romanian writer born in the late 1930s who, despite a miserable existence under Communism, resisted leaving Romania for decades, a struggle he describes in this harrowed, neurotic, nauseated memoir that paradoxically provides a good starting point for his novels and stories. Anyone who feels that too much contemporary fiction is under-fictionalized (what might as well be thinly disguised autobiography written by people whose lives are uninterestingly familiar) should read Manea. His fiction takes place in a world so disorienting and sparsely sketched that it induces a kind of vertigo where you cannot find your feet and it's often difficult to figure out just what's going on. Characters are vaguely identified and emerge from indistinct situations (the test, the fear, the failure, the disaster). They are frail, thin-sapped creatures who move about their indefinite world like somnambulists—so tired as to be nearly unconscious, or dreaming bewildering dreams (perhaps no other writer's protagonists spend so much time asleep).

Despite the unreality of his fiction, there is nothing magical about it—his stories are about life in Communist Romania. But nor is *The Hooligan's Return* strictly a memoir; it is life twisted and tugged and drawn out into wiry words.

LARISSA MACFARQUHAR

Larissa MacFarquhar is a staff writer at The New Yorker, where she has written profiles of John Ashbery, Noam Chomsky, and Barack Obama, among others. Previously she was a senior editor at Lingua Franca and an advisory editor at The Paris Review.

Hula

By Lisa Shea

1994

The epigraph of Lisa Shea's celebrated but now neglected first and only novel is from a Jorie Graham poem:

> *Nothing will catch you.*
> *Nothing will let you go.*

In its ambiguity, it's the perfect introduction to the work that follows. "Nothing will catch you": is that comfort or torment? "Nothing will let you go": is that to be celebrated or lamented? A source of solace or fear?

Hula is the kind of book that reminds us of the possibilities of the unknown even as it depicts its often terrible consequences. It concerns itself with two sisters in Virginia over the course of two summers in the 1960s. The younger girl describes life with her older sister, her largely absent mother, her tormented father.

One of the challenges of writing from a child's point of view is the problem of rendering the variety and depths of a child's emotional understanding despite the limitations of her descriptive abilities. *Hula*'s unnamed narrator offers us almost no introspection at all. In its place, she gives us what children can: sharp and evocative perceptions. It's up to us, her only audience and the people responsible for the most attention this girl gets, to tell what all these perceptions mean.

Hula is a book that suggests in clear ways why, despite its many obvious potential pitfalls, so many writers return to childhood in their work. Childhood is a strange and mysterious place. It's ambiguous, and the ambiguous is always a useful place for literature to settle itself. It's a place of lush imagination and stark fears. The strange becomes the everyday. The routine becomes oddly disorienting.

The writer Steven Millhauser has said, "I want fiction to exhilarate me, to unbind my eyes, to murder and resurrect me, to harm me in some fruitful way." I think of this when I think of how our childhoods continue to work on us. I think of this when I read *Hula* and how it continues, year after year, to work on me. "Nothing will catch you. / Nothing will let you go." Equal parts murder and resurrection. Lucky for us.

KAREN SHEPARD

Karen Shepard is the author of three novels: An Empire of Women, The Bad Boy's Wife, and Don't I Know You? She teaches writing and literature at Williams College, in Williamstown, Massachusetts.

The Human Predicament

By Richard Hughes

1961; 1973

For a maverick adolescent at a North Wales boarding school, books were both an escape and a salvation. My reading was defined by the dictates of the syllabus, the

established literary canon, and self-important borrow-
ings from my mother's shelves.

While the world of fiction was vivid to me, that of
writing was remote (although I was vaguely aware that
an old woman who lived close to my uncle in France
had kept house for a famous novelist called Proust).
Then, one day, my form master announced that, as a
change from the usual run of mountaineers and
sportsmen, he had invited the novelist Richard Hughes
to come to talk.

The audience was shamefully small, but Hughes
seemed to be unconcerned. We knew him solely from
A High Wind in Jamaica, but any hope that he would
resemble one of his pirates was dashed by the soft-
spoken, silver-haired, clerical-looking gentleman in
our midst.

Rather than regaling us with tales of adventure on
the high seas, he read from a work in progress, *The
Wooden Shepherdess*, the second of a proposed
three- or four-volume novel of the 1920s and '30s that
mixed fictional and historical characters under the
collective title *The Human Predicament*.

The reading was spellbinding, but what impressed
me most was Hughes's acceptance that, as a painfully
slow writer in his seventies, he would never live to
complete his project (thus giving me the first intimation
that the process of writing could be as meaningful as
the product), and the extraordinary humility with which
he asked his callow audience to criticize the extract.

He put forward the view, which I've sought to
embody in my own work, that the novel should be a
vehicle for moral and philosophical exploration. As I
read and reread *The Wooden Shepherdess* and its
precursor, *The Fox in the Attic*, I delight in the mixture

of richly drawn characters from across the social scale (Hughes's ear for the speech of country-house servants is matched only by that of Henry Green); the delicate painting of the English, Welsh, Bavarian, and American landscapes; and the nuanced social comedy (Gladstone's glazed face at the bottom of a Tory landowner's commode).

Above all, however, I relish Hughes's ambition in grappling with what he described as "the pattern of man's relationships with man . . . the one thing specifically human in humanity" by setting the aimless young Anglo-Welsh squire, Augustine, and the emerging demagogue, Hitler, as the twin poles of the work.

I was lucky to have the privilege of meeting Hughes and reading his books at a decisive moment of my life. Other writers may have influenced me more (that famous French novelist, for one), but none has so inspired me with his vision of a writer's calling. "Do your bit to save humanity from lapsing back into barbarity by reading all the novels you can," he advised on his seventy-fifth birthday. Make certain to include his.

MICHAEL ARDITTI

Michael Arditti is a novelist, playwright, and critic. His fiction includes The Celibate, Pagan and Her Parents, Easter, Unity, Good Clean Fun, A Sea Change, *and* The Enemy of the Good.

I—J

Il Nocchiero

Paola Capriolo

1989

In English, this Italian novel would be titled *The Helmsman*. It presents an unusual case: although no translation exists, it actually has been translated. Soon after its appearance in Italy, HarperCollins bought the English rights and commissioned a translation from William Weaver, the doyen of Anglophone translators of Italian fiction. Weaver duly delivered his manuscript, which was scheduled for publication in 1991. But his editor departed in a financial reorganization, and the manuscript vanished. Not even the translator retained a copy. The only trace is an ISBN number—evidence of a book that never was.

This mystery weirdly suits Paola Capriolo's narrative, which unfolds rapidly with enigmatic suspense. One evening Walter, a ferry pilot who customarily enjoys the sunset in the terrazza café of the Hotel Excelsior, sees a woman's arm stretching over a nearby table. Her figure is hidden so that Walter can glimpse only her bare arm, the wrist "girded by a long spiral of smooth silver that recalled a serpent." Momentarily distracted by the lighting of a lamp, he again looks in her direction, but she has disappeared. The scenario is repeated the next evening; on the third night, the woman misses their mute rendezvous. Walter's fascination drives him to make inquiries, and he discovers that she is a foreigner called Carmen, occasionally escorted by a gentleman. Once more Walter spots the silver-braceleted arm, yet when he approaches, he is disconcerted: the woman speaks his language like a native and introduces herself as Linda.

The question of Linda's identity is never definitively settled. Capriolo uses it to show how Walter's growing obsession shapes its own object. In his view, the woman's bracelet is "the symbol of a slavery that aroused in him at once a singular attraction and the desire to abolish it, to liberate her." His ambivalence is dramatized in conversations with two friends, both also named Walter, one a skeptical "student of physics," the other a mystical "cultivator of theosophical speculations." Walter ultimately marries Linda, but their intimacy does not resolve his uncertainty. "She was a beautiful, inexpressive mask," he observes, "behind which shone the ambiguous image of Carmen." As they settle into household routines, Linda becomes withdrawn, her thoughts inscrutable, and Walter considers his marriage "a crime, if not against Linda, then against the idea of beauty that she represented."

Capriolo links Walter's quandary to dissatisfaction with work. After his father's death, he had to "abandon his studies and accept employment as a pilot, so inferior to his ambitions." In the employ of "the Company," he nightly transports unknown cargo to "the Island" whereon "the Villa," a once magnificently appointed mansion, lies in shuttered disrepair. The two Walters dub him the "'helmsman,' not without irony, alluding to the mythic creature who ferried the souls of the deceased over the Stygian waters." The irony is not lost on Walter. "To work for the Company was fine and honorable," he thinks, whereas "to work for the old Captain," the rotund, good-natured superior who "at the slightest pretext rudely slapped him on the

back," seemed "a degradation." Walter's self-impor-
tance induces the worry that "his job could transform
him into a figure like the Captain, whose presence
would have been inconceivable on the white terrazza of
the Excelsior."

Unable to reconcile alluring romance with workaday
domesticity, Walter unravels. He meets the Count, the
Villa's former proprietor, whom Walter assumes to be
Carmen's escort and the key to the murky dealings on
the island. The nobleman refuses to get involved,
however, declaring with sinister resignation, "I prefer
to remember." One night, sensing the "absurdity" of
his situation, Walter is alarmed by sounds coming
from the hold. "Now they seemed like animal cries,
now human laments uttered in an unknown language,
now both in an appalling, incomprehensible union."
He identifies a woman's voice as Carmen's and helps
her to the deck, handing her the jackknife that Linda
once packed for him in a basket of fruit. The final
scene is set with luggage, boxes, and an ancient canvas
depicting Cupid and Psyche, a wedding gift that
Walter had chosen from the Company's lavish
warehouse but failed to interpret so as to avoid his
impending tragedy.

Part medieval morality play, part Kafkaesque
fantasy, *The Helmsman* spins an existential tale in
hauntingly evocative prose. Capriolo has crafted a
uniquely sophisticated page-turner that explores the
vagaries of desire as the fragile basis of identity. "With
the Villa, the island, the woman with the silver
bracelet," Walter realizes too late, "he could not get his
mental bearings, inhabited by images that eluded his
grasp." Unfortunately, the puzzling disappearance of

Weaver's translation puts readers in a similar relation to this subtle yet compelling novel.

LAWRENCE VENUTI

Lawrence Venuti is a translation theorist and historian, as well as a translator from the Italian, French, and Catalan. He is the author of The Translator's Invisibility and The Scandals of Translation. His reviews of foreign fiction have appeared in such periodicals as The New York Times and the Times Literary Supplement.

The Inhuman Land

By Józef Czapski

1949

The Polish journalist, painter, and writer Józef Czapski (1896-1993) was a remarkable figure of his times. A pacifist, he volunteered for the Polish Army in 1920, fought against the Bolsheviks, and was awarded the Virtuti Militari, the highest Polish military decoration. An aristocrat who was educated in St. Petersburg and Paris, he was captured by the Russians and spent time in their prison and labor camps. Czapski became a fearless investigator of the Katyn massacre of thousands of Polish officers and soldiers in 1940, which he survived, and of similar crimes; he testified on the matter before the United States Congress. In exile, having not returned to Communist Poland after World War II, Czapski co-founded the Instytut Literacki (Literary Institute) and the influential Polish émigré monthly *Kultura* (*Culture*) in Paris. And he never stopped painting and writing. A memoir of Czapski's incarceration in Soviet camps and a firsthand account of his negotiations on behalf of the Polish government with the Russians over their Polish captives, the book became an important document for establishing a record of the atrocities that followed the Soviets' 1939 invasion of Poland. It would be naïve not to notice that Czapski's title *The Inhuman Land* to some extent refers to Russia, or at the very least, the Russian/Soviet Empire. No doubt the horrors Czapski describes—for example, the ways in which people were tortured by the Soviet secret police in the infamous Lubyanka prison—are nothing but the continuation of the centuries-old struggle between Poland and her more powerful neighbor; he even uses the term "concentration camps" to recollect the fate of the eighteenth-century Polish insurgents, and maybe rightly so: "Xavier Kozicki . . . and five of his companions were stripped naked and given 800 blows with the knout, after which they had their nostrils torn off, and the mark of a gibbet branded with a hot iron on their foreheads."

The book can hardly be called a comprehensive picture of its era, one of the most tragic and controversial periods in Eastern European history; after all, the author was in charge of the Army Propaganda Service, under the command of General Anders. Rather, it is moving, highly personal, and subjective, an honest and passionate eyewitness tale devoted to the Polish national cause yet willing to admit to and even admire the richness of Russian culture. Czapski sympathizes with all victims of the war and of the inhuman Soviet regime, sometimes slipping into simplification but never into dull anger or hatred. As seen by this attentive and unyielding foreigner, it's also a perfect— and necessary—antidote to the official Russian version of history, described in merciless detail with a firm and unforgiving attitude: "Henri Zoltowski was arrested as a delegate of the Polish Embassy, and died in prison.

The parcels of food which his wife and children sent to him, and which they had got together by dint of selling everything they had, were still being accepted eagerly by the prison authorities more than two months after his death." The moral strength of the book lies in the fact that Czapski speaks about, and on behalf of, the silenced victims and survivors whose voices were all too often ignored in the West for a variety of political reasons, if not for pure convenience. As Edward Crankshaw ironically writes in his foreword, "the weak may no longer give evidence against the strong."

Czapski also witnessed the intimidation that the Soviet regime imposed upon its own people. A heartbreaking statement of not just Polish but Eastern European tragedy, *The Inhuman Land* is also a wonderful testimony of human spiritual resistance. Having described an eight-year-old Polish boy, Michel, who raised his arm before Stalin's picture and "shook his little fist at him" (though the boy risked being seen and punished by officials), Czapski quotes a woman who was "by no means surprised. 'It's always the same with the children. What's Stalin given these poor kids? — hunger and poverty. In the *kolkhoze* [so-called collective farms] where I was, every time they passed Stalin's portrait, they stuck out their tongues at him or shook their fists: some even spat. There was no way of stopping them.'

"The picture of that small fist raised against the all-powerful dictator is the last impression I took with me on leaving the Soviet Union."

Ekaterina Kozitskaia Fleishman

Ekaterina Kozitskaia Fleishman is the author of more than thirty scholarly works, including a book on intertextuality in Russian poetry and essays on Joseph Brodsky, late Soviet and post-Soviet culture, Russian rock, East European literature and history, and Jewry in the Slavic world.

Into Their Labours: A Trilogy *(Pig Earth, 1979; Once in Europa, 1983; Lilac and Flag, 1990)*

By John Berger

1991

John Berger is best known—in the United States, at least—for his seminal book on visual art, *Ways of Seeing*. But less known are his many novels, which include *To the Wedding*, *A Painter of Our Time*, and *G* (which won the 1972 Booker prize). Berger defies easy definition; he's a novelist, essayist, storyteller, art historian, critic, and dramatist. Trained as a painter, he distills his disparate passions—and his politics—into the philter of everything he writes.

My personal favorite is Berger's trilogy *Into Their Labours*. Each book in the trilogy stands on its own, but together the works create a gorgeous tapestry of interwoven narratives, characters, and lives. *Into Their Labours* tells the story of a mountain village in the French Alps and what happens to its inhabitants over the course of the twentieth century: how a rural peasant community breaks apart with modernization and migration to cities, and what becomes of the old traditions and how they remake themselves—or fail to—in the new cities of Europe. Berger's work has proven prescient about life in an increasingly globalized world, and the books seem as fresh today as they did when first published.

Into Their Labours concerns itself, appropriately, with work—how it is done and by whom. Each chapter offers the raw material of lives lived close to the land—blood and birthed calves, poppies and engine oil, slaughtered pigs and manure. Berger's characters are herders, butchers, street vendors, factory workers, policemen, immigrants, lovers, animals—and sometimes even the dead.

Berger's surname means "shepherd" in French, and in all his writings, he seems to have taken his namesake to heart. He gently guides his characters (and his readers) across the page; he treats them with such great tenderness and respect that one feels an odd religiosity and wonder—and love—emanating from his works. What makes Berger's characters so affecting is the voice he imbues them with, as if they were whispering directly into your ear. What they have to say is always worth listening to.

BRAD KESSLER

Brad Kessler is the author of the novel Birds in Fall and a memoir, Goat Song: A Seasonal Life, A Short History of Herding, and the Art of Making Cheese. He is the winner of the Dayton Literary Peace Prize, a Whiting Writer's Award, and the Rome Prize from the American Academy of Arts and Letters.

The Invention of Solitude
By Paul Auster
1982

Years ago, at a bookstore in Missouri, I asked an employee where to find J. D. Salinger's *Nine Stories*. I was directed to the checkout counter, behind which a shelf displayed the works of three authors: Salinger, Jack Kerouac, and Paul Auster. At first, I thought the unusual placement of these books was some kind of a promotion—an attempt to catch the attention of moody young men like myself—but the bookseller told me he had a different purpose: the store could no longer afford to keep these authors on the normal shelves, so often were they shoplifted. And so a young man seeking a book by Paul Auster had to ask for it, like a condom from a grocer's display case. Even before I opened my first Auster book, I was already a little in love with it. Like most, I began with Auster's *New York Trilogy* (*City of Glass*, *Ghosts*, *The Locked Room*), a series of sublimely disorienting, metaphysical mysteries built around noirish detective narratives. In those books, as in many of his others, Auster constructs an intricate fictional structure as a raft to allow our crossing to an otherworld—an ambiguous state between reality and fiction—where one must constantly question assumptions of authorship, the veracity of storytelling, and the limitations of language. In much of Auster's work, mystery and suspense arise as much from how the story is being told—who is telling it and how it should be understood—as from within the story itself.

In reading my way through Auster's work, I was surprised when I finally read his first book, *The Invention of Solitude*. Instead of courting narrative ambiguity and drawing attention to the story's fictional artifice, as he often does in later work, Auster begins this memoir with a self-consciously direct motive. Following the sudden death of his distant, obscure father, Auster says, "I knew that I would have to write about my father. . . . I thought: my father is gone. If I do not act quickly, his entire life will vanish along with him." Auster attempts to fulfill his earnest, straightforward mission in the book's first section, entitled "Portrait of an Invisible Man," a moving, stunning, and heartbreaking account of a son trying to rescue his father from oblivion by fixing his life into language. Auster begins this narrative with the belief that his "need to write" about his father is "so great" that the words will "come spontaneously, in a trancelike outpouring." Seeking the proper conduit to channel his story, Auster approaches his lost father every way he can: by recounting the chronology of his father's life, by describing the things his father left behind, by recalling his own interactions with his father, and, finally, by exploring his father's relationship with his own parents. In the process, Auster reveals a shocking family secret that perhaps casts a half-light onto his father's motives but ultimately fails to allow Auster to penetrate the mind of the obscure man. As Auster tells his story, he also tells of the telling of it, eventually admitting that "never before have I been so aware of the rift between thinking and writing" and wondering if "the story I am trying to tell is somehow incompatible with language."

In the book's second half, "The Book of Memory," Auster switches to other narrative forms, describing in the third person a fictional author very much like Auster himself, using the modes of philosophical discourse and literary theory to address questions of fate, chance, and the failures of language raised in the book's first half. In light of Auster's later work, this move in his first book from first person to third—from direct memoir to fiction and criticism—seems to take on larger implications, suggesting a motivating awareness behind the often metafictional, philosophical oeuvre that has followed. In trying and failing to locate and tell the full truth of his father, Auster explores the other truth he discovers in its place—a truth he has continued to confront, again and again, in so many of his strange, challenging, beautiful books: the impossible complexity of trying to transform life into words.

STEFAN MERRILL BLOCK

Stefan Merrill Block's first novel, The Story of Forgetting, *was published in 2008.*

Inventor of the Disposable Culture: King Camp Gillette, 1855–1932, by Tim Dowling

see p. 106

Joe the Engineer

By Chuck Wachtel

1983

Near the beginning of Chuck Wachtel's novel *Joe the Engineer*, Joe and his wife, Rosie, are watching *Bowling for Dollars* while eating dinner in the living room of their apartment in Woodside, Queens. They're discussing the corn on the cob that Rosie's sister bought on a trip to New Jersey. They know the corn is supposed to be *better*, somehow, than the corn they're used to, but Joe—on his third ear—doesn't think so. "It tastes just like the kind ya get in the A&P except the rows are all uneven and some of the kernels are white," he says. Then he hears the sound of someone sawing wood in a yard outside. "'Listen,'" Joe says to Rosie. "'*Testa di minghia, testa di minghia, testa di minghia . . .*'"

Joe the Engineer is Sicilian—his given name is Joe Lazaro—and *testa di minghia* is a Sicilian obscenity which for the purposes of this piece will be translated as "dickhead." It's "a phrase Joe learned at the age of five," Wachtel writes, "watching his father saw the boards that would become the bunk beds he and his brother were to share. His father asked him if he

understood what the saw was saying and Joe said, no,
he didn't understand and his father said, listen. . . . "
So his father says it again and again, *testa di minghia*,
testa di minghia, "with each rip of the saw, and soon
Joe heard it too. *Testa di minghia*. 'This is what it's
tellin ya,' his father said. 'If ya stupid enough to do shit
work for a livin' you're a *testa di minghia*.' "

Suffice it to say that Joe does shit work for a living.
Suffice it to say that he's not really an engineer. He "got
the name in high school when he decided that an
engineer was what he wanted to be. He made the
decision suddenly one night while reading Thomas
Hardy's *The Return of the Native* for an English class
and had come across the word 'engender.' He had no
idea what it meant, so he looked it up in the dictionary.
The definitions offered were 'to beget; to produce; to
cause to exist.' Having even less grasp on the word
than before he looked it up, he lost interest. His eyes
glided down the page and landed on 'engineer' . . . And
that was it. This he had use for. Simple. A definition he
could put on like a uniform."

Well, Joe realizes part of his dream, anyway. He
puts on a uniform to go to work. But the uniforms he
and his partner wear are "dark green shirts with the
letters B/Q in two-chambered patches over the left
breast pockets"—B/Q, as in Brooklyn/Queens, as in
Brooklyn/Queens Water Resources, which employs Joe
as a meter reader. His partner? Joe Flushing Avenue, a
fat ignoramus who just wants Joe the Engineer to *talk*
to him, or at least listen to his stories of sexual
conquest. And when Joe the Engineer doesn't, Joe
Flushing Avenue "takes the silence personally." At the
end of the first chapter, he gives his standard speech to
Joe the Engineer—or what passes for a speech in a

book devoid of speechifying—and somehow manages to pose the question that Joe will spend the next two hundred or so pages having to answer: "Look. It's a job. Ya get a check every week. Ya got a TV, an air conditioner, money in ya pocket. That ain't enough? Ya think ya shit don't stink?"

Suffice it to say that it ain't enough. Nothing is, and Joe can't even begin to imagine, much less articulate, what might be. Joe is the kind of man who always wants to be doing something other than what he's doing, and who always wants to be somewhere other than where he is. And yet when he's asked—usually by Rosie—if he wants to go somewhere outside the neighborhood, or do something besides watch TV and drink beers with Joe Flushing Avenue, whom he loathes, he has the same answer: "Nah." He's twenty-seven years old, a Vietnam vet, and he is at once terrified and comforted by his suspicion that not only has he proven himself insufficient to life's demands but that life has proven itself insufficient to his. And so the novel that bears his name is animated not by plot but by a sense of *wanting* that's as keen as it is inchoate. It proceeds almost like a science project, with Joe—more of an engineer, or at least more of an empiricist, than he gives himself credit for being—testing the life that's supposed to be better than his life with Rosie, Joe Flushing Avenue, and his shit job, and then wondering whether he has failed it, or it has failed him. The corn from New Jersey is no better than the corn from the A&P. The college-educated couple befriended by Rosie turn out to be striving snobs. The middle-aged woman with whom he has a desperate one-night stand wants him to stay with her for a few minutes after he "rips off his piece," and he flees. The young supermarket checkout girl Joe undresses on a handball court in the consuming darkness of a blackout insists on reciting her poetry to him. He flees from her, too. He doesn't know anything except what he does know, and what he does know is the sound that the saw makes. And as much as he tries to un-know it, to un-hear it, he can't, because it's privileged information. It's the whisper of the world, and the measure by which the world is found wanting.

If *Joe the Engineer* sounds in any way reductive, be assured that it's not—no novel is reductive whose headlong present-tense sentences disclose nothing and everything, slide easily from confusion to confusion, and nag like a toothache. No, what makes *Joe* feel almost foreign years after it was published is that it belongs to a genre that simply doesn't exist anymore— the novel of working-class complaint. Long before the people Chuck Wachtel writes about in *Joe* were wiped off the map economically, they were wiped off the map culturally, and so *Joe* stands as a kind of relic, a novel of the kind nobody writes anymore. Sure, there are the hipster-proletariat novels that Richard Price was writing before he left the Bronx, but from the very start Price's novels wanted more, in literary terms, than Chuck Wachtel will allow *Joe the Engineer* or anyone in it, particularly Joe himself. Indeed, what's striking about Joe is that it's a novel of manners among the unmannered; it's an economical novel before minimal- ism turned economy into gesture; it's an urban novel before Don DeLillo imparted an oracular obligation upon urban novels. It takes place in the summer of 1977: the Summer of Sam, the summer of the blackout, the summer the Bronx burned. But where most writers and filmmakers mine that material for inklings of apocalypse, Wachtel exploits it as merely another annoyance. "Son a Sam?" He's just something and somebody else that Joe can't figure out.

Joe was twenty-seven in the summer of 1977. I was nineteen. I was twenty-five when I first read *Joe the Engineer*, and it was the first novel I ever read where people talked exactly like the people I knew growing up on Long Island, and where the main character's answer to nearly everything was a shrug of refusal—a nasally "nah" coiled in my own DNA. I was not working-class, but my father, a Brooklynite who never graduated from high school, he knew what the saw said. We all did. I came upon the world of Joe the Engineer not only with an odd sense of recognition but of reluctant arrival. I read it with a friend who has since put together a life with his talent for working with his hands. To this day, if you ask him what the saw says, he, like me, will tell you right away: "*Testa di minghia.*" Once you hear it, you see, you're a little like Joe himself, and once you read *Joe the Engineer* you hear it for good.

Tom Junod

Tom Junod has been a writer-at-large for Esquire since 1997. He has received two National Magazine Awards and has been a finalist for nine others. His 2003 story "The Falling Man" was recently named one of the seven best stories in Esquire's seventy-five-year history.

K

Kabloona

By Gontran de Poncins

1941

In and out of print since it was first published, *Kabloona* describes the fifteen-month, twenty-thousand-mile journey that its author, France's Gontran de Poncins, made to the Eskimo lands near the North Pole. A viscount and descendant of Montaigne, de Poncins had become, according to notes in the Book-of-the-Month Club edition, disenchanted with "the selfishness of our world, the ungenerosity of man to man," and had taken to wandering in places like China, India, and the South Seas to see if he could discover any alternative. "Surely of all things in the world the rarest is a civilized man at peace with himself," de Poncins wrote with typical acuity in the preface to *Kabloona*. His trip to the far north was an attempt to see if that barren area could in some way provide the contentment he sought.

Open to experience rather than threatened by it, willing to let things happen and able to convivially describe them when they do, de Poncins extends a pleasing and profound sympathy to the Eskimo as he develops an understanding of their communal way of life. "The important thing was hospitality, ownership was nothing," he discovered. "Human life in the Arctic would vanish without this solidarity among men. It is the community that remains alive here, not the men."

De Poncins's admirable character makes *Kabloona* the singular adventure it is. Almost majestic in his ability to see himself as he is seen by others—the book's title comes from the derogatory Eskimo term for white man—de Poncins produced a book that is disarming and enchanting in its insights and poetic honesty. "In this Arctic have I found my peace, the peace I was never able to find Outside," he wrote. "Outside it wanted war and flood to give man this sense of brotherhood; here it was a commonplace of life." To read this memoir is to be grateful that Gontran de Poncins left a record of his journey, fresh as the instant he wrote it, for us to savor and pass along.

KENNETH TURAN

Kenneth Turan is film critic for the Los Angeles Times, director of the Times Book Prizes, and film critic for National Public Radio's Morning Edition. He is on the board of directors of the National Yiddish Book Center, and his other books include Sundance to Sarajevo: Film Festivals and the World They Made, and Never Coming to a Theater Near You: A Celebration of a Certain Kind of Movie.

Kaputt: A Novel

By Curzio Malaparte

Translated from the Italian by Cesare Foligno

1944

Ever since I first read *Kaputt*, I have been tormented by Curzio Malaparte's description of meeting Ante Pavelić, the Croatian Fascist leader in World War II. The Italian war reporter noticed a wicker basket on Pavelić's desk that seemed to be filled with shelled oysters "as they are occasionally displayed in the windows of Fortnum and Mason in Piccadilly in London." He politely inquired if the oysters came from the Dalmatian coast. "It's a present from my loyal ustashis," Pavelić replied. "Forty pounds of human eyes."

Malaparte (whose nom de plume was a play on "Bonaparte") was, as we might say today, "embedded" with the Nazis. As a correspondent for Italy's *Corriere della Sera*, he was able to tour the Eastern Front behind Axis lines. From this vantage, he recounts the casual, even flippant, brutality of the German war machine. The book is filled with the horrifying, indeed surreal, images of the war: half-buried bodies with their outstretched arms serving as signposts; German soldiers laughing at their starving Russian prisoners feasting on fellow inmates in order to survive; Jews strung up on trees next to their dogs (their "Jewish dogs").

Published in Naples in 1944, *Kaputt* was a sensation at the end of World War II. I own a ragged English-language paperback from that time that boasts "over a million copies sold." But the book was carefully subtitled "A Novel," making it a profoundly troublesome work. Malaparte, as we know from his newspaper reports, actually did meet Pavelić. But the anecdote about the eyeballs (still a staple of Serb propaganda) is likely hyperbole. Other key episodes of the book were also invented. He never did, apparently, tour the Warsaw Ghetto in his Italian officer's uniform and console the suffering Jews by telling them in French that "*un jour vous serez libres, vous serez heureux et libres*" (one day, you will be free, you will be happy and free). You have to wonder about the sort of person who would make that up.

The book, assembled from a smuggled manuscript, is an irreplaceable artifact of World War II. Not only was Malaparte an eyewitness to a morbid culture, he was also a product of it—a mercurial personality with a talent for reinventing himself. An early Italian Fascist—later expelled from the party and banished by

Mussolini to the island of Lipari—he was a Communist at the end of his life (and is perhaps best remembered today for Casa Malaparte, the house he built on Capri that was featured in Godard's *Contempt*). There are questions about whether he rewrote parts of *Kaputt* when it became clear that the Allies would win the war.

For a journalist, the fascination of the book lies in how the blending of fact and fiction yields such a powerful and enduring result. (In this, he is a precursor of that other great war reporter Ryszard Kapuscinski.) For, despite being an unreliable and self-aggrandizing narrator, he captured the perverse imagination and aesthetics of that broken world. In one of his central insights, he writes of the Germans: "Their cruelty is made of fear; they are ill with fear."

JAMES BONE

James Bone, the longtime New York correspondent for the Times (London), is a former war reporter who has covered conflicts in Afghanistan, Haiti, Iran, Nicaragua, Northern Ireland, and Panama, as well as the 9/11 attack on New York. His great-grandfather was Britain's first official war artist.

The Key

By Junichiro Tanizaki
1956

The way I came upon this erotic novella is as memorable to me as the book itself. I was in my mid-twenties and visiting my father in Salt Lake City. We were wandering through a favorite bookstore when he pulled the book from a shelf; he looked at it for a moment, and then in his slow, quiet tone told me that I should read it. I examined the cover—a line drawing of a naked Japanese girl with long dark straight hair draped carefully over her breasts. It seemed so exotic to read a sexy Japanese novella in the midst of a Mormon Mecca.

The juxtaposition of the intimacy and quiet voyeurism explored in Tanizaki's *The Key*, mixed with the mysterious traditions and exclusivity of the Mormon faith, made me feel like the ultimate outsider, the true observer, a voyeur, both in the city I was exploring and the book I was reading.

As I delved into its pages, I was quickly taken with the simplicity of the prose and structure of the novella. The book is told in the form of parallel diaries. The story follows the dissolution of a thirty-year marriage. The wife is no longer sexually interested in her husband, so he concocts a plan to both arouse her and himself: to bring a lover into their lives. The lover satisfies her physically, while the husband experiences his erotic pleasure through his voyeurism and as the instigator of the affair.

The husband and wife record their exploits of the previous evening in their dairies. As they record them, each suspects the other of reading the entries; the intimacies they convey in their respective diaries appear to be intended for the eyes of the other, though neither will confess that this is the case.

To read *The Key* is to be involved in an erotic fantasy—you're watching two people make love, you're going through their lingerie and their love letters, and eavesdropping on their secret conversations. You can't resist; you're on the outside, but never has the outside felt so intimate.

JESSICA STRAND

Jessica Strand has written on food and lifestyle for numerous publications. She's also written eight books on entertaining: five cookbooks, two cocktail books, and a design book for kids. More recently, she has been researching and writing about the evolution of the women's movement in the years since the publication of Betty Friedan's The Feminine Mystique.

Kingdoms of Elfin

By Sylvia Townsend Warner

1977

As a kid I was never interested in elves and fairies and hobbits, never went near Tolkien or his kind. But in the 1970s, a friend turned me on to a remarkable series of stories by Sylvia Townsend Warner that ran in *The New Yorker* and which changed my thinking entirely. I knew Warner in her realist mode—she'd written "A Love Match," the most stunning story about incest I've ever encountered. (It's in her 1966 collection "Swans on a Summer River," and it's a classic.) But she worked in many modes, and in 1977, at the end of her long and prolific life, she collected sixteen of her singular stories about the world of fairies in *Kingdoms of Elfin*.

These tales are, by definition, fanciful, but there's nothing sugary or sentimental about Warner's brand of whimsy, nor is there an ounce of fat on her surgically precise prose. As she explains, with matter-of-fact assurance, "The various tribes of fairies are erroneously supposed to be immortal and very small. In fact, they are of smallish human stature and of ordinary human contrivance. They are born, and eventually die; but their longevity and their habit of remaining good-looking, slender and unimpaired till the hour of death have led to the Kingdom of Elfin being called the Land of the Ever-Young." These creatures can fly, but it's considered bad form among the aristocracy: only the servant class utilizes its wings. The fairies are invisible to human eyes, unless they choose otherwise. They don't cry, have no theology, have no sense of remorse, live underground, and have a habit of kidnapping human infants, whom they raise for amusement, leaving changelings in their place.

In the wonderful opening story, "The One and the Other," a mortal boy named Tiffany grows up to become the Queen of Elphane's lover. Another tribe, in Wales, has the power to move mountains—although the mountains always return to their former setting. These kingdoms (which are, in fact, all matriarchies, ruled by queens) are spread across Europe, from Germany and France—which has the most ornate, refined elfin court life—to Lapland and the Balkans, and the marked differences among the fairy tribes seem to mirror the differences in the human worlds above ground.

There's enormous wit here, and a sly sense of satire, but the stories defy easy categorization: a tale may start in a comic mode and take a savage and startling turn. Warner, in her impeccably well-mannered English way, was a deeply subversive writer, and her tales of the frivolous, playful, promiscuous, and ruthless elfin worlds force us to regard our own human realm from a bracingly fresh perspective. Not that there's anything the least bit didactic about these flights of very peculiar fancy. They create their own world, and the prose is its own reward. This is not a book that you devour in one sitting, or want to rush through to get to the end: the stories aren't very long, but they are so rich, so beautifully written, and so dense that you can only take them in one at a time, like a box of very dark and satisfying chocolates. The first bite is sweet, but the aftertaste can be wondrously tart, even bitter.

Perhaps the neglect that has befallen *Kingdoms of Elfin*, which was never released in paperback, is due to the misapprehension that a book about fairies must be written for children. This one is strictly for grown-ups.

DAVID ANSEN

David Ansen was Newsweek's movie critic from 1977 through 2008, and he continues to write about movies. He has written television documentaries on Groucho Marx, Bette Davis, Greta Garbo, and Elizabeth Taylor, and is a member of the New York Film Critics Circle, the National Society of Film Critics, and the Los Angeles Film Critics Association.

Kusamakura

By Natsume Soseki
1906

This is the book that made me want to become a professor of Japanese literature. Natsume Soseki (1867-1916) is that rare bird, a novelist who won both critical acclaim and mass popularity: for many years his face graced the one-thousand-yen note. When his works were first translated in the 1950s and '60s, he was presented to English-speaking readers as the last great psychological realist of the nineteenth century, the heir to Flaubert and Stendhal. But that view downplayed the great strangeness that warps all of Soseki's fiction. As this novella amply demonstrates, he is much closer to being the first great modernist author of the twentieth century, forebear to James Joyce, Lu Xun, and Virginia Woolf.

Here, Soseki employs Kafkaesque tactics. He ditches the standard language of realism for a craftier writing style that mixes classical and modern Japanese, not to mention Chinese. Moreover, he refracts our modern world through the prisms of classical and folk traditions—haiku, Chinese poetry, and ink-brush paintings, among others. A thirty-year-old painter flees the city for a rustic hot-spring inn, where he vows to become utterly nonhuman in his detachment. The first thing he does after making this resolve, though, is trip over a rock, and his adventures have only begun. Alternately funny, philosophical, sexy, and poetic, the story is written in something close to stream-of-consciousness mode. Nothing much happens. Yet everywhere seemingly tranquil surfaces throb with pent-up tectonic tension, and war and death hover constantly just offstage. We encounter a remarkable metafictional lecture on how to read novels, one that anticipates William S. Burroughs's experiments with cut-up prose (the narrator himself cites Lawrence Sterne's *Tristam Shandy*), and we receive a rather dubious explanation of how a painter chooses his subject matter. We also meet the mysterious Nami, a beauty with a knack for unnerving the hero whenever he seems about to regain his tranquil poise. She is unmistakably doomed—but to what?

There are two widely available translations of what Soseki called his "haiku novel": Alan Turney's 1965 version, titled *The Three-Cornered World*, and Meredith McKinney's 2008 rendering, which retains the original Japanese title (a poetic phrase borrowed from haiku meaning "grass pillow," that is, to sleep in the open air while on a journey). Both are excellent;

McKinney skillfully mirrors the texture of Soseki's original language, while Turney captures the overall spirit of the work in sparkling English prose.

MICHAEL BOURDAGHS

Michael Bourdaghs teaches modern Japanese literature and culture at the University of Chicago. He is the author of The Dawn That Never Comes: Shimazaki Toson and Japanese Nationalism. His short stories have appeared in many literary journals, including Avery Anthology.

L

The Last Time I Saw Paris

By Elliot Paul

1942

I was still in high school when Elliot Paul's *The Last Time I Saw Paris* was published, and I read it immediately. It was a detailed portrait of life on the rue de la Huchette, which Paul stumbled onto in 1923 and continued to live on or visit for almost two decades. Affectionate without being sentimental, he identifies the shopkeepers, the hoteliers and their customers ("one weirdly assorted family"), minor officials, priests, the girls in the brothel, workers, and drones—all of whom were articulate and opinionated. It was a Paris to be envied. When I came back to the book, as I often did, I discovered that it was not so much the picture of a community as of the loss of one. The richness of the '20s collapsed in the '30s when the larger political world intruded—the Spanish Civil War, the defeat of the Popular Front by Rightists, the appeasement of Hitler and Mussolini—and old differences turned lethal, lives were lost, families split, businesses collapsed. The book ends as the Nazis march into Paris. The last words belong to Hyacinthe Goujon, whom Paul and the readers met when she was a precise and precocious child, and who died with her mother and grandfather in a group suicide, leaving a last message for Elliot Paul: "I cannot be accused of self-destruction. It is not Hyacinthe who dies, but the life all around her."

GERALD WEALES

Gerald Weales is an octogenarian with a long memory. He is an emeritus professor of English at the University of Pennsylvania. A former drama critic for The Reporter and Commonweal, he is the author of many books on theater and film, as well as a novel and several children's books.

Forgotten Memoirs

Laughing Torso
By Nina Hamnett
1932

The Square Sun
By Stefan Knapp
1956

Artists' memoirs rarely provide insight into the creative process. Classics of the genre offer other pleasures: vignettes of notorious contemporaries, snapshots of a particular métier from a participant's point of view—in short, history at first hand. Both Nina Hamnett and Stefan Knapp had seen enough of life by early middle age to write a book about it. Their engrossing if neglected memoirs depict differently the effort to maintain equilibrium in a hostile world. The authors' circumstances differ wildly, but both books indelibly capture the tenor of their time and place.

Born in 1890 in Tenby, on the coast of Wales, Hamnett was trained at London's Slade School, and she first traveled to Paris when she was twenty-four. A lively lass, always up for a bit of fun, she quickly met the denizens of bohemian Montparnasse and joined their ranks with gusto. A model as well as a painter, Hamnett was also a sexual adventuress who became a minor celebrity in a milieu with no shortage of them. Amedeo Modigliani and Roger Fry painted her portrait; her book's title refers to a ten-inch-high marble based on her youthful, gamine frame, sculpted by Henri Gaudier-Brzeska in 1914 and now at the Tate.

A headlong rush through Hamnett's first forty-two years, *Laughing Torso* was a best-seller both in Britain and America. The reader would scarcely suspect that by the time it was published its author was well past her prime. Hamnett's flame burned brightly, but it had begun to flicker by 1925. In May of that year, Fry wrote to a friend: "What a collapse . . . she's suddenly become a coarse heavy middle-aged *rouée* and all the queer satyrlike oddity and grace of her is gone forever. She's quite repulsive." Her book limns a hardscrabble existence kept afloat on rivers of booze, but it glosses over such nettlesome autobiographical details as her many simultaneous affairs and her bisexuality. Scant mention is made of the author's many exhibitions, both in Paris and London, before and after World War I. But their insouciance and what-the-devil indecorum make these reminiscences a propulsive, irresistible read.

Hamnett's voice is enchanting, dizzy, and deadpan, simultaneously self-effacing and in-your-face. Her tone veers from frenzy to ennui, matching Hemingwayesque affectlessness to borderline non sequiturs, and suggesting stream-of-consciousness recollections, lightly edited. Its rhythms are captivating. She recounts the embarrassment of running into acquaintances at the selling desk of the neighborhood pawnshop; she asks Aleister Crowley about his sexual encounter the previous evening; she teaches sea chanteys to Georges Auric, hoping that the composer might finally finish the third act of *Les Matelots*; she leads Satie's funeral procession. In print, Hamnett is a shameless name-dropper; the book's index references three hundred personages. "Joyce," she writes, "said I was one of the few vital women he had ever met. I don't know if that is true, but I have very big lungs and can make a great deal of noise if encouraged."

The book's photographs include a few of Hamnett, a beguiling woman with bobbed hair and a bemused yet alert expression. Her book ends with her return to London, where she fell into alcoholism and poverty, spending decades drinking at the Fitzroy Tavern. In 1956, she dropped forty feet from her apartment window (probably by accident), and she died from the resulting injuries a few days later.

Stefan Knapp's comparatively workmanlike autobiography, *The Square Sun*, was published the year of Hamnett's demise. The title refers to a different high window, in a cell in Kherson Prison, near Odessa, Ukraine. There Knapp spent three months in the fall of 1939, having been rounded up at the age of eighteen by Soviet soldiers who overran his Polish village. That incarceration was followed by two years in a Siberian labor camp, where endless toil was rewarded with black bread. Knapp's harrowing memoir of unimaginable hardship and hard-won subsistence was published seventeen years before Aleksandr Solzhenitsyn's *Gulag Archipelago*. The brutality of camp life seems to have stoked rather than sapped Knapp's creative drive, suggesting a common source in the will to survive.

Years later, Knapp would settle in London and become a painter and sculptor, working in a Cubist-Surrealist mode employing forms derived from the human figure. Known in the U.K. for public mural projects, he also traveled to the U.S., where his experimentation in large-scale enamel techniques led, in 1960, to what was then considered to be the world's largest painting, a 50' x 200' mural on the side of a (now demolished) department store in Paramus, New Jersey. That was a far cry from the pigments he had devised in the Kherson prison: red from blood, yellow from onions, blue from laundry soap.

Knapp was nothing if not resourceful. After being released from camp in 1941 and declared a Soviet citizen, he made his way across the frozen hinterland by train to Moscow in the uniform of the Red Army. Along the way, he ate roots and, when lucky, dogs. He crossed the Caspian Sea to Persia, where there was food but little soap, then shipped to Bombay, Cape Town, and, eventually, Glasgow. He joined the Royal Air Force and earned his wings in December 1943. By the following summer, the Allies had taken Naples, and Knapp found himself stationed there: "Famine or no famine, the Opera in Naples was excellent." Scenes from *Rigoletto* rang in his ears as he flew his Spitfire over German positions north of the city, shells exploding around him. For the sake of the war effort, Knapp was expected to stifle his ire at the British public for its naïve embrace of the dictator at whose command he and countless others had suffered so profoundly. But by then his antinationalist convictions were galvanized: "Flying taught me one thing: frontiers are fiction. The world is one from 40,000 feet. . . . It seems pretty futile to chop up the Alps and call one part one thing and another part something else. . . . How foolish, how petty to try and split the grain of the granite, to etch a line across the running waters, to clutch at one slanting ray and claim it as your own."

Both Hamnett and Knapp were capable if unremarkable artists, in step with the prevailing pictorial idiom of the day. Neither their work nor their memoirs are "timeless," but are very much products of the remarkable times they witnessed. Their writing crackles with keen observation and penetrating description borne of empathy with their surroundings. These books are vividly etched portraits—of the authors, and of their eras.

<small>STEPHEN MAINE</small>

Stephen Maine is a painter, an art critic, and a curator. A regular contributor to Art in America and artcritical.com, he has also written for Art on Paper, artnet.com, artecontexto, and The New York Sun. Maine teaches in the M.F.A. Fine Arts program at the School of Visual Arts in New York, and is a manager in the art department of the Strand Book Store.

Left Hand, Right Hand!

By Sir Osbert Sitwell

1945–50

Written somewhat in the manner of the *roman-fleuve* pioneered by Proust, Sir Osbert Sitwell's autobiography was very successful in its day, and published by Macmillan in five beautifully designed volumes as follows: *Left Hand, Right Hand!* (1945), *The Scarlet Tree* (1946), *Great Morning* (1948), *Laughter in the Next Room* (1949), and *Noble Essences* (1950). Sitwell may be said to have been privileged, not only as a member of the upper classes—with a stately home in Derbyshire and a castle near Florence—but also as a man whose life (1892–1969) moved from the country-side of nineteenth-century England, through Diaghilev, Picasso, and the beau monde, and into the Swinging

Sixties. He served in World War I, endured World War II, and (with his sister, Edith, and brother, Sacheverell) contributed a brilliant, rococo strain to the modern movement in English literature. He is interested in all human types and stations, but a droll twinkle is never far away. Expansive yet lean, graceful yet vivid and highly original, the result is the greatest English-language autobiography of the twentieth century—a wonderfully sustained and absorbing marvel of mandarin prose.

DUNCAN FALLOWELL

Duncan Fallowell is a novelist, travel writer, and cultural commentator. He has written novels (Satyrday, The Underbelly, and A History of Facelifting), travel books (To Noto and One Hot Summer in St. Petersburg), and the biography of a transsexual, April Ashley's Odyssey.

Le Peau de Chagrin

By Honoré de Balzac

1831

Though declared by Harold Bloom to be one of Balzac's eight canonical works, *Le Peau de Chagrin* (*The Wild Ass's Skin*) may be the novelist's least read masterpiece. For my own part, it's one of the top-ten best stories ever told. The book is packed with unforgettable set pieces, from the opening scene in the most sordid of Parisian gambling dens to a suicide that gets sidetracked by an encounter in a curiosity shop whose recesses, receding endlessly in room after room of increasing gloom, conceal a horde of lost art treasures (and, not incidentally, the talismanic skin of the title) to an all-night orgy featuring a bevy of the most infamous courtesans of the author's day—all this within the first third of the book. At less than three hundred pages, this may be the shortest, fastest-paced novel Balzac ever wrote, and surely the most fantastic. The protagonist of the tale is a young poet and scholar, Raphael de Valentin, driven to despair by his obsession with Fedora, "the woman without a heart," a society belle who ruins him to the point where he throws his last sou, and all his hopes, onto the roulette wheel. The book opens with a coat-checker crying, "Your hat sir, if you please!" The author observes that what one really checks at the door, when one is desperate enough to join the dead souls gathered around a gaming table at nine o'clock in the morning, is one's soul. Balzac calls the coat-checker's cry "a parable," which is what the rest of the ensuing story is intended to be: a parable of what happens to the soul—that inner poet in all of us—when it gives in to the irresistible materialistic temptations of society. The magical skin that distracts Raphael from his suicidal intention is engraved with an inscription that begins, "Possess me and thou shalt possess all things. But thy life is forfeit to me." Our hero destroys himself with extravagant pleasures and the fulfillment of all his worldly ambitions, as surely as if he had succeeded in drowning himself in the Seine on the first page.

Balzac considered the novel, which he wrote when he was thirty and which became his first big literary success, to be a philosophical work, dramatizing his theory that the individual human will is the most powerful, and the most potentially destructive, force in nature. To some extent, the hundred novels that poured from his pen over the next twenty years were all case studies derived from this primary symbolic drama. The allegory itself is powerful, but the lurid element of the supernatural, combined with the supreme realist's eye for descriptive detail and the telltale gestures of character, add up to a story far more hypnotic than any treatise. The final third of the book builds to a heartbreakingly tragic and revelatory climax, an intersection of love and death that, for all its melodrama, mirrors the story of the fate of youth, and the final trajectory of every human heart.

The title of the book is a pun. "Chagrin" in French denotes a species of wild donkey native to Africa; it also means "grief." The novel has the most eccentric epigraph ever: no words, just a snaky squiggle lifted from one of the stranger pages of *Tristram Shandy*; it has what is surely the most astonishing dueling scene ever written; it has the most memorable one-liner ending I know, equal to any poem. It's as low-down and entertaining as an action movie, as bold in every emotional stroke as an opera, as existentially deep as any volume by Kierkegaard. The hero is the sensitive idealistic youth in all of us, and the heroine—well, she's just one of the many exquisite, piercing, unforgettable, and complete surprises of this incomparable tale.

WILLIAM WADSWORTH

William Wadsworth is the former executive director of the Academy of American Poets, and is currently Administrative Director of the Columbia University Graduate Writing Program, where he also teaches. His poems and essays have been published in The Paris Review, Tin House, The New Republic, and The Yale Review, among other magazines and journals, and have appeared in anthologies, including The Best American Poetry 1994, The Best American Erotic Poetry, and the Library of America anthology of American Religious Poems.

The Letters of Jean Rhys

Edited by Francis Wyndham and Diana Melly

1984

One afternoon in Harvey's on Forty-fifth Street, I noticed that one of the fading hardcover books flung on a shelf as decor was *The Letters of Jean Rhys*. Waiting for the salesman, I sat down to read it. When he arrived, I dropped the book into my handbag as though it were mine.

During the composition of these letters, Rhys was writing (or worrying about writing) *Wide Sargasso Sea*. Eventually we learn that she has interpreted herself as the madwoman in Mr. Rochester's attic in Charlotte Brontë's *Jane Eyre*, a girl from the West Indies who comes to cold England and goes mad. (Notice the similarity between the nom de plume Jean Rhys and the name Jane Eyre.) In real life, Rhys's third husband is arrested for embezzlement, and following his stint in jail, they shuffle through rural England from hotel to cottage to hotel, sometimes sharing a single room. All the while she is trying to write. She complains of fatigue, illness, relentless rain, dampness, piercing wind, a sense of darkness. She apologizes for her circumstances. There is no money. She writes with the help of whiskey, or laments the lack of it. In one windy village, neighbors accuse her of witchcraft.

Rhys writes with a quirky edge, inventing scraps of song and lacing her comments with flights of metaphor: "the book is there like an egg in its shell, but it's as fragile as an egg too, till safely on paper." She writes by hand in lined notebooks and on bundled sheets of paper, admitting that only she knows "how they go." She is always seeking a typist. She shreds one of her chapters, mistaking it for something else. At last, her publisher sends a stenographer.

To anyone with illusions about the makers of masterpieces, this book is for you.

SARAH ARVIO

Bio on p. 101

Letters Writ by a Turkish Spy

By Giovanni Paolo Marana
1683

On April 15, 1683, Giovanni Paolo Marana, a Genoese political refugee, presented a draft manuscript to Louis XIV in Paris titled *L'esploratore turco e le di liu pratiche segrete con la Porta Ottomana: Scoperte in Parigi nel regno di Luiggi [sic] in Grande, L'anno 1683, Tomo primo,* wherein thrived an unprecedented character, an enlightened Renaissance spy with a delightful sense of humor. Marana's fictional innovations provoked an extraordinary wave of imitators, from Defoe and Montesquieu to Swift, Greene, and Conrad, and his literary device of incorporating letters into his narrative was repeatedly pirated in books claiming to be "the secret history" or "authentic memoirs." And, of course, the success of this new genre led to a craze for espionage fiction that continues to this day.

Due to the repressive nature of his time, little is known about Marana's life, but his writing reveals the homesick heart murmurs of an unrequited lover in exile. He was born in 1642 to a once noble family near Genoa, received a liberal education, and was jailed for four years after being involved in a conspiracy to deliver Genoa to the Duke of Savoy. After his release, in order to document his case, he journeyed to Spain, whereupon his writings were seized and he was forced to abandon his country for France.

The manuscript that Marana presented to Louis XIV contained thirty letters that, recalling Cervantes in *Don Quixote*, he claimed were originally written in Arabic: "Found in a corner of an abandoned lodging, twelve months after the author, by all accounts, had mysteriously vanished." The supposed writer of these letters, Mahmut, "had lived in Paris undetected for forty-five years from 1637-1682." Marana assured the court of the significance of his discovery, which "contained relations of war and peace and discoursed not only of the affairs of France, but those of all Christendom." His made-up story not only provided him with the cloak of translator but it allowed him to publish his writing with the King's permission. A second and a third collection, although delayed by royal censors, followed in 1684 and 1686. Following Marana's death, the authorship issue became further complicated when the English version was extended to eight volumes.

Six hundred letters in total provide familiar aspects of everyday life and reveal the many difficulties and intrigues that affected Mahmut at Constantinople, and which expose his true identity: "Low stature, of an ill-favour'd Countenance, ill-shap'd and by Nature not given to Talkativeness." He confesses to a twenty-year infatuation with a Greek woman named Daria. Once they are reunited, he learns that he was responsible for her husband's death.

Originating in Italian, being published in French, and ultimately gaining several more volumes in English gave Marana's cosmopolitan hero popularity beyond borders. The later author or authors of *Letters Writ by a Turkish Spy* never allowed Marana's gift of readability to lapse, a fact demonstrated best when Mahmut describes the nature of his longing for Constantinople in the final volume: "In describing this imperial city, I have imitated the painters, who, when they would draw a beauty to the life . . . following the conduct of a wild and strong fancy, they dash their pencil here and there, as that volatile faculty inspires them . . . curious in delineating every little singularity. So I, in portraying this queen of cities, this superlative beauty of the whole earth, draw my strokes at random . . . this I do not perform all at once (it were too great a task) but even like them, by fits and starts, as I find my opportunities."

While his hero thrived, Marana stayed faithful to his fancy by disappearing to an unnoticed and forgotten corner of our culture. Nevertheless, in 1684, the year that the second collection of the *L'espion du Grand-Seigneur* was printed in Paris, Louis XIV had Genoa bombarded, as history records, "without any just cause."

SEBNEM SENYENER

Sebnem Senyener, born in Izmir, Turkey, is a novelist living in New York. Her first novel takes its title from Letters Writ by a Turkish Spy. Her other novels are February 30th, Death of the Belly Dancer, and The Merchant of Character.

Life and Fate

By Vasily Grossman

1959

For two decades, Vasily Grossman's monumental novel of the Soviet Union had a half-life as a samizdat text. On completion in 1959, not long before Grossman's early death, the book was seized by Soviet authorities, who told Grossman that it could not be published for at least three hundred years. Even his typewriter ribbons were confiscated. We did not have to wait that long, because Andrei Sakharov secretly photographed draft pages preserved by Semyon Lipkin, and the writer Vladimir Voinovich managed to smuggle the photographic films abroad. The first edition was published in Switzerland in 1980 and became available in English in 1995. Many readers, like me, first became aware of it in the footnotes to Antony Beevor's history of the end of the Third Reich, *Berlin: The Downfall*, or had it pressed upon them by an eager friend. Journalists seem to have been early adopters.

The novel is set during the battle of Stalingrad, but it is not a war epic. It is a total denunciation of the very idea of the Soviet Union, told through the various members of a Jewish family fighting on the front, held in prison for crimes against the state, or working in a physics lab where anti-Semitism is part of the system. In one monumental chapter, a mother in Auschwitz writes an imaginary letter to her son.

Life and Fate is written in that maligned style, socialist realism, but out of it comes the great life-changing lesson for the reader: that ideology is nothing compared with individual human acts, whether heroic or banal. A soldier preparing himself for his first kiss gently removes a louse on the collar of a girl soldier's uniform. In the gas chamber, an unmarried woman holds the hand of a child she does not know and reflects that this is the only time she will be a mother.

Life and Fate is a vast undertaking for the reader. It took me three weeks to complete and three weeks to recover from the experience, a time in which I read nothing. This is the twentieth century's *War and Peace*.

LINDA GRANT

Linda Grant is the author four works of nonfiction and four novels, including The Clothes on Their Backs, shortlisted for the 2008 Man Booker Prize, and When I Lived in Modern Times, winner of the Orange Prize for Fiction.

Lessons in Life and Leisure

A Life of One's Own

By Joanna Field (Marion Milner)

1934

An Experiment in Leisure

By Joanna Field (Marion Milner)

1937

Can a book change our lives? *A Life of One's Own* is certainly one that could help us to think differently and more deeply about them. As a young woman in London in the 1920s, Joanna Field (the pen name of Marion Milner) felt as if she had been living her life in a state of half-dreaming, unfulfilled and often discontented, but without really knowing why. She decided to keep a journal. In the first instance, she recorded what made her feel happy, and then investigated what she could learn from what she had written. Milner had qualified as a psychologist (in later life, she became an eminent psychoanalyst), and she brings a scientific, methodical approach to her investigations. Yet her style is intimate, human, honest, her voice youthful. She keeps her diary for many years and makes the discovery that the ways of attending to things—of looking, moving, and experiencing—bring joy, and that this "feminine" approach to the universe is just as valid as a more "masculine," competitive, or striving one.

She reveals that "by a simple self-chosen act of keeping my thought on one thing instead of dozens, I had found a window opening out across a country of wide horizons and unexplored delights." Pushing herself toward endless goals had been keeping her away from what she'd really wanted. Joanna Field has continual insights on this journey; for instance, that delight comes when one stops trying, that there are two ways of looking (with a wide or narrow focus), and that adults can gain clues from the way children think. She describes the ups and downs in this "getting of wisdom," but what comes through is the adventurousness of the whole endeavor. Her findings shed light on various areas of life, including relationships, religion, and creativity.

This book has a sequel, *An Experiment in Leisure*, first published in 1937 and currently out of print. Here Milner/Field starts from interests that fill, or have in the past filled, her spare time, and asks what they can tell her. An examination of such passions as her love of nature, books, and travel, and her interest in witchcraft, for example, leads her to an in-depth exploration of otherness and the darker aspects of oneself, as well as comparisons between the laws of action and those of imagination. She highlights the creative process and how blockages and other difficulties can be surmounted when they are completely accepted. Only at the point of surrender, of giving up, does the knowledge of how to surmount the difficulty grow. She does not attempt to solve the problems of existence, but describes experience as "this thing which was always more than all that could be said about it—and yet in order to know it you had to be continually trying to say things about it." *A Life of One's Own* and *An Experiment in Leisure* are necessary books, worth rereading or consulting often— potential friends for the path of life.

Moniza Alvi

Moniza Alvi has published six collections of poetry, the most recent of which are Split World: Poems 1990-2005 and Europa. She lives in London and tutors for the Poetry School.

Life Supports: New and Collected Poems
By William Bronk
1981

I can't help but go back again and again to *Life Supports*, the collected poems of William Bronk — though these are not poems to calm or ease the anxious heart. The world we wish to know is, according to Bronk, not only unknowable but not even the world. Nevertheless, he insists, "Something wants to be said / wanting the partialness, as if to say: / place, I want place, want I, / want other place, other I, I want." Bronk grew up in Hudson Falls, New York, and remained there in adulthood, taking over his father's coal and lumber business and living in his childhood home until the end of his life. In his poems' sentences, phrases unravel, implode, sing with their own ambiguities. Over and over in this collection, Bronk shows himself to be the embodiment of what he says we are: makers — despite the nothing there is to make. "There is no order we can live with," he writes. "There is nothing else."

Under-read yet intimately treasured, Bronk is a great American poet.

Victoria Redel

Victoria Redel has written five books of fiction and poetry, including The Border of Truth, Loverboy, and Swoon.

Lights Out in the Reptile House
By Jim Shepard
1990

Jim Shepard's *Lights Out in the Reptile House* was published long before Abu Ghraib, black-site prisons, renditions, Guantánamo, and waterboarding became a shameful and terrifying part of history after 9/11.

The novel is set in a brutally repressive land. Its fifteen-year-old protagonist, Karel Roeder, has two passions: the iguanas, geckos, snakes, and other reptiles he cares for in the zoo, and Leda—a strong-willed, idealistic girl who sends him reaching for the stars with love.

The boy beats himself up for being the "King of Hesitation," someone ceaselessly saddened by his own mediocrity, the kind of young man whom the state hopes to foster, someone who will not interfere, which in a time of totalitarian rule isn't easy. In other words, he is a kind of Everyman.

Lights Out in the Reptile House is fueled by Shepard's characteristic fascination with the incredible. Early on, Leda, who becomes the boy's moral compass, leads him on their first date through a cave so narrow the two must navigate it on their backs, feet first. They hear a rustling, followed by the smell of guano. Down the tunnel, a huge wind builds and bats explode into a torrent, "unbearably thick and furious in the darkness," rushing over them and crawling under their clothing.

There is the stunning retelling of a local tsunami disaster—the Roof of Hell—generations before Karel was born, "the way whole buildings were driven through the ones behind them like parts of a collapsing telescope." In a Faulknerian scene nearly paralyzing in its barbarity, the zoo is set on fire and its last survivor, Seelie, a Komodo dragon riddled with bullets, "a foreclaw up," tumbles into an embankment.

In this nightmare world where citizens disappear and fear rules, there remain saving graces of humanity even if some arrive in unexpected form: a small translucent gecko pressing itself against a window, its pale palms and belly somehow suggesting vulnerability and mercy. And, remarkably, in a world where torturers believe they can "make martyrdom impossible," in a place "without witnesses or testimonies," Karel understands, with Leda's help, something about the sanctity of the individual that allows him to resist.

Upon publication, *Lights Out in the Reptile House* seemed like a chilling fable that reminded us of political horrors far from our land, of past terrors like the Soviet gulags or the Argentine *desaparecidos*, to name two of history's multitude of state-sponsored atrocities. Reading this courageous novel again makes me wonder whether Jim Shepard meant it as a warning to his own America—a warning that now reads like a rebuke.

GARY ZEBRUN

Gary Zebrun, a Lambda Literary Award finalist, has published two novels, Someone You Know and Only the Lonely.

Little America

By Henry Bromell

2001

After the World Trade Center attacks, when George W. Bush asked (rhetorically, mind you, not really caring), "Why do they hate us?," I thought I knew, having just read a novel by my friend Henry Bromell called *Little America*.

Published in the spring of 2001, it concerns the attempts of a historian, Terry Hooper, to decipher the events of a particular year—1958—in a particular Middle East nationette, Kurash (imagined by Bromell as a hypothetical representation of other nations in the region). It is the late '90s, and Terry, now fifty, is perturbed in his conscience about what he suspects his father, Mack Hooper, has done, and, in a larger sense, what he suspects his country has done. Bromell weaves together Terry's investigation and the events he discovers in an extremely graceful but suspenseful narrative. I wasn't the only reader impressed by the package—Joan Didion called it "the best and smartest novel I've read in a long time."

The gist of Terry's story is betrayal. In 1958, Mack Hooper is sent out by Allan and John Foster Dulles to control and manipulate the new young king of Kurash, the grandson of the king originally imposed upon the Kurashians by the British, and propped up there for several decades. The British are now on their way out, and the Americans plan to take over, using the king and his country to foil the designs of the Soviets and the Egyptians (Nasser and his pan-Arab League present the principal danger to American designs). Bromell is explicit in his portrayal of American fears. In the late fifties, the Soviets are riding a tide of success, and seem to be expanding their influence all over the world. The Americans fear they are in a losing battle with the ideology of Communism, and are willing to do just about anything to stem that tide.

The young king's fatal flaw, from the point of view of geopolitics, is that he isn't important enough to stand in the way of the Dulles brothers' schemes. Toward the end of the novel, Bromell shows that, when they finally do discuss him, the Dulleses spend only ten minutes on him before moving on to more important matters. But what Bromell does, and what the novel itself is designed to do, is to show that to the Kurashians, to the king himself, to ten-year-old Terry, and to the CIA operatives in the Kurash office, what goes on in Kurash is all important, important enough to shape many lives and much Middle Eastern history. Because the Dulles boys think the way they do, and because the Kurashians think the way they do, profound resentments are inevitable and important. The answer to the question "Why do they hate us?" in my reading of *Little America* was a nuanced and tragic one. I of course thought Bromell's book should be, could be, and would be a best seller. Silly me.

There were signs that the book was being taken seriously in certain places. Bromell heard through the grapevine that Richard Helms was reading it. A friend of mine with lots of former-spy friends called one of them and said, "I've just been reading about your life." She sent the book to her friend, who subsequently ordered fifty copies. But that was that. Just when the book should have hit the best-seller list and provided answers to some of our big questions, it died.

I've been thinking about *Little America* for almost eight years, so I went back and reread it. I was not disappointed. Bromell uses the resources of the novel (character, plot, narrative technique, dialogue) in a beautifully sophisticated way to both inform the reader and move her. But *Little America* is more than a novel. Bromell's childhood was spent not in Kurash but in Iran. I know this because he told me long ago, when we were friends in our twenties. His sense of what we as a nation did there, and how we screwed up there, is informed and evenhanded. He has a strong empathy with every character and a terrific take on the inter-locking relationships they have that cross all sorts of lines and boundaries. Americans are frequently guilty, one generation after another, of not knowing how current events got to be what they are. Were it not so obscure, *Little America* could correct that flaw with regard to the Middle East.

JANE SMILEY

Jane Smiley is the author of many novels, including A Thousand Acres, Horse Heaven, *and* Ten Days in the Hills, *as well as several works of nonfiction, most notably* Thirteen Ways of Looking at the Novel, *an anatomy and history of the novel as a form.*

The Lonely Londoners

By Samuel Selvon

1956

Samuel Selvon emigrated from Trinidad to London in the 1950s, and it was a stroke of luck for literature that he did. His novel *The Lonely Londoners* is about the West Indian immigrant community in Britain's capital at a time when "the English people starting to make rab about how too much West Indians coming to the country: this was a time, when any corner you turn, is ten to one you bound to bounce up a spade." Spades (a derogatory term for blacks) are at the center of Selvon's fictional world, and *The Lonely Londoners* might easily take its place in the canon as a study of race relations in postwar Britain, a portrait of modern urban life, and the grandfather of the multicultural fiction boom of late-twentieth-century Britain. Selvon begets Hanif Kureishi, say, who begets Zadie Smith.

But the reason to read *The Lonely Londoners* is that it is lyrical and endearing and human. The hero, Trinidadian-turned-Londoner Moses Aloetta, wins you over from the first page, when he sets out to meet a compatriot fresh off the boat train to offer him guidance in this cold, strange land. And Selvon wins you over from the first line, which pays homage to the opening of another great London-fog novel, *Bleak House*, but using the rhythms of West Indian-inflected English: "One grim winter evening, when it had a kind of unrealness about London, with a fog sleeping restlessly over the city . . ." This is *The Lonely Londoners'* guiding idiom, and Selvon's style is so immersive that one could be forgiven for coming away from the book with the impression that England is an outpost of the West Indian empire, and the Queen's English is but a quirky variant on the syntax of West Indian speech.

At its core, *The Lonely Londoners* is a novel about the elusiveness of belonging. Moses is a ten-year veteran of London, but he is still puzzled and pained by the fact that as a black man he is only "tolerated" in English society. He longs for the warmth of his homeland, but every year he is seduced by the English spring and the long days of summer. He feels beaten down by the city, isolated and alienated, yet he is the hub of his social universe; every Sunday the whole immigrant community, it seems, congregates around his chair. Selvon can't solve any of these contradictions, any more than Moses can. But he writes about them so compellingly that even as we acknowledge Moses's loneliness, we sympathize with it, connect with it, and feel less alone.

RADHIKA JONES

Radhika Jones is senior arts editor at Time and Time.com, where she writes about books. She holds a Ph.D. in English and Comparative Literature from Columbia University.

The Long Walk

By Slavomir Rawicz

1956

While visiting Poland in 1983, I met a man who told me about *The Long Walk*, by Slavomir Rawicz. The man bet me a hundred zloty (roughly ten dollars) that if I read the first twenty pages, I wouldn't be able to put the book down. Needless to say, I lost the zloty, and much sleep, before finishing this most astonishing and riveting memoir. When I returned to the States, I bought ten copies and gave them to friends. At the same time, I discovered a subculture of *Long Walk* obsessives.

The book begins with an introduction by Ronald Downing, a reporter for the London *Daily Mail*, who in 1956 was researching sightings of the yeti, or Abominable Snowman. He went to see Rawicz, who was living in England. Rawicz was purported to have seen some unusual animals while in the Himalayas. Rawicz told Downing that he would tell him what he had seen, but only in the context of a larger story. So astounded was Downing by Rawicz's tale that he agreed to help him write *The Long Walk*.

The story begins in 1939. Rawicz, a twenty-five-year-old Polish cavalry officer, was captured by the Russians and sent to the notorious Lubyanka prison, where he was tortured by the KGB. After confessing to false charges of espionage, he was sentenced to twenty-five years in the Gulag. Rawicz and thousands of other prisoners were stuffed into unheated cattle cars, in which they began a harrowing monthlong journey eastward on the Trans-Siberian Railway. The last eight hundred miles were spent on foot, with the prisoners chained together behind trucks as they trudged through the Siberian winter. Rawicz scraped by as a prisoner, suffering severe deprivations. Eventually, he and six other prisoners engineered an escape from the camp with the unlikely help of the commandant's wife. And that is when the "long walk" to freedom—four thousand miles long—really begins.

In an epic saga of survival and grit, the escapees set out to walk southward, with the goal of finding freedom in English-occupied India. In vivid detail, Rawicz describes their odyssey through Siberian forests, Mongolian villages, the Gobi Desert, the Himalayas, and Tibet. This is a story of defiance in the face of seemingly insurmountable odds, a story of human perseverance that ranks right up there with *Endurance*, by Alfred Lansing, and Jon Krakauer's *Into Thin Air*. *The Long Walk* is a haunting and unforgettable classic of survival literature.

As of this writing, Peter Weir (*The Year of Living Dangerously, Master and Commander*) is directing a film version of the story, starring Colin Farrell and renamed *The Way Back*. As for the Abominable Snowman . . . read the book. But hold on to your zloty.

STEVE HOFFMAN

Steve Hoffman was for twenty years the Creative Director of Sports Illustrated. In 2009 he formed Hoffman Noli Design, a design, branding, and consulting company in Brooklyn. He remains a contributing editor to Sports Illustrated.

Lost Diaries and Dead Letters

By Maurice Baring

1910; 1913 (published in a single volume in 1988)

I have a taste for those clever little books which have now all but disappeared—arcane works of parody and pastiche. *Lost Diaries and Dead Letters* is a spin on these forms. Baring has written alternative history in the form of letters and diaries. But, rather than imitating, say, Shakespeare, he rewrites the backstage life of his characters in the style of a twentieth-century soap opera.

Maurice Baring was the fifth son in the ennobled Baring family of Barings bank fame. He was a decorated Royal Air Force pilot in World War I and then went on to write. He was a famed practical joker and staunch anti-intellectual; he despised literary criticism. The interesting thing is that his work throws light on the strengths and weaknesses of the authors he tackles far better than any lengthy work of literary criticism could.

In *Lost Diaries and Dead Letters*, there are letters between Shakespeare's literary agent and Lord Chamberlain regarding the licensing of the plays; letters from Camelot; and those between the warriors and wives at Troy. Lady Macbeth writes to Lady Macduff ("My dearest Flora"), explaining the death of Duncan and inviting her to come and stay: "P.S. Don't forget to bring Jeamie. It will do Macbeth good to see a child in the house." And Goneril writes to Regan, telling her the whole dreadful saga of her mad papa, King Lear: "P.S. Another thing Papa does which is most exasperating is to throw up Cordelia at one every moment. He keeps on saying: 'If only Cordelia was here,' or 'How unlike Cordelia!' And you will remember, darling, that when Cordelia was here Papa could

not endure the sight of her. P.P.S. It is wretched
weather. The poor little ponies on the heath will have
to be brought in." He includes imagined diaries by,
among others, William the Conqueror: "London—
Everything sadly in need of thorough reorganisation.
Have resolved to carry out the initial reforms at once:
1. Everybody to put out their lights at 8. Bell to ring for
the purpose. The people here sit up too late, drinking.
Most dangerous. 2. Enroll everybody in a book." And
Mark Antony on his campaign in Egypt: "Enobarbus
worrying me to death to fight on land. Cleopatra won't
hear of it, and I am quite certain she is right. A
woman's instinct in matters of strategy and tactics are
infallible; and then—what a woman!"

It's all very clever, very camp, and very funny.

FIDELIS MORGAN

Bio on p. 29

Lost Weddings

By Maria Beig

1990

Most of the writers I know are dying to learn of
overlooked writers they should be reading, and have
one or two examples they themselves are looking to
share. Often the neglected in question are well-known
in their native countries yet obscure over here. Charlie
Baxter initiated me into the joys of Javier Marías, for
example, while I passed on to him the good news about
Marta Morazzoni. When it comes to important writers
overlooked in America, though, it's hard to find
someone farther off the radar than Maria Beig.

Beig was apparently notorious in Germany in the
1980s because of the violence her work did to the

cherished and still-sentimentalized notion of *Heimat* in the two most common uses of the word, the individual home and the provincial homeland. Beig debuted as a sixty-two-year-old retired knitting teacher from a rural backwater, and her portraits of country life, rather than offering the traditional trope of Common Folk Eking a Hard Living from the Earth, turned out to be so quietly withering that she stopped giving readings after her final one was broken up by shouts of "*Nestbeschmutzer*!" ("Nest-soiler!") We all *aspire* to be *Nestbeschmutzers*, but every so often a Maria Beig pulls it off.

Lost Weddings, her second book, makes clear why her neighbors were upset. It's a novel of four concise and delicately overlapping life histories. Four women—two beautiful, two plain—who live in and around the same village but who've been handed lives of such dray-horse isolation that they barely register one another's presence.

Some are able to imagine normal lives for themselves; some are not. The four narratives unfold the particulars of each woman's bad—or, in their world, ordinary—luck. They help their mothers raise their siblings; they become their brothers' farmhands. They come within a hair of happiness, or a hard kind of fulfillment, or at least a safer sinecure. One by one their opportunities—mostly male—evaporate. Eventually they find themselves to be more and more in the way. "Do you think I want to end up like you, and have to beg one day for bread and milk?" a favorite niece asks one of them at one point.

Family in this world represents a settling for what little there is. Intermittently, there's eroticism; occasionally there's kindness; almost never is there tenderness. Parents are constantly scolding. Small children are shuttled among extended relatives. Self-pity has no utility, so you do without it.

Maria Beig's prose renders all of this with a sharpness as evocative and non-lyrical as childhood memories of unpleasantly hard work. Climaxes are elided, narratives shanghaied by minor characters, and loss is rendered with a startling simplicity. In her rural Germany, you begin with almost no expectations, and then discover that you've set those expectations too high. And yet indefatigably you return to remembered joy and tenderness, using it to negotiate further decades of a circumscribed life.

JIM SHEPARD

Jim Shepard is the author of six novels, including, most recently, Project X, and three story collections, including Like You'd Understand, Anyway, which was nominated for the National Book Award and won the Story Prize. His short fiction has appeared in, among other magazines, Harper's, McSweeney's, The Paris Review, the Atlantic Monthly, Esquire, Granta, The New Yorker, and Playboy. He teaches at Williams College.

Love, Loss, and What I Wore

By Ilene Beckerman

1995

In the crowded bazaar of memoirs, I cherish a little book that came across my desk a dozen years ago called *Love, Loss, and What I Wore*. A fashion-conscious woman named Ilene Beckerman painted her life growing up in New York City in the 1940s, '50s, and beyond, in swift strokes—with charming color sketches of once-beloved outfits, accompanied by a few concise words about the memories they sparked. She didn't dwell on life's losses—the deaths, the divorces—but hers seemed especially poignant, planted like little bombs among the details of a sharkskin blouse or a favorite navy dress with a detachable cape collar. Like a gourmand remembering long-ago feasts, Beckerman recalled the delicious swishing sound made by a plaid taffeta birthday dress; the eternity it took to hem the yellow-striped circle skirt she sewed with her best friend in high school; and the expensive Chinese brocade dress she wore one New Year's Eve, when she found her first husband kissing the party's hostess at midnight. Maybe I love the book because I still have every party dress I ever owned (after my mother died, I found the childhood ones she packed in a trunk, wrapped carefully in tissue). I've often given this slim volume to friends (women only, of course). Its virtue lies in its understatement—and that, as its stylish author knew, is the key to true chic.

CATHLEEN MCGUIGAN

Cathleen McGuigan is a contributor to Newsweek, where she writes about architecture, design, books, and other cultural subjects. Her articles have also appeared in The New York Times Magazine, Smithsonian, Harper's Bazaar, and Rolling Stone, among other publications. McGuigan was a Loeb Fellow at Harvard University and is currently an adjunct professor at the Columbia School of Journalism.

M

Marius the Epicurean
By Walter Pater
1885

Marius the Epicurean is a book that stands alone, outside the perimeter of literary novels, books of philosophy, essays on aesthetics, or historical writings. Walter Pater's imaginary portrait of Marius relates the coming-of-age of a young man during the time of Roman Emperor Marcus Aurelius. Pater's prose richly unfolds the "sensations and ideas" of Marius, who is "bent on living in the full stream of refined sensation."

A correct understanding of the term "Epicurean" is essential to understanding the title, the character of Marius, and the point of view of Pater, the author and first-person narrator. "Epicurean" has adapted, in contemporary times, to have a mildly negative meaning that differs considerably from Pater's comprehension. An Epicurean for Pater was not a hedonist but one who seeks fullness and insight in life—an arbiter and lover of beauty, an individual devoted to making the most of life in the brief years allotted to him.

"[Marius] had a strong apprehension also of the beauty of the visible things around him; their fading, momentary graces and attractions. His natural susceptibility in this direction, enlarged by experience, seems to demand of him an almost exclusive preoccupation with the *aspects* of things; with their aesthetic character, as it is called—their revelations to the eye and the imagination: not so much because those aspects of them yield him the largest amount of enjoyment, as because to be occupied in this way with the aesthetic or imaginative side of things is to be in real contact with those elements of his own nature, and of theirs, which, for him at least, are matters of the most real kind of apprehension."

Marius the Epicurean was a key book for Oscar Wilde, a fact reported by numerous critics, but more illuminating is its profound influence on connoisseurs such as Bernard Berenson, Kenneth Clark, and John Pope-Hennessy, as well as the stylistic influence it exerted on the writings of Joyce and Eliot.

In *Marius*, Pater makes an important aesthetic distinction: "Let us eat and drink, for tomorrow we die!—is a proposal, the real import of which differs immensely, according to the natural taste, and the acquired judgment, of the guests who sit at the table."

WILLIAM WYER

William Wyer sells rare books in New York City. He won the 1957 third grade broad jump at Groveland Elementary School.

The Marriage of Heaven and Hell
By William Blake
1790–1793

Although Blake is certainly celebrated in our literary culture, if often reflexively, I think *The Marriage of Heaven and Hell* is insufficiently esteemed as a source of unique yet oddly accessible philosophic and theological speculation.

Neither poem nor essay, it is best characterized as a kind of visionary blurt unlike anything else in the world. And it delineates better than any other single work the spiritual problems and projects of the two hundred years that have followed its creation. It was written at the end of the eighteenth century, and when I read it again now — post-Christianity, post-Enlightenment, post-Romantic, post-Nietzsche, post-Freud — it seems that everything I learned when I first read it at college still exists somewhere in me. An expression and elaboration of the most profound issues, in detail and writ large, of being a mature human being, it seemed then to signal the possible end of one of my many adolescences.

Framed as a series of visions — near-hallucinations — it attacks and subverts reason, that bland, boring possession of which humans are so proud, but which Blake demonstrates is really an affliction. "Without Contraries is no progression," the text says (more interestingly than Hegel), then, with a downpour of bizarre images, of turnabouts, reversals, underminings, it proves it.

The section entitled "The Voice of the Devil" is a profound reframing of the ancient tension between body and mind, and soul. Devils and Angels shift identities in it, as didactic instruments and as moral concepts. Among its other refashionings: "Man has no Body distinct from his Soul; for that call'd Body is a portion of Soul discern'd by the five Senses, the chief inlets of Soul in this age. Energy is the only life and is from the Body and Reason is the bound or outward circumference of energy. Energy is Eternal Delight." Isn't that pretty much where we are now? Might not energy be the ultimate, nonjudgmental solvent by which everything else can be fairly valued?

The introduction to the section entitled "Proverbs of Hell" begins, "As I was walking among the fires of hell, delighted with the enjoyments of Genius; which to Angels look like torment and Insanity, I collected some of their Proverbs . . . " and there follows a compendium of gnomic adages and parables about psychology, spirituality, sexuality, practicality; many memorable, unforgettable.

Here are a few of the best known: "The road of excess leads to the palace of wisdom." "Prudence is a rich ugly old maid courted by Incapacity." "He who desires but acts not, breeds pestilence." "Eternity is in love with the productions of time." (Stunning!) "If the fool would persist in his folly he would become wise." "Prisons are built with stones of Law, Brothels with bricks of Religion." "The nakedness of women is the work of God." "The tygers of wrath are wiser than the horses of instruction."

The rest of the work is an enactment of Blake's other visionary method, a frankly prophetic elaboration of his ideas. The several sections demonstrate different kinds of consciousness, different ways of thinking about and visualizing the adventures of the human spirit. "The Prophets Isaiah and Ezekiel dined with me . . . " begins one of the "Memorable Fancies," and there ensue various reenacts of ancient quandaries and conflicts, many of which still boil at the center of our own dilemmas, bedeviling us as they have everyone, always. This is another genre of Blake's genius, less easily digested, perhaps, and less immediately illuminating, but endlessly intriguing in its demonstration of a singular, overflowing spirit.

C. K. WILLIAMS

C. K. Williams's Collected Poems was published in 2006. His ten books of poetry include The Singing, winner of the 2003 National Book Award, and Repair, which won the Pulitzer Prize in 2000. The winner of the Ruth Lilly Poetry Prize, a Guggenheim Fellowship, two NEA Grants, a Lila Wallace Fellowship, and

prizes from PEN and the American Academy of Arts and Letters,
he teaches in the Creative Writing Program at Princeton University.

Martin Dressler: The Tale of an American Dreamer

By Steven Millhauser

1997

Whenever I introduce my students to the work of
Steven Millhauser, they react as if I've shown them The
Way, for Millhauser makes writers feel they can do
anything at all if they'll only invest craft, thoroughness,
and an infinite originality. In fact, if more young
writers followed his example, we would have more
books that celebrate the imagination and fewer that
read as thin riffs on autobiography.

Millhauser won the Pulitzer Prize for *Martin
Dressler: The Tale of an American Dreamer.* As
the subtitle suggests, this is a story patterned on
our national narrative, in which a young man of
humble means rises in the mercantile world purely
on the strength of his drive, integrity, and willingness
to—yes—dream. But Millhauser is too interesting
a writer to simply puncture that dream, and there's
little irony here, no judgments on the cheapness
of human appetites. Martin Dressler is not a robber
baron, corrupted by money, sex, and power.
Instead, he's a genuine visionary whose sincerity of
purpose is well matched by Millhauser's elegiac and
surprising prose.

Martin Dressler is also one of the loveliest books I
know about New York. The late-nineteenth-century
setting suggests the city itself as a place where miracles
are standard practice, and as Martin's fancies grow
more extravagant we see the city expanding in similar,

if not exactly parallel, ways. The Brooklyn Bridge is built, changing the way working people travel to Brighton Beach. Uptown is conquered, and in one of my favorite brief passages, Central Park is begun. Millhauser seems to be proposing a world in which dreams are within reach, yet as the New York of the novel grows more like the city we know today, a realm borne only of the imagination arises in the book's final chapters: tantalizing, wistful, and incomparably real.

DAVE KING

Bio on p. 84

A Mathematician's Apology

By G. H. Hardy

1940

Big fat tomes with millions of characters whose names sound alike seem to get all the attention in the world of literature—*War and Peace*, *Don Quixote*, the telephone book. What I go for, however, are those pamphlet-length works that can be read in less than a lifetime—especially ones rich in anecdotes that can be repeated at dinner parties. That's why I love *A Mathematician's Apology*, by G. H. Hardy, an Englishman who claims he was, "at best, for a short time, the fifth best pure mathematician in the world." But who's counting? Hardy was, apparently. According to C. P. Snow's introductory biography to the 1967 edition, which is longer than what follows it, at age two our apologist entertained himself by enumerating, with pencil and paper, the integers from one to several million, and, while at church, mentally factored the hymn numbers. As an adult, he despised the sight of his reflection to such a degree that he would cover the mirrors in his hotel rooms. This charming, dark, droll, and, yes, short discourse (153 pages) is less about number theory and the Riemann Hypothesis than about mathematical exquisiteness, the pleasures of creativity, and the sorrows of someone who has become an old man in what is "essentially a young man's game" — someone, whose life, by his reckoning, is finished. By the way, I, who truly do have a lot to apologize to mathematics for (I think negative numbers should just buck up), had no trouble following *A Mathematician's Apology*.

PATRICIA MARX

Bio on p. 41

McTeague

By Frank Norris

1899

It could not begin more prosaically: "It was Sunday." A dull-witted dentist takes his regular supper of soup, meat cooked rare, and two vegetables. Five hundred pages later, it could not end more dramatically: the dentist, destroyed by jealousy, dying under the Death Valley sun, handcuffed to the body of his rival. In *McTeague*, Frank Norris shows he's the literary grandson of Melville and the pen-brother of Stephen Crane and Theodore Dreiser. He was one of America's first twentieth-century writers, although he wrote just before the turn of that century. With his muscular prose and his attraction to violence and his love of cold irony, Norris anticipates Hemingway, Mailer, and Cormac McCarthy. But Norris had luck as bad as his doomed protagonist McTeague. Published in 1899, the novel misses all the surveys, lists, and course syllabi on twentieth-century literature. Even worse, in 1902, at the age of thirty-two, at the brink of greatness, Norris died of a ruptured appendix. Buried with him in the Oakland cemetery is all the potential and promise we heap on young writers. For more than a century, admirers have tried to keep the novel alive. In 1924, Erich von Stroheim adapted it into the great silent film *Greed*. In 1992, William Bolcom's opera premiered. The novel isn't entirely forgotten. It has always remained in print. Yet it has never been widely recognized for what it is: an American masterpiece.

David Ebershoff

David Ebershoff is the author of the novels The 19th Wife, Pasadena, and The Danish Girl and a short-story collection, The Rose City. His fiction has won a number of awards, including the Rosenthal Foundation Award from the American Academy of Arts and Letters. Ebershoff currently teaches in the graduate writing program at Columbia University. For many years, he was the publishing director of the Modern Library and is now an editor-at-large at Random House.

Michael Kohlhaas

By Heinrich von Kleist
Translated from the German by Frances H. King,
David Luke, and Nigel Reeves
1811

This novella often appears in a volume called *The Marquise of O and Other Stories*. One of many books first commended to my attention by my older brother, Don, this is a wonderful story, sweetly told, about a horse dealer who gets crosswise with the privileged and powerful of his day and, after a prolonged and active resistance, succumbs. It is exquisite reading in every detail. A secondary pleasure is discovering how E. L. Doctorow used this work in service of his novel

Ragtime, which was later turned into a not-so-great American movie. I encourage you to read this book—and skip the rest.

FREDERICK BARTHELME

Frederick Barthelme is author of sixteen books, including the memoir Double Down: Reflections on Gambling and Loss, co-authored with his brother Steven; Painted Desert; Bob the Gambler; and The Law of Averages, his collected stories. His novel Elroy Nights was named a New York Times Notable Book of the Year and was a finalist for the 2004 PEN/Faulkner Award.

Midpoint and Other Poems

By John Updike

1969

I'm writing this not long after John Updike's death. I tend to judge the worth of writers by how much I want to borrow from them. For me, Updike's worth was enormous. I hasten to recommend to any reader of this essay the rereading of any of Updike's early short stories or his first novel, *The Poorhouse Fair*, written a few years after he graduated from college. All reveal a sublime talent. But I especially recommend a slim book of verse called *Midpoint and Other Poems*. When I read this work back in the day, there was no doubt in my mind that Updike would become something like the writer he became. But who could have guessed that he would have written as much as he did? Small wonder he was never the golfer he wanted to be.

Instead of analyzing Updike's work—his stories were, after all, short on metaphor and long on style and story—let me instead tell you a story he told me, some years back. Updike was one of my early writer-heroes. He was a small-town boy from Shillington, Pennsylvania (he later moved with his family to nearby

Plowville, Pennsylvania), and wrote eloquently—and emotionally—of growing up in small-town America. He was bright, well-educated, and had enormous early success. By the time I was sixteen, Updike, at twenty-three, was already writing for the Talk of the Town page in *The New Yorker*, a magazine that seemed to me, as a young man, sophisticated beyond my wildest dreams. Updike seemed to be *The New Yorker*'s young prince. I saw him on the street the very first day I lived in New York City, having just moved from small-town Massachusetts. I introduced myself to Updike and was gobsmacked when he told me that he was moving from New York, the very next day—to Ipswich, Massachusetts.

"But, I've just come from there! Why would you move there?"

"Because everybody in this city's doing something more important than I am!" he explained.

At age 69.99, I've just begun to understand what Updike was saying. But I digress. Here's the story.

Updike had agreed to attend his fortieth high-school reunion. Several months before the actual event, he'd dutifully sent in his check—thinking it would be a good idea somehow to see what his former classmates had become, and maybe even brag a bit about what he'd made of himself. In any case, his reservation form and check arrived in Shillington, Pennsylvania, and the local newspaper quickly heralded the news that the acclaimed novelist, Shillington's own John Updike, would be in town, at SHS's reunion. Updike told me that everyone who attended—himself included—looked "simply awful." Age had been nobody's friend . . . well, almost nobody's. One woman—one of Updike's former high-school girlfriends—looked amazingly young, robust, sexy. Her hair was still blond, and bobbed. Her skirt was short, revealing strong, thin, shapely legs. In no time, he reported, she was sitting on his lap, whispering to him, running her fingers through his thinning gray hair. Cutting through a blend of amusement, astonishment, and arousal, Updike popped The Question to his old flame: "Mary-Ellen"—I've changed her name—"how on earth is it possible that everybody looks the way they do while you look the way you do?" To which she replied, "I lost seventy-one pounds for this reunion, John."

Rabbit, rest in peace.

ISRAEL HOROVITZ

Israel Horovitz is the author of more than seventy plays, including The Indian Wants the Bronx, Line, The Primary English Class, Park Your Car in Harvard Yard, My Old Lady, and The Widow's Blind Date. His screenplays include Author! Author!, The Strawberry Statement, and Sunshine. He divides his time between the United States and France, where he is the most-produced American playwright in French theatre history.

Minor Characters

By Joyce Johnson
1983

When the novelist Joyce Johnson set out to write a memoir, she had a sensational subject—her love affair, when she was barely twenty years old, with Jack Kerouac, just as *On the Road* changed American culture forever.

She's writing the book twenty years after the fact, at the end of the 1970s, when telling the truth about women's lives is a brand new idea, and so she has a way into the story. She'll begin with her own life and those of her women friends, "minor characters" in the

lives of these rebellious young men on their way to
becoming great.

For the girl who appears in accounts of Kerouac's
life as Joyce Glassman, it all began years before she
met him. She was thirteen and an only child living
with her parents on the Upper West Side when she and
her best friend took a bus downtown to Greenwich
Village, coming upon an eating place called the
Waldorf Cafeteria. "I'd hang out around the edges of
the crowded tables, listening, looking, not really
participating. Ideas flashed by like silver freight trains
that wouldn't stop at your station to unload but had to
push on to a vanishing point in the distance. What was
Jungian? Existentialist? Abstract Expressionist?"

Looking back, she can name the fascinating talkers
who make "the Waldorf sound like the Deux Magots
of Eighth Street: ee cummings, W. H. Auden, Maxwell
Bodenheim, Delmore Schwartz. . . . Obscure younger
people too, like Allen Ginsberg, who moved downtown
to the Lower East Side before he followed Jack's route
westward in pursuit of Neal Cassady—and certainly
before his wanderings, Jack himself. . . ."

In the way of lives, our heroine will soon find
herself at the center of that alluring world. She enrolls
at Barnard, drops out, and eventually meets Allen
Ginsberg, through her best friend Elise Cowen, who's
had a brief affair with him—he's not yet famous or gay.
A year or two later, when Joyce is twenty, the phone
rings: "Hello. I'm Jack. Allen tells me you're very nice.
Would you like to come down to Howard Johnson's on
Eighth Street? I'll be sitting at the counter. I have black
hair and I'll be wearing a red and black checked shirt."
He's an older man, but a boy really, and Johnson paints
a vivid portrait of the guy who calls her cat "Ti-Gris,"

leaves town six weeks after he's met her, comes back and leaves again, and writes her reams of letters from the road.

Minor Characters reads like a novel, and, as in all great memoirs, it's the drama of the author's re-remembering that makes the story, the tension between the adult writing and the person in the past she is writing about. It's her achievement that one feels present both among the characters of bohemian beat New York and in the life of Joyce Johnson, an aspiring novelist who quits her secretarial job at Farrar, Straus to follow her boyfriend Jack, watching him become wildly famous as she comes of age. In less capable hands this book would be a catalog of oft-repeated Beat episodes. As it is, *Minor Characters* is as incisive and delicious an account of a time, place, and cultural zeitgeist as *The Autobiography of Alice B. Toklas*.

HONOR MOORE

Honor Moore is the author of three collections of poems, Red Shoes, Darling, and Memoir, and two works of nonfiction, the memoir The Bishop's Daughter, a finalist for the National Book Critics Circle Award in 2009, and The White Blackbird: A Life of the Painter Margarett Sargent by Her Granddaughter. She is the editor of Poems from the Women's Movement and of Amy Lowell: Selected Poems, both from the Library of America.

A Month in the Country

By J. L. Carr
1980

A young man in his twenties spends the summer in the countryside. He has fled from his life, his future a looming question. This is a familiar story. That he has failed at love, or so it seems, doesn't appear an extraordinary detail either, given the usual trajectory of the bildungsroman (especially of the "summer job" variety). Yet Tom Birkin, the hero of J. L. Carr's *A Month in the Country*, is a recent veteran of World War I, with a facial tic, a stammer, and a ruptured marriage a few souvenirs of his ordeal "Over There." It is the summer of 1920. Birkin, a Londoner, stumbles north to the Yorkshire countryside—"stumble" is his word; he uses it twice in the first three sentences to describe his unsteady arrival from the train into the quiet town of Oxbody. His mission is to uncover and restore a recently discovered medieval mural in the local church. And so the hot, still season unfolds, the Vale "heavy with leaves, motionless in the early morning," and "Birkin up on a scaffolding slowly and methodically unveiling a masterpiece beneath a coat of whitewash." A fine skein of Judgment (with a capital J) laces through *A Month in the Country*, yet in truth the theme of this well-paced, bucolic novel is less that of judgment than of restoration, as the comings and goings of the small town's denizens slowly and methodically nurture Birkin's wounded spirit. Over many tins of tea and church suppers, over many visits by curious locals, Birkin falls for the beautiful young wife of the stern minister, Keach. "Summertime!" he declares. "And in love! No, better than that—secretly in love, coddling it up in myself." Yet the lovely Alice is not to be his; the crescendo of their mutual attraction, against the backdrop of the great painting, peaks and passes in a split second of indecision. "I should have lifted an arm and taken her shoulder, turned her face and kissed her. It was that kind of day. It was why she'd come. Then everything would have been different." The summer turns to fall. Alice and her husband leave the town. Birkin lingers a few days more until, his work done, he sets off across the meadow toward his adult life and back to his estranged wife, unhooking the binder twine on the gate, never looking back. And so it remains a summer idyll; true to such, Birkin's month in the country is full of redemptive powers yet remains a luminous dream—its redemptive force lying in its temporary nature. "And I thought, perhaps you did well to leave early. It may not have lasted."

A Methodist schoolteacher, James Lloyd Carr was fifty-five when he retired, without a pension, to try his hand as a novelist. *A Month in the Country*, published in 1980, was his fifth book of fiction. He was sixty-eight. The novel (nearly a novella at a hundred pages) had a discreet reception upon publication, but went on to be shortlisted for a Booker Prize, win the 1980 Guardian Prize for Fiction, and seven years later become a film starring Colin Firth and Natasha Richardson. Despite some attendant fanfare, the novel remains a modest gem, a quiet and evanescent ode to the healing power of love, even a lost love, and to the redemptive power of art—its discovery as much as its creation.

JEANNE McCULLOCH

Jeanne McCulloch has been an editor at The Paris Review and Tin House Magazine, and was the founding Editorial Director of Tin House Books. Her work has appeared in The New York Times Book Review, Vogue, The Paris Review, O Magazine, and other publications.

More Home Cooking, by Laurie Colwin

see p. 163

A Mother's Kisses, By Bruce Jay Friedman
see p. 312

Mrs. Caliban

By Rachel Ingalls
1983

This fierce, short novel tells the love story of two damaged beings—Larry, a half-human creature who escapes from a research lab, where he was subjected to sadistic and humiliating experiments, and Dorothy, an unhappily married woman crushed by the deaths of her two children.

The prose is simultaneously rich and simple, capable of limning deep emotion and of peeling back the surface layer of people and circumstances to expose the complexity and ambiguity below. On one level, the book is a satire of traditional marriage; on another, it's a fantasy of a brave new world in which a natural and uninhibited man can put on a flowered apron and cheerfully help with the housework, then make love to his wife "on the living room floor and on the dining room sofa and sitting in the kitchen chairs, and upstairs in the bathtub."

On a deeper level, the book is also a meditation on freedom and dignity, love and violence and suffering. Shakespeare's Caliban was a "thing of darkness," a being devoid of reason and grace; Larry the monster man has both, as well as an eagerness to learn what it means to be human. In their short time as lovers, Larry and Dorothy foster and encourage what is best in both of them, and the pain of their separate lives momentarily recedes. But the writer never lets us forget the monstrous and destructive side of Larry's nature. In

escaping from the research lab, Larry tore the head off
of one scientist and dismembered another. His second
act of violence tips the story inevitably toward tragedy.
In the end, no one is saved. But the book has accomplished what Chekhov once suggested art must do—it
has asked the right questions, it has formulated the
problem correctly. What is human and what is
monstrous in what we do? How do we become less
alien to one another? What kills and what heals?

PAM DURBAN

*Pam Durban is the author of a collection of short stories, All Set
About with Fever Trees, and two novels, The Laughing Place and
So Far Back. Her short story "Soon" was included in The Best
American Short Stories of the Century. She is the recipient of a
National Endowment for the Arts Creative Writing Fellowship
and a Whiting Writer's Award, and she is the Doris Betts
Distinguished Professor of Creative Writing at the University of
North Carolina.*

Murderers Sane & Mad

By Miriam Allen deFord

1965

Before 1966—when the publication of Truman
Capote's *In Cold Blood* endowed it with an air of
legitimacy—American true-crime writing was
generally regarded as a disreputable, sub-literary
genre. And in fact it *was*: the product of talentless
hacks pounding out nonfiction sensationalism for
sleazy pulp magazines, and the kind of lurid paperbacks sold on revolving racks in Greyhound bus
stations. As with every other form of popular writing,
however—sci-fi, fantasy, detective fiction, westerns,
etc.—there has always been a select number of
genuinely gifted artists in the field of true crime whose

work, while unrecognized by the larger reading public, is prized by aficionados.

One of these was Miriam Allen deFord (1888–1975). A full-time freelancer for most of her long and exceptionally prolific career, deFord produced everything from histories and biographies to light verse, adventure novels, and a study of notable bastards (*Love Children: A Book of Illustrious Illegitimates*). By her own admission, however, true crime was her favorite genre. "I'm interested in the psychology of the criminal," she once remarked, "and if he's a real person, naturally it's more interesting." Her articles, published in periodicals ranging from the venerable literary journal *Prairie Schooner* to newsstand pulps like *Front Page Detective*, attracted an avid following but remained uncollected until the mid-1960s, when the influential editor and reviewer Anthony Boucher urged "some sensible publisher" to issue a volume of her true-crime pieces. In 1965, the British house Abelard-Schuman, heeding Boucher's call, published an anthology of thirteen of deFord's articles under the title *Murderers Sane & Mad: Case Histories in the Motivation and Rationale of Murder*, reprinted in the U.S. as an Avon paperback the following year minus the scholarly-sounding subtitle.

Shunning the overheated prose and gratuitous titillation that characterize the worst examples of the genre, deFord's essays combine crisp writing, solid research, and sharp insight into homicidal behavior. Her subjects range from such classic criminals as the Jazz Age "thrill-killers" Leopold and Loeb to modern serial murderers like William Heirens (famous for the lipstick-scrawled message he left at one crime scene, "Catch me before I kill more") and the necrophiliac

British psychopath John Christie. A deeply informative, darkly entertaining page-turner, *Murderers Sane & Mad*, long out of print, is a genre classic that richly deserves rediscovery.

HAROLD SCHECHTER

Harold Schechter is Professor of American Literature at Queens College, CUNY. Among his more than thirty published books are the true-crime volumes Deviant, The Devil's Gentleman, and The Serial Killer Files. He is the editor of True Crime: An American Anthology, published in 2008 by the Library of America.

The Music of the Swamp

By Lewis Nordan

1991

The sentence was a paragraph-long freight train of a thing, which was fitting since it was about a freight train. I encountered it in a literary magazine and read the story that it began without pause, tracking that locomotive with its straining, greasy engine and the clickety-clacking of its consonants and vowels. When I reached the end I thought to myself, I hope that this story makes it into a book and that everything else in it is just as marvelous and magical and surprising. My wish came true: the story, "Train, Train, Coming Round the Bend" made it into a thoroughly wonderful collection, *The Music of the Swamp*.

All of the stories feature scenes and events in the life of Sugar Mecklin and his family in the Mississippi Delta. Nordan Southern-fries magic realism and the result reads like the love child of Gabriel García Márquez and Flannery O'Connor. Blue smoke wafts off a bowl of gravy; there's a woman in a glass-topped coffin buried under the family's house; a girl standing in a cabbage patch spontaneously begins to sing an aria and will be silenced only when struck on the head with the side of a hoe. But throughout, it is not the fantastic images and situations that latch on to the reader, it's the language and the timing of the sentences. Word by word, here is the music of the swamp, and it's just as lush and funky and ripe as the landscape.

MICHAEL CHITWOOD

Michael Chitwood has published six collections of poetry and two books of prose. He teaches at the University of North Carolina at Chapel Hill.

N

Nausea

By Jean-Paul Sartre

1938

When I told a friend that my subject for this essay was
Jean-Paul Sartre's first novel, *Nausea*, he made a noise
of disgust—a quick, sharp exhale through his teeth—
and said, "*Nausea*. The very essence of pretension."
Then (get this) he said he'd never even read it, and
asked me what it was about.

I told him it was about my hometown.

To be clear, I did not grow up in Bouville, the
fictional coastal town where Sartre sets *Nausea*, nor
did I grow up in Le Havre, the town on the English
Channel in northwest France where Sartre was
teaching when he wrote the novel, and I certainly
didn't grow up in Paris, where Sartre lived the rest of
the time. I grew up on the Texas Gulf Coast, in a
flyspeck of a redneck town called Highlands. And I
went to high school and then a junior college named
after Robert E. Lee in the nearby industrial town of
Baytown, where Exxon operates one of the largest-
capacity oil refineries in the world. Wherever you are in
Baytown, you can look up and see a refinery in just
about any direction. Discharge torches ten stories high
burn off excess chemicals from the refining processes,
and storage tanks, like giant hatboxes, are strewn
across the land as far as the eye can see. A sign with a
giant Exxon tiger counts the days since the last fatal
accident. As I grew up, the Plant, as it is simply known,
dominated life in that town, and say what you will
about particulate pollutants released into the

atmosphere, those chemicals do make for dazzling sunsets. The novelist Paul Auster once washed up in Baytown as a merchant marine and would later describe a "sad and crumbling little place."

And mister, you don't know anything about the very essence of pretension until you've sold cable TV door-to-door in a Baytown, Texas, summer.

I guess you could say my heart wasn't really in cable sales. But my schedule was otherwise fairly free at the time, this being the summer of 1980. I was seventeen and had almost no sense of the future and no idea of the outside world, just a gnawing, vague, deep unhappiness.

And then one ordinary day I found this book.

There was this guy in a beat-up white van who would come to pick me up every evening and drop me off with my list of names and addresses in the sad hope of selling folks on cable and earning a meager commission. Name was Ben Webber. He'd leave me in a different neighborhood every day. I hated selling, and to tell the truth, I actually just liked driving around with Ben, who was interesting to talk with, a sort of a stranger in a strange land. By Baytown standards, Ben and his brother, Will, and father, Barney, made for a truly weird family. That they all seemed to speak a bunch of languages and took in Amir, an Iranian student who somehow found himself studying at Lee College, definitely marked the Webbers as something unusual. We had a small going-away party when Carter deported all those students during the hostage crisis. Fearing he'd be killed if he returned to Iran, Amir was headed to Madrid, and seemed to be relieved to be getting out of Baytown. I remember being envious.

So Ben and I were driving around one day before my shift, past pawnshops and gun shops and ice houses, on a road that took us right through the heart of the Plant, and I absentmindedly popped open the glove box, pulled out a paperback, and started reading:

"Something has happened to me, I can't doubt it any more. It came as an illness does, not like an ordinary certainty, not like anything evident. It came cunningly, little by little; I felt a little strange, a little put out, that's all. . . . And now it's blossoming. . . .

"For instance, there is something new about my hands, a certain way of picking up my pipe or fork. Or else it's the fork which now has a certain way of having itself picked up, I don't know."

From then on I was hooked. I slipped the book into my bag—stole it, actually (sorry, Ben, that's where your book went)—went home that night and read until I had finished the entire saga of Antoine Roquentin, who in diary form was recording the dissolution of his mind. He called it a "sweetish sickness," this nausea that came over him in waves as he became increasingly and acutely aware of his existence, and of the ominous indifference of the physical world, and as the regular things—objects, routines, women—that he had once clung to for meaning began to fail him.

I couldn't sleep that night. I felt hopped up on this new discovery, and was aware that this was something very special, a bulletin from the wide world telling me I was not crazy, I was not alone. Its effect was almost narcotic. A book—*a book!*—shot me through with a joy so pure. I would read for a while, mispronouncing all the French words, and then stop and just look at the physical book, turning it over in my hands, make a pot of coffee, read some more. This guy Sartre knew what he was talking about. Surely he had been to Baytown.

I did not know what existentialism was; I had never heard the word, and I couldn't even pronounce it. I had no school of thought, nor the vocabulary, to explain why this book mattered to me, why it moved me. It just did. It jangled something that I already had inside, put words to a feeling that comes with discouraging regularity, whether you're in coastal France or coastal Texas. Or, you know, all the places in between.

It is not exaggerating in the slightest to say that this book changed my entire outlook on life and how to live it. I would read *Nausea* every summer for about fifteen years, the same torn and ragged paperback. The purloined copy is the only copy I have ever owned, and it occupies a special place on my shelf. I still pick it up every now and again, still mispronouncing all of the French. But now when I read it, I visualize Roquentin not at a café or boarding house in Bouville, Le Havre, or Paris. Instead, he lingers at the Waffle House, loiters at the half-empty mall, and in the evenings retreats back to a trailer parked in a cow pasture.

It feels somehow more accurate.

MARK WARREN

Mark Warren is the executive editor at Esquire. He is the author of The Good Fight: Hard Lessons from Searchlight to Washington, with Senator Harry Reid of Nevada.

New Days: Poems of Exile and Return

By June Jordan

1974

On the cover of this book, June Jordan wears a big Afro and a smile. I consider *New Days* to be the collection that marks the turning point in her career. These poems carry more weight than what most African-American poets were writing in the late '60s. Jordan's voice is not just urban, it's sensual, sassy, hilarious, and, yes, political. She bends the language toward blackness, and sets the table for all the academic discussions around Black English. I can still see my mentor and literary critic, Stephen Henderson, in his Howard University office, putting down the half smoke he was eating to talk about Jordan's "Getting Down to Get Over." He claimed it to be one of the best poems by a contemporary African-American poet. How many times since that day have I quoted the last lines of the poem?

> teach me to survive my
> momma
> teach me how to hold a new life
> momma
> help me
> turn the face of history
> *to your face.*

The last poem in *New Days* would become the title poem for Jordan's more popular and successful collection, *Things I Do in the Dark*. She autographed my copy of *New Days* in 1975. It's the same year we became close friends and started writing poems to one another. How blessed to fall in love with a woman after falling in love with her book.

E. Ethelbert Miller

E. Ethelbert Miller is a literary activist. He is the board chair of the Institute for Policy Studies and the director of the African American Resource Center at Howard University. His most recent book is The 5th Inning, a memoir.

First Class Mailer

Advertisements for Myself

By Norman Mailer

1959

I sometimes think of how certain artists who are no longer with us would have been right at home with new media. Confucius would be a master at Twitter; Ernie Kovacs, with his short bursts of TV surrealism, embodied the YouTube spirit. On the basis of his penetrating and often maddening omnibus *Advertisements for Myself*, I would argue that Norman Mailer could have been the quintessential blogger. In the late fifties, Mailer wanted nothing less than to make "a revolution in the consciousness of our time." Like the best blogs, this wide-ranging collection of prose in different guises was alive to the possibilities and contradictions of the present. And has there ever been a title that better captures the raison d'être of the entire blogosphere than *Advertisements for Myself*?

Advertisements was promoted as being "unlike any other book you have ever read" in 1959, about midway between two defining poles of Mailer's legacy, *The Naked and the Dead* (1948) and *Armies of the Night* (1968). After two failed novels in the early fifties, Mailer embraced new forms of writing to articulate a fiery journey of self against the creeping postwar conformism. Instead of attempting to write the Great American Novel, he responded to the moment, adapting his literary skills for an existential urban adventure. In 1955 he cofounded *The Village Voice*, first bringing the Beat sensibility of Ginsberg and Burroughs to counterculture journalism. Many of his *Voice* columns were mixed into his *Advertisements* bouillabaisse, giving the nation a first taste of what was subversively cooking in Greenwich Village.

One of the motifs running through all the diverse literary stuff in *Advertisements*—short stories, political essays, drafts, letters, interviews, poems, plays, and miscellany—is Mailer's autobiographical exploration of the emerging hip sensibility, a defiant stand against the enveloping fear in American life. Mailer defined the hipster

philosophy in the "The White Negro," the seminal essay
that became a lightning rod for cultural controversy and is
examined from many different angles in *Advertisements*.
He argues that a true hipster needs to absorb "the
existentialist synapses of the Negro," thereby gaining an
understanding of the danger and ugliness of modern life.
Much of *Advertisements* feels like an improvisatory bebop
session, with Mailer soloing on all the instruments.
Throughout these ruminations, Mailer is probing the role
of masculinity and violence in contemporary society, ideas
that would consume him throughout his career.

Advertisements also exposed the entanglements of the
New York literary scene with an unprecedented brutal
honesty. We are given a view through an open window into
the jealousies and feuds among the literati. Mailer's
assessment of his fellow writers was often devastating,
leading to the severing of numerous friendships. Although
he valorized the Beat attitude, he found Jack Kerouac
lacking "discipline, intelligence, honesty, and a sense of the
novel." He was equally caustic about fifties favorite J. D.
Salinger, whom he dismissed as "the greatest mind ever to
stay in prep school." Bloggers strive for unbridled opinion,
but few have made the put-down such an art form.

Mailer gave several tables of contents for his unusual
anthology, which encompassed some of his earliest
collegiate writing, and he included an italicized commentary
throughout the book, which he used for personal reflection—his own "advertisement" of consciousness. You
could read the book chronologically, experiencing the
evolution of an artist's sensibility. Or you could read it by
genre, perusing the fiction first and then proceeding to the
essays and journalism. Mailer implicitly acknowledged that
the reader has freedom over how to read the work,
anticipating a pre-Internet participation between writer and
the audience.

Advertisements for Myself was ahead of its time; the
hardcover sold only nine thousand copies. But the
paperback has flourished in print ever since, inspiring
writers who want to intersect with their era. Few artists
have melded with the zeitgeist as Mailer did with postwar
America. His warnings about the coarsening and deadening

of the spirit have proved prophetic. Mailer was never a fan
of technology, especially online communication: "I think
the Internet is the greatest waste of time since masturbation
was discovered." Yet his *Advertisements*, rebellious and
self-mocking, serve as the exemplary guide for any writer,
especially for bloggers who want to be dynamically
engaged with the 24/7 present. We need the digital author
who can peer into our national soul and give such a
profound diagnosis. Let's face it—Mailer's compendium
could also be subtitled *Advertisements for Ourselves*.

RON SIMON

*Ron Simon has been curator of radio and television at the Paley
Center for Media since the early 1980s. An adjunct associate
professor at Columbia University, at New York University, and at
Hunter College, he teaches courses on the history of media. Simon
has contributed to many books, including The Encyclopedia of
Television and Thinking Outside of the Box.*

Northern Mists

By Carl Ortwin Sauer
1968

Carl Ortwin Sauer's *Northern Mists* is an account of
pre-Columbian European explorations of Atlantic
waters from the Azores north to the Faeroe Islands and
from Finisterre west to Iceland, Greenland, and what
the Vikings called Vinland and we call the Maritime
Provinces of Canada and the New England coast.
Sauer's scholarship is deep, unhurried, and careful. He
is never pedantic or clotted; he is never tendentious or
excessively speculative; and he has a wonderful eye for
the beautiful fact. Excellent scholarship, though, is only
one of *Northern Mists'* many virtues. Sauer, a student
of geography (the German word *Erdkunde*, the science
of the earth, captures much better the nature of his
enterprise), who for much of his long and distinguished
career chaired the geography department at the

University of California at Berkeley, was widely
admired outside his field—most famously by poets such
as Charles Olson and Robert Duncan, and for good
reason. He had a visionary feel for his governing
subject, the interaction of humans with their land- and
seascapes. He was unmatched at re-creating—out of
fugitive, often legendary, sources, enigmatic fragments
of archeological evidence, documented natural
phenomena, and his own well-examined intuitions
about human and natural migration—visually alert,
subtly dramatic narratives of small, intrepid human
figures negotiating their enormous terrestriality. The
prose of *Northern Mists* is foursquare and pure, the
focus is specific, empirical, often minute, but the effect
is one of continuous imaginative discovery and
amazement, like the amazement the Irish monks and
the Scandinavians blown a thousand miles off their
courses must have felt when they came upon the
unknown lands in the west.

Vijay Seshadri

Vijay Seshadri is the author of Wild Kingdom *and* The Long
Meadow. *His poems, essays, and reviews have appeared in leading
periodicals, and his work has been acknowledged with a number
of honors. He teaches at Sarah Lawrence College.*

Not Since *Carrie*: Forty Years of Broadway Musical Flops

By Ken Mandelbaum

1991

A gem of a theater-world book—and much more
successful than the shows it reports on—Ken
Mandelbaum's *Not Since Carrie: Forty Years of
Broadway Musical Flops* is a breezily readable, insidery

look at tuners that may have looked good on paper but were veritably unwatchable on stage. Mandelbaum takes you from misguided "star flops" (Robert Preston as Ben Franklin, Anthony Newley as Chaplin) to misbegotten film adaptations (a musical of *The Yearling* with real wildlife, but a turkey nonetheless) and beyond, entertainingly relaying what went wrong while making you almost wish, out of morbid curiosity, that you'd seen these shows.

The gold standard here—as witnessed by the book's title—is *Carrie*, the grisly 1988 musical based on Stephen King's story of a weird girl who uses telekinesis to avenge her fellow prom-goers. That show sank into deserved camp obscurity, but Mandelbaum's book cries out for a wider audience.

MICHAEL MUSTO

Michael Musto writes the popular long-running entertainment column La Dolce Musto in The Village Voice, as well as the blog La Daily Musto. He has written three books—Downtown, Manhattan on the Rocks, and La Dolce Musto—and is a regular commentator on cable channels everywhere.

O

The Old Bunch

By Meyer Levin

1936

One of my favorite "secret" books is Meyer Levin's *The Old Bunch*, a sprawling and at times brilliant novel of Jewish American life in the first half of the twentieth century. Students of Jewish American fiction tend to jump from early writers whose roots remained in the Yiddish-speaking world (Henry Roth, Isaac Bashevis Singer, and Abraham Cahan, for example) to the mid-century masters: Bellow, Malamud, and Roth. But there are others worth noting. And for anyone interested in Jewish American life before the Holocaust became part of our consciousness and before Israel became a nation—a time when many other noted literary journals refused to publish Jewish writers— Meyer Levin is one of the authors I would recommend.

Levin is best (if at all) remembered for his sensational novel *Compulsion*, a fictional account of the famous Leopold and Loeb murder and trial. Yet *The Old Bunch*, a realistic treatment of the second generation of Chicago's West Side Jews, is his masterpiece. Although the theme of assimilation and the concomitant crisis of identity would dominate much of Jewish American literature in the second half of the twentieth century, Levin was one of the first to describe a generation of Jews who felt themselves lost between worlds old and new. These were the children of immigrants who eagerly abandoned the traditions of their parents and grandparents in order to join mainstream American society as quickly as possible.

Most moved without remorse toward a future that ignored the past. A few, however, felt a deep sense of loss. And it is their stories that resonate with today's readers throughout the novel.

I met Meyer Levin only once, in the late 1970s. He was in his seventies and dividing his time between Manhattan and Israel, where he would move permanently a short time later; he died there in 1981. I was writing a critical biography of him, and it was perhaps one of the only times his work received any critical attention. Although I had expected him to be excited about the prospect (as modest as it may have been), that was not the case. He was cordial, but clearly troubled that such homage had taken so long to be paid. To understand his life, one needs to know that he was perpetually shunned by the literary powers that be—those he labeled the "New York literary mafia." Despite being one of the first to discover *The Diary of Anne Frank*, and one of the forces in having the work published in English, he was given little credit. His dramatic adaptation of the memoir was ignored in favor of a very similar one produced by Lillian Hellman. (Few remember that Levin later won a court case claiming that his version was appropriated.) So nearing the end of his career and having published more than a dozen novels, he was bitter—and I suspect not particularly well-off financially, despite his many literary accomplishments.

But *The Old Bunch* remains a testament to Levin's literary skills: his ability to recreate a specific time and place and to make his readers care about the people who inhabit that milieu. The novel deserves to be remembered, to be read, and to be enjoyed. In my view it ranks with some of the best of the American novels of the period: those of Dreiser, Norris, and Farrell, if not Steinbeck.

STEVEN J. RUBIN

Bio on p. 16

On Killing: The Psychological Cost of Learning to Kill in War and Society

By Dave Grossman

1995

In the animal kingdom, while it is not uncommon for members of the same species to engage in fierce combat, it is quite rare, whether the animal is insect or mammal, carnivore or herbivore, for the conflict to result in a death. Two lions may battle ferociously over turf, but ultimately one will surrender and the other will walk away. *Homo sapiens* is one of the few species in which conflict results in fatal outcomes with some degree of regularity. Throughout human history, murder, massacre, tribal conflict, racial and religious hostility, war between and among nations, and acts of terrorism have led to incalculable carnage, pain, and sorrow. Death by our own hands appears to be a natural element of the human condition.

In *On Killing: The Psychological Cost of Learning to Kill in War and Society*, Dave Grossman challenges the inevitability of humans killing each other, arguing persuasively that despite our history, humans, like other members of the animal kingdom, have a powerful, innate resistance to intraspecies killing. Extensive data and analysis of a number of parameters, including battlefield conditions, ammunition consumption, "firing rate," "hit rate," and "kill rate," extracted from studies dating to the Napoleonic Wars, present compelling evidence supporting his thesis. Numerous studies indicate that the firing rate—the percentage of soldiers willing to fire their weapon in a typical combat situation—is less than twenty percent. Interviews with former soldiers corroborate the data. Where lines of soldiers are firing at each other at point-blank range, the number of casualties per round of ammunition is less than ten percent. The typical soldier, after lining up a human target in his sights, more often than not finds it impossible to pull the trigger, even when his own life is at risk. When he does pull the trigger, he routinely fires over the enemy's head.

The book explains the data that appears contradictory. German soldiers during World War II had firing rates considerably higher than twenty percent. These soldiers, however, were convinced that non-Aryans were of a different species and, consequently, the intraspecies resistance to killing was not triggered. In addition, Pavlovian conditioning techniques can create a reflexive "quick shoot" response. This can be coupled with repetitive practice under simulated circumstances during training, further mitigating the psychological resistance to killing through a process of denial, i.e. confusing the actual act of killing with the habitual simulations.

After the Korean War, the United States military developed new training techniques for combat troops based on sophisticated conditioning methods that proved highly successful, producing vastly increased kill rates during the Vietnam War. Modern weaponry used in recent wars also establishes a large physical and emotional distance between the soldier and the target, creating an ambiguity as to who is responsible when people die. However, the book explains that neither of these factors nor the training techniques eradicate the psychological predisposition against killing. Soldiers subject to effective training strategies do kill, but the deeply ingrained aversion then manifests itself in other, often debilitating maladies, in particular, post-traumatic stress disorder, which, according to Grossman, afflicted between 400,000 and 1.5 million Vietnam veterans.

The book addresses the phenomenon of killing in considerable breadth and depth, and highlights some of the remaining questions. One incongruous fact is that there appear to be outliers—two percent of the male population—who do not *seem* to have a natural distaste for killing. How much of this is due to their environment? An important environmental question in today's world is to what extent will violence in the media—television, news outlets, movies, and video games—lead to more psychological inoculation against nonviolence?

The unanswered questions do not significantly diminish the book's central thesis or optimistic outlook, asserted in an early chapter:

> There can be no doubt that this resistance to killing one's fellow man . . . exists as a result of a powerful combination of instinctive, rational, environmental, hereditary, cultural, and social factors . . . and it gives us cause to believe there just may be hope for mankind after all.

Perhaps in the not too distant future, instead of pursuing improvements in our ability to conduct warfare, we will seek ways to adapt to our inherent revulsion to killing and figure out how to resolve human conflict without resorting to fatal violence.

GEORGE CAMPBELL JR.

George Campbell Jr. is president of the Cooper Union for the Advancement of Science and Art, an all-honors college that awards every admitted student a full-tuition scholarship. Dr. Campbell, a physicist, is a director of Con Edison, Inc. and Barnes and Noble, Inc., and a trustee of Rensselaer Polytechnic Institute.

One Woman in the War: Hungary 1944-45

By Alaine Polcz

2002

In the photograph on the cover, a young woman walks on the steel rail of a railroad track, holding out her arms in a balancing act while wearing a short white summer dress. This is Alaine Polcz, an upper-middle-class Hungarian girl and the cherished daughter of the Chief Counsel from the Transylvanian city of Kolozsvár (today Cluj, Romania), sometime in the early 1940s. The railroad scene is as idyllic as the landscape of fertile lands—but we suspect that a train will eventually come, knowing that the tracks are not made for humans to walk.

In the early summer of 1944, Alaine marries her fiancé, a young writer and non-commissioned army officer just back from the Soviet front. In a matter of a few weeks, her life is entirely overturned by the unexpected. She discovers that her husband, János, is indifferent to her body and her personality, that he drinks and has affairs. She contracts gonorrhea from him, though she receives the doctor's diagnosis incredulously. Nazi troops have freshly occupied Hungary, their unreliable ally, and the SS and their Hungarian collaborators begin to raid Jewish homes. As Hungarian citizens, they no longer have immunity, and are deported to makeshift transit camps. Alaine and her circle provide asylum and false papers for many, but the larger tragedy cannot be averted. As she prepares to leave for the imagined security of Budapest, an Allied bombing raid nearly kills her in a shelter by the railway station.

Ultimately, in late 1944, she ends up in bucolic Csákvár, in Transdanubia, on an Esterházy estate, where her mother-in-law is employed as a housekeeper in the baronial mansion. János has returned into the wilderness of war-stricken Budapest. The women do not suspect that the area will soon be the site of one of the most bitterly fought armored battles of World War II, where the front will alternate for two months and the neighboring city of Székesfehérvár will change hands eleven times between the Soviet and Nazi armies. As soldiers move in—German officers shattering the mirrors of the Esterházy mansion for fun—Alaine begins to work as a nurse in a Hungarian field hospital. The Soviets are approaching Csákvár, but Alaine and her mother-in-law refuse to escape to the West. They take refuge in the Roman Catholic parsonage—which soon becomes the local headquarters of the Soviet officers. Stuck in the house, Alaine and other women fall prey to the soldiers, who rape them regularly, and in groups, for weeks on end.

It is rare that a woman writes about war in this way, from the inside, as a sufferer and as an acute observer, and about rape, that unspeakable, nonsexual experience of aggression. Alaine survived through will, instinctive strength, and a strong but understated faith, and even a spiritual and emotional empathy for some of the desperate soldiers who abused her. Conversely, her mother-in-law, a religious woman, rejects God at some point during the successive rapes. An estimated 140,000 Hungarian women were treated in a similar manner by the Soviet army in 1944 and 1945. These events are set alongside further scenes of privation and humiliation that reveal what many unsuspecting civilians had to endure during World War II in Central Europe, the precariousness and worthlessness of human life that their imaginations could never have contemplated, absurd moments of humor, grotesque attempts at survival, and humane gestures of companionship and support.

This memoir was written more than forty-five years after the events. To set these things on paper before 1990, even privately, in Soviet-occupied Hungary would have brought a severe prison sentence. Yet this is not a bitter book. It is not about loss but about triumph. It is not an insufferable book, nor an appeal for pity. It is an impartial account with the solidity of the best fiction writing. Polcz must have needed the triumph of a career and a successful second marriage to be able to write this account. Unable to bear a child after contracting severe tuberculosis in the aftermath of the war, she became a child psychologist, and in the late 1980s she founded the Hungarian hospice movement. She wrote excellent common-sense books about psychology, and became a respected figure in Hungarian intellectual life. Some of this second story can be learned from the introductory essay of the translator, Albert Tezla.

Alaine Polcz also had to protect her second husband, the major novelist Miklós Mészöly, by not publishing the intimate details of her ordeal too early. (He was made aware of much of it, and he helped her to recover physically and mentally, remaining a loyal partner to her throughout the rest of his life.) Finally, after Hungary's liberation, when she and her husband were in old age, the time had come for Polcz to be publicly relieved of her burden, her writing of this book serving also as a rite of expurgation for the other survivors and victims who could never speak.

Gyula Kodolányi

Bio on p. 98

Opium

By Jean Cocteau
Translated from the French by Margaret Crosland and Sinclair Road
1930

Opium has long been replaced by other drugs of a more vicious nature, but its literary associations are august. Cocteau's contribution is a jerky, jazzy 1920s notebook, published with his own distinctive line drawings in the modernist style. It has never achieved the popularity of its great predecessor, De Quincey's *Confessions of an English Opium-Eater* (1822), which is more oceanic in its method. But, just as De Quincey's is one of the great texts of Romanticism, so Cocteau's should be regarded (though never is) as one of the great texts of Surrealism, since it arises explicitly where the conscious, subconscious, and unconscious overlap: Cocteau's ornate self-awareness and yearning for abandon here find some ideal reciprocity. Written as the "Diary of a Cure" during a stay in the clinic at Saint-Cloud, its medical usefulness is hardly a factor (e.g., "Tobacco is almost harmless"), and it is better approached as a work of literature. It contains all sorts of fascinating ideas on the nature of reality, inspiration, and intoxication, with ghostly walk-on parts from Victor Hugo, Mallarmé, Raymond Roussel, Eisenstein, Buñuel, and others. Incidentally, Cocteau was no more cured than was William

Burroughs, but the essential was achieved: to manage the compulsion so that creation might continue.

DUNCAN FALLOWELL

Bio on p. 200

Our Horses in Egypt
By Rosalind Belben
2007

I first knew of this book through another writer, who whispered its name to me as if it were a password and I had mysteriously been admitted into a secret club. I read the book immediately—it exists in a strange and exotic realm of its own, its paths sometimes difficult to follow, its creatures haunted and eccentric—and I was, as promised, drawn into its idiosyncratic world with astonishment and awe. It is the story of a young Englishwoman, widowed in World War I, who in 1921 takes her six-year-old daughter and the child's nanny with her to Egypt in the hope of finding her hunter, Philomena. One of thousands of horses requisitioned for the war by the government, Philomena has seen brutal service with the Dorset Yeomanry in Palestine, and is, at the end of the war, abandoned in Egypt, along with twenty-two thousand other horses.

There are other novels, of course, where the life of an animal is imagined. As a child, I was a distraught reader of animal stories (*Black Beauty*, *The Yearling*, *Perri*, *Tarka the Otter*), so I knew what to expect when I began to read *Our Horses in Egypt*. Like those earlier books, it is sometimes unbearably sad. Full of quirks and oddities, it is also humorous and gruff,

mannered and exuberantly original. Read it, and
welcome to the club.

SUSANNA MOORE

*Susanna Moore is the author of the novels The Big Girls, One
Last Look, In the Cut, The Whiteness of Bones, Sleeping Beauties,
and My Old Sweetheart, which won the Ernest Hemingway
Foundation/PEN Award for First Fiction and the Sue Kaufman
Prize for First Fiction from the American Academy of Arts and
Letters. Her nonfiction travel book, I Myself Have Seen It, was
published by the National Geographic Society.*

P

Pale Fire

By Vladimir Nabokov

1962

I suppose it doesn't speak very well for American cultural life that a novel as famous as *Pale Fire* can be thought a fit subject for an "insider's guide." However that may be, I have been besotted with the book for decades. As a musician, I have always been surprised that despite Nabokov's well-known aversion to music his books have such an elaborately contrapuntal air. And in none of them is this clearer than in *Pale Fire*, with its two main strands of narrative (one in the poem, the other in the footnotes) weaving in and out of each other until their catastrophic collision in the assassination of the wrong target. But that's not all: like an ambiguous harmonic field, the book is filled with delicious uncertainties, the chief of which is the question of the very identity of the narrator. I can't get enough of it.

Charles Wuorinen

Charles Wuorinen's many honors include a MacArthur Foundation Fellowship and a Pulitzer Prize for Music; he was the youngest composer to have received the award. His compositions encompass every form and medium, including works for orchestra, chamber ensemble, soloists, ballet, and stage. Wuorinen is a member of the American Academy of Arts and Letters and the American Academy of Arts and Sciences.

The Passionate Playgoer

Edited by George Oppenheimer

1958

Brooks Atkinson, the most respected of all *New York Times* drama critics, called *The Passionate Playgoer* the most civilized book about theater he knew. Civilized, yes, but also the most enjoyable. This remarkably diverse anthology of theater essays, reviews, profiles, poems, commentary, and backstage blarney brings to vivid life the greatest decades of Broadway, from World War I through the 1950s. Actors, playwrights, producers, audiences, press agents, and critics get their due in more than one hundred entries collected by George Oppenheimer, who was for many years the drama critic of *Newsday*. Nearly all the material Oppenheimer assembled in this book first appeared as ephemeral magazine articles, and the collection is presented as his scrapbook from a lifetime of reading and theater-going. The comments of that era's greatest American theater personalities can be found here, from Arthur Miller to Moss Hart, Robert Benchley to S. J. Perelman, Ethel Barrymore to Gypsy Rose Lee. Accounts of Hippodrome vaudeville brush up against Eugene O'Neill. You'll find Elia Kazan's notes on staging *A Streetcar Named Desire* and a spiritual, poignant farewell to theater by one of the most remarkable American stage designers, Robert Edmund Jones. In a timeless parody of drama critics, Frank Sullivan's alter ego, Mr. Arbuthnot (the cliché expert), pontificates that "In this reviewer's opinion, *The Gay Mortician* was powerfully wrought, richly rewarding, utterly engaging, eminently satisfactory, wholly convincing, beautifully integrated, admirably played, and fairly obvious." There is Stark Young on Laurette Taylor's still-influential performance in *The Glass Menagerie*, and—a true hidden treasure—an ironic, unsigned *Daily Worker* review of *Life with Father*, which concludes that the play "may be good propaganda, but it's bad art."

Long out of print (but easily found in either its original 1958 hardcover or a 1960s paperback edition), *The Passionate Playgoer* has over time become much more than the pleasant theatrical celebration Oppenheimer intended. From the distance of our twenty-first century, this remarkable collection is a sharp-eyed return to a time when the American theater really mattered and was part of this nation's common culture. Today it would be impossible to create a book like *The Passionate Playgoer*, not only because the theater has been overshadowed in America but because this kind of theatrical writing no longer exists in any contemporary sense. And yet the book lives on as much more than an exercise in nostalgia. It's an unexpected call from the past to keep the theater important, clear-eyed, and fresh, to never lose sight of a living art's human foibles and creative impact, even in depressed times.

ROBERT MARX

Robert Marx has served as the director of the theater program at the National Endowment for the Arts and the New York State Council on the Arts, and was executive director of the New York Public Library for the Performing Arts at Lincoln Center. He is an essayist on theater and opera, has produced Off-Broadway plays, and is the voice frequently heard on the intermission features of the Metropolitan Opera's radio broadcasts.

Pedro Páramo

By Juan Rulfo

Translated from the Spanish by Margaret Sayers Peden

1955

"I came to Comala because I had been told that my father, a man named Pedro Páramo, lived there." Read the first paragraph of Juan Rulfo's great novel, and you will be drawn into the writer's world, a strange place that is at once real—presented in compelling concrete detail—and utterly fantastic. The narrator, whose name, Juan Preciado, we learn only late in the tale, is dispatched by his dying mother to go to the village of Comala, find his father, and reclaim what is theirs. He does so, and on the way meets a burro driver who says he is also Pedro Páramo's son. They enter Comala. There the mystery deepens and takes over the narrative—and the reader.

We are in a village, presumably in rural Mexico in the late nineteenth century. We are in the busy, beautiful town of the mother's memories, lyrical passages printed in italics that accompany Preciado on his journey. We are in a wasteland (the name "Páramo" means "barren plain"). The story unravels in contrasts. Preciado's memory of his mother's voice: "*Every morning the town trembles from the passing carts. They come from everywhere, loaded with niter, ears of corn, and fodder.*" Preciado's perception: "Empty carts, churning the silence of the streets. Fading into the dark road of night. And shadows. The echo of shadows."

And that's traditional storytelling compared with what happens next. Villagers invite Preciado to their homes. They talk about the place and about Páramo, who turns out to be an evil man. The narrative acquires a dreamlike quality: tenses, personal pronouns, and points of view change abruptly; they are not to be depended upon. Nothing is. The villagers are dead. Only the past is alive. One character says: "This town is filled with echoes. It's like they were trapped between the walls, or beneath the cobblestones. When you walk you feel like someone's behind you, stepping in your footsteps."

When I read and reread this book I find myself continually asking, How does he manage this? How was this done? My edition runs to a mere 124 pages. In that short space, Juan Rulfo has given us a novel of passion, brutality, misery, revolution, and blood revenge. Examine his method—the shifting tenses, the attenuated dialogues—and the achievement of his effect remains as mysterious as the story itself.

GRACE SCHULMAN

Grace Schulman is the author of six books of poems, including The Broken String, Days of Wonder: New and Selected Poems, and The Paintings of Our Lives. Among her honors are the Aiken Taylor Award, the Delmore Schwartz Memorial Award, a Guggenheim Fellowship, and New York University's Distinguished Alumni Award. Editor of The Poems of Marianne Moore, she is Distinguished Professor of English at Baruch College, CUNY. She is a former director of the Poetry Center, and former poetry editor of The Nation.

People of the Puszta

By Gyula Illyés

1936

Physical deprivation humiliates, and therefore also injures us mentally and morally. Deprivation of the freedom of mobility and deprivation of work are equally destructive, and they can eat out our guts. Yet in societies where such states are a common lot, human life is just as rich in variation and genius as elsewhere. Love, solidarity, will, and talent find their apt articulations in these closed and oppressed human environments, too, where resentment is seated deep.

These are typical themes of the 1930s in the Atlantic world, and they found many outstanding expressions in Europe and in the Americas. Majority opinion in the Atlantic world has liked to believe since the '60s that poverty and deprivation belong to the Third World. Yet with the financial and economic crisis that began in the fall of 2007, we may see developments that will force us to once more look into the woes and spiritual resources of the poor.

People of the Puszta, by Gyula Illyés (1902-1983), is a beautiful statement of the committed literature of the '30s, a casebook for sociologists and anthropologists; yet it is also a classic statement on the human predicament, and one of the monuments of twentieth-century Hungarian writing. Into the naturally unfolding description of a *puszta*, in this case a large agricultural estate in Hungary before World War II, are woven enchanting threads of an autobiography. Illyés, who emigrated to Paris from Budapest at age eighteen, returned five years later to the remote and isolated scenes of his childhood in Tolna county. His father had been employed as chief machinist on estates, and thus a foreman among hundreds of farm servants and their swarming families, who were paid in kind and rarely had the opportunity to move up to the higher rungs of society, such as the landed peasantry, craftsmen, or town clerks. The book synthesizes the incisive vision of a young modernist poet bred on French culture and democracy, with memories of the child, fresh insights into Hungarian traditions, and the love and disgust for a world that had hardly changed. Among the many compliments the book received throughout the world, the Australian novelist Gerald Murnane recorded that he was so moved and captured by the book that it prompted him to learn Hungarian.

Illyés was to grow into a towering figure as a poet and prose writer, yet *People of the Puszta* remained his early peak: in it we hear the youthful yet mature voice of a master, worldly-wise yet revolted. The prose is lucid and balanced, poignant and economic in its metaphors, its irony ranging from the tender to the savage.

GYULA KODOLÁNYI

Bio on p. 98

Pictures from Italy

By Charles Dickens

1846

Dickens was already famed as a novelist when he published his two travel books. *American Notes* (1842) is better known, but *Pictures from Italy* is more magical. It might be considered a key work in the transition from Romanticism to nineteenth-century realism, but the former wins out, especially in the original edition, with vignette illustrations by Samuel Palmer (who had spent his honeymoon in Italy, from 1837 to 1839). The book was the result of a tour through France, Switzerland, and Italy taken by Dickens and his family, with an extended period of residence in Genoa. At times, his cleanliness-is-next-to-godliness morality is severely tested, but this only inspires the prose to ever more fabulous, more precise confections; for this is an Italy in the throes of a kind of voluptuous anarchy, after the defeat of Napoleon but before the coming of Garibaldi and statehood. A mythic but deranged vitality haunts the ruins of Renaissance greatness; Byron, not Thomas Cook, still rules, and the air of having strayed into a nightmare—lit by flashes of witchy comedy and elusive, beatific visions—is very strong. Beggars, brigands, and crumbling castles; violent weather and waves of malaria; pagan carnivals and pious madness; squalid inns, terrible roads, and appalling food; semiderelict, Usher-esque palaces or collapsing convents out of Piranesi—all climax in Rome, the greatest ruin of all, where every so often one of the sights hovers like a tantalizing dream of perfection. This is Dickens at his most psychedelic.

DUNCAN FALLOWELL

Bio on p. 200

The Pillow Book

By Sei Shonagon
Translated from the Japanese by Ivan Morris
1002

The Beauty I have chosen to retrieve from obscurity is Sei Shonagon's enchanting and mesmerizing work *The Pillow Book*. It is a document as open and vulnerable, as mortal and flawed as it is possible to write—a collection of impressions, passing things, memories, anecdotes, portraits, reveries, descriptions of nature, small narratives, opinions, and tributes, written more than a thousand years ago in Japan by a woman who served as lady-in-waiting to the empress during the last decade of the tenth century. In this evening book there are so many things to admire, so many beautiful set pieces, so many intriguing fragments, and so many marvelous details that, but for their record here, would be lost to us. Laced with verse and literary references, *The Pillow Book* is remarkable in the way it is capable of rendering this one figure, Sei Shonagon, the motion of her mind, her hand, and her world with such vibrancy and verve. She is right there, and her world is right there too. She is alive in the way many on the page are not.

She renders the crystalline quality of memory and the contours of multiple complex emotions with intelligence and candor. Her powers of observation, her veracity and curiosity, her engagement with the world all afford great pleasure. She looks outward as much as inward, reporting with great acuity on all she sees and does. She is a miniaturist, and it is possible to be stalled by the beauty of the sentence, the beauty of the unit, her eye for the occasion; but then, wanting more, one moves on to be nearer the next bit of wonder.

Her honoring and elevating of the ordinary, the incidental, the peripheral moves me greatly. All the things we have come to believe as true, largely through the Western male canon, everything we have been told again and again as to what the real story is, and where the real story resides, Shonagon elides, and everything we have come to believe should be left outside the story, Shonagon leaves in.

There is a kind of abandon, a desultory, haphazard quality to the progress of the narrative, the way the scenes come to us, that feels uncannily contemporary, fluid, in flux, and early on it becomes clear that part of the drama of the project becomes the drama of witnessing a woman in the act of creating herself.

There is an incredible poignancy in watching this woman forever in progress—even now. A snippet of story might be followed by a glimpse into the life at the Court, and that followed by an acerbic opinion, or the description of clouds or a gift. All this might be followed by a list (oh, have I mentioned the lists yet?), and all of this unfolding in the most intuitive, natural, and intelligent ways, and making, I'm afraid, much of the literature that will follow seem contrived or simplistic or grandiose or silly. With this structure comes a great freedom—oh to quickly change tenor, direction, subject, tempo, dynamics in the way she does here! It is these motions, perhaps, that I treasure most.

I do not want to forget the lists. Here are a few: Things That Fall from the Sky, Pleasing Things, Things That Give a Pathetic Impression, Splendid Things, Shameful Things, Things That Have Lost Their Power, Things Worth Seeing.

If one allows it, a book like this—so spacious, so generous, so unlikely, so meandering—reframes the contemporary reader's notions of what traditional narrative is and what is possible within its wide parameters. Great freedom is afforded here within a flexible, elastic structure. *The Pillow Book* answers a question people have asked me for years: "Don't you think it necessary to write in more traditional ways before you begin to experiment?" Shonagon is all experiment. It was only we Westerners who, sometime much later, invented a bourgeois fiction and inadvertently made its "tradition" law, and it may prove eye-opening for some to see that this tradition, which so many now strive to keep, elevate, and preserve, is not so traditional after all.

Shonagon moves blissfully, serenely through the literary terrain unencumbered by prescriptions, languishing in word and world. Though we are separated by everything—time, and distance, and language—*The Pillow Book* does what great art does: it reaches out to us from unfathomable distances, pulls us toward it, cleaves to us, and changes us in small, inexplicable yet indelible ways.

She continues to reach toward me, to extend her invitation; thanks to her artistry and her openness, I still reach toward her. After a few pages I am slyly caught off guard again, startled again by my affection, my admiration, my closeness to this woman already one thousand years dead. Has anyone ended a book so beautifully before, I wonder? "It is getting so dark," she writes, "that I can scarcely go on writing; and my brush is all worn out. Yet I should like to add a few things before I end . . ."

CAROLE MASO

Carole Maso is the author of nine books: the novels Ghost Dance, The Art Lover, AVA, The American Woman in the Chinese Hat, and Defiance; two collections of prose poems, Auerole and Beauty Is Convulsive; a book of essays, Break Every Rule; and a memoir, A Room Lit by Roses.

Portrait of a General: Sir Henry Clinton in the War of Independence

By William B. Willcox

1964

George Washington is the subject of at least a thousand biographies, but his principal opponent during the Revolutionary War, British general Henry Clinton, is the subject of only one. Clinton served in the top positions of command longer than anyone on either side except Washington, and he was far more aggressive than the Howe brothers, whose feelings of friendship for Americans made them hesitant to crush the Continental army. Clinton was seemingly the ideal man to put down the American rebellion. However, while he handed the Americans their worst defeat of the war when he captured Charleston, South Carolina, Clinton's inaction during the pivotal Saratoga and Yorktown campaigns helped doom the British war effort. In this penetrating psychological study, Willcox examines why Clinton was unable to marshal his own abundant talent and Britain's overwhelming military strength to more decisive effect. *Portrait of a General* is essential reading for anyone who wants to understand not only how Washington won the war but also how the British lost it. Willcox reveals the human dimension of military strategy and tactics—how a leader's internal conflicts can play out on the battlefield, giving his personality a powerful impact on the course of history.

BARNET SCHECTER

Barnet Schecter is the author of The Battle for New York and The Devil's Own Work.

A Princess of Roumania

By Paul Park

2004–2008

Paul Park's four-novel series—collectively called *A Princess of Roumania*, after its opening volume—isn't obscure to certain readers; it was nominated for a World Fantasy Award, and its author is well known in the sci-fi/fantasy realm, where large numbers of readers unfortunately, but perhaps understandably, never venture. In praising Park, critics and authors such as

Ursula LeGuin, Jonathan Lethem, and Michael Dirda
bring up Philip Pullman for comparison; Park's work,
however, is in certain ways much more interesting.
Pullman's imagination is tremendous, and his purposes
gripping, but his novels are often powered by the
standard devices of adventure fiction. There's nothing
standard about Park's series, even as it tells of a
girl's perilous journey from home and safety toward
the recovery of her inheritance. For one thing,
the safe, familiar place where her quest begins—the
Berkshires of Massachusetts—is revealed to, in fact,
be imaginary. (Since long before *Narnia*, children have
been traveling from commonplace homes to fantastic
lands; this is the first novel I know of where home is
the place that's unreal.)

In subsequent volumes—*The Tourmaline*, *The
White Tyger*, *The Hidden World*—Park creates an
astonishingly detailed and convincing alternate Europe,
where the Romania of our experience (and its dreary
history in this century) becomes the kingdom of Great
Roumania. The Ceauşescus, squalid dictators in our
world, are there an ambitious aristocratic clan led by a
baroness who rose from the theater—an enchantress in
every sense, unstoppably evil yet never less than
appallingly (and appealingly) human. Park's mature
and detailed portrait of the manners, hierarchies, and
crosscurrents of a complex society resembles a Tolstoy
novel infused with magical science: journeys to the land
of the dead, entrapped homunculi forced to speak the
truth, the souls of the dying momentarily morphed into
small beasts or birds. Not for one page of this alternate
vision do we forget the real Europe of the twentieth
century; the darkness of Park's creation is different yet
recognizable. Terrifying, magisterial, and written with

great sureness, this series is like nothing else I know. It deserves a readership well beyond the bounds of the fantasy realm.

John Crowley

John Crowley is a recipient of the American Academy and Institute of Letters Award for Literature and the World Fantasy Lifetime Achievement Award. His work includes Little, Big, the Ægypt cycle (The Solitudes, Love & Sleep, Dæmonomania, Endless Things), The Translator (winner of Italy's Premio Flaiano), and Lord Byron's Novel: The Evening Land. He teaches fiction writing and screenwriting at Yale University.

A Puerto Rican in New York and Other Sketches

By Jesus Colon
1961

One of my favorite books of all time, a scrappy 202-pager, is *A Puerto Rican in New York and Other Sketches*, by Jesus Colon, a writer who has one of the most human and humane voices I've ever encountered in any kind of literature, Latino or otherwise. I found my copy in one of those now extinct Fourth Avenue bookstores—the best few bucks I've ever spent.

Jesus Colon writes about everything that pops into his head—about food, music, books, and ordinary folks he's known during his life in New York. Plainspoken, down-to-earth, and funny (with a knack for touching, tossed-off lines), his portrait of New York City as he found it as a newcomer from Puerto Rico in the 1920s, and onwards for four decades, is as good as it gets.

Through sketches with titles like "On the Docks It Was Cold," "Hiawatha into Spanish," and, long before my own novel about the Mambo epoch of the 1950s came out, "The Origin of Latin American Dances (According to the Madison Avenue Boys)," this wonderful writer—who died in 1974 and has since been recognized as a founder of the Nuyorican movement (think humanist lyric hip-hop)—has given us a book that all writers and readers will love, not only for its subtle, hip crafting but for its beautiful, no-nonsense heart.

OSCAR HIJUELOS

Oscar Hijuelos, the author of six novels, is the first Hispanic-American writer to win the Pulitzer Prize for fiction, which he did in 1991 for The Mambo Kings Play Songs of Love. His awards include a National Hispanic Heritage Award, the Raúl Juliá Award from the Repertorio Español, and the Rome Prize in Literature, as well as NEA and Guggenheim Foundation grants, and an honorary doctorate in letters from CCNY.

The Pursuit of Love

By Nancy Mitford

1945

The Mitford sisters grew up in England between the two wars, daughters of minor aristocrats; their only brother died young, while serving in the armed forces. Educated at home, the six sisters careened from their parents' country estate to become a Francophile novelist; a horse-and-hound enthusiast; a famously beautiful debutante, who divorced an heir to the Guinness fortune to marry the leader of Fascist forces in Britain; a naïve but devoted companion of Hitler who shot herself (but survived) when war was declared between Britain and Germany; a Communist who eloped to fight with her young husband in the Spanish Civil War and who eventually became a celebrated muckraker in San Francisco; and a duchess well known

for her excellent cookbooks. Their remarkable lives
threaten to overshadow their literary accomplishments.
Nancy, the eldest, was a best-selling novelist in her day,
although her books now are considered little more than
autobiographical hyperbole, sharpened by the notorious Mitford wit. In fact, her classic *The Pursuit of
Love* is a novel I return to again and again—not for its
barbed humor but for the author's craft and for the
surprise of its rare tender moments. In Mitford's hands,
the travails of finding love are both hilarious and
sincere. We follow a romance-stricken child through
absurd marriages, beginning in her young adulthood,
to love's ultimate playing field, Paris, until war
intervenes. The book is a triumph over sentiment;
readers might be shocked (though amused) to note how
blithely husbands and children are abandoned. But
running through all this evidence of love's carnage is
a strong thread of true feeling, of friendships that
endure and sustain, and of the great spirit required to
pursue love, whatever the cost. The book's most
profound revelation is given to an unlikely source of
wisdom—a delightfully flippant character known only
as The Bolter for her habit of skipping town in search
of her next affair. But, at least with this reader, her
words remain.

Those who enjoy *The Pursuit of Love* might also be
interested in other of Nancy Mitford's novels, including
Love in a Cold Climate and *Pigeon Pie*; Jessica
Mitford's memoir, *Hons and Rebels*; and Mary S.
Lovell's recent biography of the clan, *The Sisters: The
Saga of the Mitford Family*.

NALINI JONES

Bio on p. 33

R

Ravelstein

By Saul Bellow

2000

The erudite cheese-cube nibblers to whom the fates and legacies of authors are unfortunately assigned will, when they get around to him for one final ruling, have a lot to say about Saul Bellow. The numerous wives, the consuming, uniquely Mitteleuropean Jewish paranoia, the intellectual name-dropping: all of it will compute into some form of intellectual batting average or ERA to juxtapose against that of the contemporaries with whom he vied for the mantle of great American novelist—Updike, Roth, and Mailer all leading the pack.

Bellow will be lionized for his fuming *Herzog*, the sprawling *Augie*, and the virtually unassailable (to me, at least) *Humboldt's Gift*, which capped the most prolific era of his career while initiating the most futile one. Nearly a quarter-century of unremarkable, often vindictive, and forgettable work commenced, tarnishing a reputation built upon the exact opposite.

But with the consequence of his own mortality looming, the old hand, then eighty-five, redeemed himself with *Ravelstein*—a tender, tangential, swift repository for a life's collection of people-watching anecdotes and academic gossip. What's more: sex scenes that didn't make you cringe and imagine a disrobed man approximating your own grandfather; a long-overdue tolerance of homosexuality; an ode to a beloved friend rather than a dismantling of a foe; an unexpected and fearless posture toward life's end. A miraculously complete novel, spare enough to remind us how a great writer can punctuate the white spaces between the words and lines with unspoken observations, *Ravelstein* is a final home run echoing a career of true literary virtuosity.

JONATHAN KELLY

Jonathan Kelly, an associate editor at Vanity Fair, lives in New York and always will.

Really the Blues

By Mezz Mezzrow
1946

Among the many excellent books about jazz—Alan Lomax's *Mister Jelly Roll* (1950) is one, Charles Mingus's *Beneath the Underdog: His World as Composed by Mingus* (1971) is another—stands the extraordinary autobiography *Really the Blues*, by the jazz clarinetist Milton "Mezz" Mezzrow (1899–1972), written with the help of Bernard Wolfe. Mezz, born of a poor Jewish family on the South Side of Chicago, is better known for this book, now a classic text on jazz, especially New Orleans jazz, than for his clarinet playing. Still, he played and recorded with the likes of Sidney Bechet, Buck Clayton, Louis Armstrong (his idol), and Eddie Condon. Loving jazz as he did, and jazz being primarily an African-American art form, Mezz identified with and sought the company of black musicians. He became so immersed in jazz culture that he imagined and lived his life as though he were black. He married an African-American woman, and while in prison, on drug charges, he demanded to be placed in the black cellblock, where he soon organized a band. Despite the poverty and struggles recounted here, this is an optimistic book, and the reader (unless in possession of a hard head and a cold heart) smiles with nearly every page.

Really the Blues is valuable for both its individual story and the history it relates, but for me, it was for the language that I read and reread this book. Mezz speaks in a jazz argot so infectious that I had to type out quote after quote: "Sugar plums became salt mackerel fast in that town," and "We began to rehearse like mad, and walked around so chesty we would have made Miss Peacock pull a fade-out." So captured was I by Mezz's language and rhythms that I made a poem out of his words and titled it "In the Parlance of Mezz." The poem concludes with a line emblematic of his buoyant spirit, one uttered shortly after he was released from prison: he's a "skin full of contentment, a bundle of happiness in a blue serge suit."

Barry Wallenstein

Barry Wallenstein is the author of Visions & Revisions: The Poets' Practice *and of six collections of poetry:* Beast Is a Wolf with Brown Fire, Roller Coaster Kid, Love and Crush, The Short Life of the Five Minute Dancer, A Measure of Conduct, *and* Tony's World. *He has made six recordings of his poetry with jazz collaborations, most recently* Euphoria Ripens. *He is an emeritus professor of literature and creative writing at the City University of New York and an editor of the* American Book Review.

Rivers & Birds
By Merrill Gilfillan
2003

I have read six of Merrill Gilfillan's books several times and have never understood why he's not massively famous. My mind has grown a little infirm with age, but I don't recollect being this steadfast with any other contemporary author. I finally met him last year, after having read him for about fifteen years, and discerned a clue to his relative anonymity: he is the most modest and least pushy writer I have ever met.

Another clue came from my "mind doctor," whom I visit on occasion in New York City. He mentioned it was difficult at times to treat patients with no viable contact with nature. This is understandable, as, in my own seventy-year lifetime, the ratio of rural to urban has reversed. In my late thirties, it was seventy-five percent rural and twenty-five percent urban, and now it's the opposite. This means that, through no particular fault of their own, urban dwellers are unlikely to be familiar with the *matter* of Gilfillan's work. Social scientists use a particular term, "geopeity," to describe people's obsession with their own locale to the exclusion of all other places. Bruce Springsteen's fondness for the Jersey Shore would likely be not shared by Montanans.

Not that there is a trace of the bumpkin in Gilfillan—who has also lived in New York City and is addicted to classical music, fine food, and wine—and he is not to be confused with the hundreds of recently arrived environmental writers, many of whom try to write about wilderness without being truly familiar with the flora and fauna in a woodlot.

Though Gilfillan is profoundly knowledgeable about the natural world, I prize him foremost as a literary stylist, though to a certain degree these two qualities are inseparable. The best of writers seem thoroughly informed about their habitat—which includes the historical, botanical, sociological, and geographical—and their own particular literary tradition, which is found by not excluding influences of other traditions.

Gilfillan enlightens and enlivens the landscapes he visits, whether Montana, Colorado, Wyoming, New Mexico, Ohio, or West Virginia. He is an uncanny student of the intricacies of nature, which consequently receive the nondidactic prose they deserve.

His more recent *Rivers & Birds* is a good place to start, and then you will wish to move backward through *Grasshopper Falls*, *Chokecherry Places: Essays from the High Plains*, *Burnt House to Paw Paw: Appalachian Notes*, *Sworn Before Cranes*, and *Magpie Rising*. These are relatively short books, requiring no more than an evening's reading before you are drawn back to them for a rereading. And they are quietly elegant—hushed, in fact, in an age of the tuba of politics, the cymbals of finance, and the snare drums of the media. There is a grandeur in quietness that must be learned, a restorative that has become a secret. Gilfillan has mastered quietness.

Time reveals a great deal of clumsiness in our assessment of contemporary literature—all of the questionnaires, polls, and Casey Kasem–type Top Forty lists betray a hankering for the most recent flavors and are also shot full of the geopiety of the Eastern Seaboard. Gilfillan will tell you about a country you never knew.

Jim Harrison

Jim Harrison is the author of thirty books of poetry, fiction, and nonfiction. His latest novel is The English Major, *and his new book of poems is* In Search of Small Gods. *He is a member of the American Academy of Arts and Letters.*

The Road to Xanadu: A Study in the Ways of the Imagination

By John Livingston Lowes

1927

Very few books change one's life. Of the ones that do, most are youthful infatuations that later come to seem as foolish as that mad fling with a lover you'd never in retrospect want to spend an evening with. Hesse's *Steppenwolf*, the Alexandria Quartet of Lawrence Durrell, much of Tom Robbins—all were as transfixing to me when I was unformed as they were unsettling when recalled later. They only speak to a half-moon phase in my life.

The Road to Xanadu, by John Livingston Lowes, on the other hand, has remained alive inside of me with a shine and a solidity that I entirely trust. It's a great book precisely because it's an unlikely and unrepeatable one that came about in spite of its author rather than because of him. A professor and Chaucerian scholar, Livingston Lowes was browsing in a library just after World War I when he came upon an allusion that reminded him of something he'd encountered in Coleridge's "Rime of the Ancient Mariner." Then he came upon something else that Coleridge had clearly been reading just before he drew his mysterious vision out of the subconscious.

Very soon, the medievalist professor was abandoning his ostensible subject and traveling deeper and deeper into the passages of Coleridge's imagination, seeing how a phrase that stuck in the mind here coalesced with a footnote the poet had found there and, marinating in the unconscious, produced the dream-like haunting that became Coleridge's poem about possession.

It's rare for a work of literary criticism to take leave of everything rational and to surrender to currents and dream-patterns it can't begin to explain. It's rarer still for a man of reason and critical intellect to give himself over so fully to a distraction that carries him along like a dream and a compulsion. The result is one of the greatest travel books ever written, if you consider "travel" another word for "transformation." Every now and then, to this day, I hear from a friend in Bangkok about his secret passion for the little-known work, or learn how a man who foresaw the World Wide Web came to his vision of inner links through *The Road to Xanadu*, and I am thrilled to think that one seemingly forgotten classic is still changing lives as it did for me thirty years ago, when all I wanted was to flee the land of literary criticism and be out on the open waters of intuition and invention.

Some people take hallucinogens; others turn to Livingston Lowes.

PICO IYER

Pico Iyer has written nonfiction books on globalism, Japan, literature, and forgotten places, and novels on Cuba and Sufism.

The "Robinson" Poems (from *The Collected Poems of Weldon Kees*)
Edited By Donald Justice
1960

I love the four "Robinson" poems of Weldon Kees, a poet who vanished one day in 1955 near the Golden Gate Bridge: "Aspects of Robinson," "Robinson," "Relating to Robinson," and "Robinson at Home," all published in *The New Yorker* in the 1940's. Robinson is as lean as the shadow that falls from his razor's edge. I imagine him with Weldon Kees's mustache, a Camel cigarette dangling from his mouth. Robinson's mirror reflects nothing but its own black glass. The pages of his books are always blank. Robinson even had a *first* wife. But she has no more substance than Robinson, who is the writer's own narrowed self. The words Robinson lives with are never really his. "His sad and usual heart," Kees tells us, is "dry as a winter leaf."

JEROME CHARYN

Jerome Charyn has written thirty-seven books, including three memoirs about his childhood, The Dark Lady from Belorusse, The Black Swan, and Bronx Boy, the first two of which were named New York Times notable books. His novel Darlin' Bill received the Rosenthal Award from the American Academy and Institute of Arts and Letters. Charyn lives in New York and Paris, where he teaches film at the American University of Paris.

S

A Sand County Almanac: And Sketches Here and There

By Aldo Leopold

1949

For every hundred readers of *Walden*, there is perhaps one person who has heard of Aldo Leopold. By the middle of this century, it is likely that those odds will be less skewed. Leopold has Thoreau's gift of making us care for anything that catches his attention. He also has a brilliant turn of mind and phrase for dramatizing a scientific observation then infusing it with an ethical urgency. A devoted reader of Thoreau himself, Leopold supplies two things the pioneering American naturalist lacked: a scientific education and a theory of the natural world rooted in ecology rather than the anthropocentric theories of the New England Transcendentalists. In one of his most moving essays, Leopold describes how, as a young forester, he and his friends shot a wolf. They enjoyed the kill, but they also took a high-minded view of eliminating wolves. Fewer wolves, they reasoned, meant more deer for human hunters. Instead, the extinction of natural predators led to uncontrolled growth in the deer herd, starvation, and the destruction of habitat.

The title of that essay, "Thinking Like a Mountain," means exchanging a human perspective for one based in the landscape. The mountain knows the real consequences of the hunters' misguided zeal. The mountain understands that humans are members of the ecosystem, not aliens divinely gifted with control over it. In a series of final essays, Leopold incorporates the mountain's superior perspective into an environmental code—The Land Ethic—that establishes justice for all members of the ecosystem, not the human ones alone.

JAMES H. S. MCGREGOR

Bio on p. 96

Season of Migration to the North

By Tayeb Salih

1966

The best books come to you unexpectedly. It is not so much that you discover them but that they discover you. In the case of *Season of Migration to the North*, the book flew to me across a thousand miles and a couple of decades like the arrow it keeps invoking, released by a librarian closing up shop in a desert. The book lay dormant on my bookshelf until the day it literally fell into my hands as I was shifting a blunderbuss of a novel everyone else was talking about. I opened this slim novel and was completely captivated by the voice on the page.

The story is simple: a Sudanese student returns home after many years in London and discovers a predecessor, Mustafa Sa'eed, who is hiding a disturbing English past, full of death and revenge. The violence of misperception in culture, tradition, and sexuality is explored with tremendous poetic force and honesty. It takes some troubling risks, exploiting even as it exposes the brutality of Mustafa Sa'eed's world both at home and abroad, but the writing is hypnotic. We move effortlessly from a village on the banks of the Nile to Knightsbridge in cosmopolitan 1920s London, and discover that people everywhere are "just like us . . . they are born and die, and in the journey from cradle to the grave they dream dreams some of which come true and some of which are frustrated." Except that some end up killing, or are killed.

First published in Arabic in 1966, and in English in 1969, by Heinemann's African Writers Series, the novel was much acclaimed, but it did not gain as wide a readership in English as it deserved. In 2003, as a Penguin Modern Classic (the first Arabic novel to be included in the series), it was given a second chance. And when Tayeb Salih died in 2009, at the age of eighty, his book was reissued once again.

Romesh Gunesekera

Romesh Gunesekera's first novel, Reef, was short-listed for the 1994 Booker Prize. He is also the author of The Sandglass, winner of the BBC Asia Award, and of Heaven's Edge, which, like his collection of stories, Monkfish Moon, was a New York Times Notable Book of the Year. His novel, The Match, was described by the Irish Times as a book that "shows why fiction is written—and read." In 2004 he was made a Fellow of the Royal Society of Literature. He was born in Sri Lanka and lives in London.

Sex in History

By G. Rattray Taylor

1954

One book I know that has received considerably less than its due is G. Rattray Taylor's 1954 study (not to be confused with a book of the same name by Reay Tannahill). Taylor has used psychoanalytical concepts to break down cultures into two forms, which he calls Patrist and Matrist. The Patrist cultures, originating in Northern Protestant countries such as England and Germany, put God the father and masculinity at the center of consciousness. The Matrist culture flourishes in southern Catholic countries and worships the feminine principle, as most powerfully personified in the figure of the Virgin Mary. If the most overwhelming fear and loathing among Patrists is homosexuality, among Matrists it is incest. Taylor's apparently simplistic concepts hold up surprisingly well when applied to literature. For example, compare the Swede Strindberg's misogynistic writings, and his terror of being thought feminine, with Dante's adoration of Beatrice. Or in religious terms, compare the attraction of the Puritans to the plain, blunt, masculine male with the female worship found in Italian, French, and Spanish cultures. Shakespeare was surely a Patrist, just as Leonardo was surely a Matrist. Taylor has not invented invincible concepts with his Patrist-Matrist dualism, but he has contributed highly functional and usable ones.

ROBERT BRUSTEIN

Robert Brustein is founding director of the Yale Repertory and American Repertory Theatres, and founded the ART Institute for Advanced Theatre Training at Harvard. Twice winner of the George Jean Nathan Award for criticism, he is the author of sixteen books on theatre and society, including The Truant Muse. His seven original dramatic works include two plays about Shakespeare, The English Channel and Mortal Terror. Brustein belongs to the American Academy of Arts and Letters and has been inducted into the Theatre Hall of Fame.

Shadows on the Hudson

By Isaac Bashevis Singer

1998

Don't look to me to anoint any of Isaac Bashevis Singer's novels or stories "his best," just as I dare not enter the fray as to whether he was the best of the Yiddish writers or just the luckiest of them. But I will say this: if Dostoyevsky had been a Polish Jew living in New York in the twentieth century, he might have written Singer's *Shadows on the Hudson*. It's that kind of dark, sprawling, brilliant novel infused with the kind of biting humor that emanates from anguish and despair. The novel spans two years and is populated— haunted—by a vast cast of characters who, having survived the Holocaust (the Holocaust being, of course, the shadow cast over them all), now live in material comfort and spiritual desolation on the Upper West Side. Trying to survive the fact that they survived, all of the characters cope—or don't ("I'm dead and buried. I'm a corpse with a telephone")—in their own way: turning to God, turning away from God, chasing money, eschewing money, embracing sex, turning away from love, and knowing sorrow in all its configurations.

Shadows on the Hudson has too many plots and subplots to book-report, but the central story, such as there is one, belongs to Hertz Grein. A mathematical genius in Poland, he works on Wall Street. Married to Leah and profoundly entwined with Esther, his mistress, Hertz is in love with the also married Anna. Early on in the novel, at a gathering at her father's apartment, Hertz tries to convince Anna to leave her husband and run off with him. The exchange between them is quintessential Singer, wry and wise and, the more you think about it, amazing, in that you've never thought of this before. He tells her: "There's still love in the world."

"Yes, but there's something that's stronger than love."

"What's that?"

"Laziness. . . ."

What is quintessential to the mood of this novel is what Anna's husband says to Hertz: "Before you, you see a dead person. Dead in all respects except that the heart still beats to no end or purpose."

Written and serialized in the *Forward* in the 1950s, *Shadows on the Hudson* was translated into English and published seven years after Singer died. Seven years postmortem isn't likely to be the height of any author's popularity, and Singer's work set in New York was, by and large, never as popular as his folk tales of the shtetl; the exotica of, and nostalgia for, a world and a way of life that had disappeared made for safer reading. The New York stories were, perhaps, a little too close to home. But now that world, too, is gone, equally foreign or foggy in the memory of the next generation of readers as Jewish life in Poland was to their parents. That the Upper West Side of New York is no longer slightly shabby, that there are no longer cafeterias on Broadway, does not, however, make *Shadows on the Hudson* a safer read. That it is sometimes an unwieldy novel, occasionally flabby, does not render it any less sharp. I first read *Shadows on the Hudson* a decade ago, and it has haunted me—*the heart still beats to no end or purpose*—ever since.

Binnie Kirshenbaum

Binnie Kirshenbaum is the author of two story collections and six novels, the most recent of which is The Scenic Route. She is the chair of the M.F.A. program at Columbia University.

The Ship

By Jabra Ibrahim Jabra
1969

One of the first books I remember seeing in my mother's library was Jabra's Arabic translation of *Othello*. Like Shakespeare's tragedy, Jabra's novel *The*

Ship depicts sexual jealousies, suicides, and East-West stereotypes. Unlike Shakespeare's Moor of Venice, however, the characters in *The Ship* love, remember, and die while on a cruise from East (Beirut) to West (Marseille). Setting for a doomed affair between an Iraqi architect and his now-married former lover, trigger of a Palestinian businessman's sad memories of a dead friend and a lost homeland, and refuge to a political prisoner who cannot forget his torture, the ship is above all a literary device bringing together a number of Arab intellectuals whose mundane lives seem well-established on land but remain unfinished on the Mediterranean, where they intersect and transform.

Narrated from various points of view, *The Ship* deftly orchestrates past and present, and portrays a host of fascinating, willful women. It is not a perfect novel; at times its diction and style feel too florid and lyrical. But in an age when literature from the Arab world faces the danger of a religious perfect storm, as many Western pundits flatten Arab culture into religion, Jabra deserves to be read more widely. A novelist, poet, literary essayist, and painter, he was an aesthete who relished the richness of the Arabic language and put it to remarkable use.

ALA ALRYYES

Ala Alryyes is an associate professor of Comparative Literature and English at Yale University. He is the author of Original Subjects: The Child, the Novel, and the Nation.

A Short History of Decay

By E. M. Cioran

Translated from the French by Richard Howard

1949

Sir Robert Walpole said, "Whoever neglects the world
will be neglected by it," which explains why the
philosopher Emil Cioran isn't very famous. Born in
Romania in 1911, he flirted with fascism in his youth,
rejected it, and moved to Paris on a scholarship in 1937.
Unlike those other Parisian Romanians the Bibescos,
Ionesco, or Tristan Tzara, he lived reclusively, and with
some material difficulty, too—a remote high priest of
the Latin Quarter. Cioran has described his books as
"abstract autobiography." Others have misleadingly
called him a pessimist. He can take cynicism to
ridiculous lengths and he flickers in irony; he is a
Socratic dandy whose books are spare, aphoristic,
luminous, and thrilling. *A Short History of Decay* was
the first of his books to be written in French, and it
won a prestigious prize, after which Cioran refused all
further awards on principle. It's a good place to enter
his world of extravagant, perverse austerity: open it
anywhere and experience an amazing rush to the brain.
Cioran, who died in 1995, is our most macabre
humanist and also a master of French prose, so it is
fortunate that he should have the doyen of translators,
Richard Howard, to beguile his readers in English.

DUNCAN FALLOWELL

Bio on p. 200

Simplicius Simplicissimus

By Hans Jacob Christoffel von Grimmelshausen

1669

I have been unable to share my own pleasure reading Grimmelshausen's *Simplicius Simplicissimus* (also known as *The Adventures of a Simpleton*) with others, as the book is so little known. Over the years this seventeenth-century German novel has been translated in bits and pieces, often less than brilliantly, and only sometimes as a whole. Also sometimes in expanded editions, yet never quite in a form that resonates with contemporary readers. Perhaps the author's full name and the book's title, each a separate mouthful—along with the general lack of familiarity Anglo-Saxon readers have with German literature—have been impediments to the work becoming better known. I'm quite certain that it is not only the greatest German fictional work of the seventeenth century but a classic of world literature as well.

Set against the background of the horrific Thirty Years' War, the novel was exceptionally rude for its time, telling its tale in a picaresque style that realistically and humorously revealed an age, an early example of what later came to be known in German as a bildungsroman, a story of growing up. Abbreviated, the protagonist's name could be said to be Simplex, a kind of simpleton, and the story follows him from his innocent childhood into his somewhat jaded adulthood. Dragooned into a soldier's life, Simplex tells his tale in the first person singular. He is at once a court jester, a soldier, a rogue, a thief, and an enthusiastic philanderer. From what we know of the author's life, Grimmelshausen was more than a little connected with his main character and, in addition to his many peculiarities, never in fact wrote under his own name. He practiced obfuscation for many unproved reasons, so much so that until the nineteenth century the public thought his amazing book had been penned by one Samuel Greifnson von Hirschfeld, with his main character being called by another of Grimmelshausen's pen names! Yet this epic of love, war, thievery, poverty, and eventual wealth became an instant success almost as soon as it was published.

A novel of extraordinary color, gallantry, and honor, *Simplicius Simplicissimus* tells us more about life in the times it describes than many better-known books. Like all great fiction, it also tells us about life itself. Picaresque novels, as a genre, headed north from Spain and were probably known by Grimmelshausen, but the sensibility of Simplicius is entirely Northern European. One cannot, for example, imagine Brecht's *Mother Courage* without being sure that Brecht hadn't read Grimmelshausen.

Having looked at numerous flawed translations, I once commissioned a new one. My chosen translator was the late distinguished scholar Bayard Quincy Morgan. He allegedly completed the translation just before his death; his family claimed to have mailed it to my office in New York, but it never arrived. Having seen early sample chapters, I think it might well have been the best ever version of this marvelous book. No carbon was ever found. Oh, to have had computers in the early '70s! Later, I failed once again, this time as a Penguin publisher, to convince colleagues to translate it; the book was considered too obscure. Readers today are, however, left with very good work by Stephen Mitchell. Although theoretically available, few bookshops carry it, and it is still hardly known in the Anglo-Saxon world.

One last note: this masterpiece was written in a language that at the time must have been revolutionary in the German lands, a language that was all at once common, intimate, and rude. We feel we are on the march and in the boudoir with our hero, and we feel we betray no one at all as our hero swears his loyalty and commitment, his sword and purchasable honor, first to one army and then the other. It was a warring time and soldiers' lives were for rent, with little circumstance and pomp but a great likelihood of grisly and meaningless death. So, au fond, *Simplicius Simplicissimus* is a novel of survival in a beastly era. One cannot help but to reflect that it's always beastly in whatever time we live. Thank heavens, therefore, for the humor and humanity of Grimmelshausen's tale.

PETER MAYER

Peter Mayer is president of The Overlook Press/Peter Mayer Publishers, Inc., which he founded with his father in 1971. At the time, Mayer was head of Avon Books; from 1978 to 1996, he was CEO of Penguin Books.

Single Lady

By John Monk Saunders

1931

John Monk Saunders was a handsome and dashing flier in World War I. He was married to King Kong's inamorata, Fay Wray, and he behaved recklessly and romantically most of the time. But in between all this, he wrote novels of exquisite beauty, including *Single Lady*, which I first read in serial form in *Liberty* magazine. Since then, it has been three-quarters of a century that I've been hoping for someone to ask me if there is an underappreciated book about which I feel passionate!

Its central character is a mysterious young beauty whose name is Nikki. She is based on Wray, but when First National filmed it, Helen Chandler played Nikki, enchantingly. She appears out of nowhere at the Ritz bar and is adopted by four former fliers: Cary, Shep, Bill, and Francis the Washout. Actually, they are *all* washouts, smashed by the insanity of war. To the unseeing eye, they are just a bunch of drunks, but delve deeper and you will fall in love with each of them—especially Shep, who stays drunk because there were lice under his bandages in the army hospital, and the only way he can quiet his "tic" is to keep mildly tight.

Critics dismissed *Single Lady* as pseudo-Hemingway, but not in the whole life's work of tough old Ernest will you find characters of such sweetness and vulnerability and, yes, nobility as these five train wrecks from World War I. There is a scene in Père-Lachaise cemetery that surpasses almost everything else I've ever read for tender and sensitive dialogue. You will adore Shep—and Nikki and Cary and Bill and Francis the Washout. And I don't think you will ever forget them.

HUGH MARTIN

A native of Birmingham, Alabama, Hugh Martin began his career in New York as a vocal arranger. With Ralph Blane, he wrote the score of Meet Me in St. Louis *for Judy Garland. Two of its songs,*

*"The Trolley Song" and "Have Yourself a Merry Little Christmas,"
have become classics.*

A Day in the Life

A Single Man

By Christopher Isherwood

1964

The Test

By Dorothy Bryant

1991

Fiction's equivalent to the sonnet may be the single-day
narrative. Joyce's *Ulysses* would seem to disprove this
notion, yet most diurnal stories are short and tight. Think
of Howell's *The Day of Their Wedding* or Solzhenitsyn's
One Day in the Life of Ivan Denisovich. Even Woolf's *Mrs.
Dalloway* isn't *too* long.

Two overlooked yet outstanding exemplars of the form
are Christopher Isherwood's *A Single Man* and Dorothy
Bryant's *The Test*. These California tales will resonate for
any contemporary reader. At the center of both are cars
and the people who drive them. In Isherwood's novel, a
friend asks the protagonist, George, why he doesn't return
to his home country—merry old England—and our hero
replies that even ancient villages have become suburban-
ized. In Bryant's story, a daughter arrives one morning to
take her elderly father to his driver's-license-renewal exam.
Like all single-day stories, both of these novels use the
twenty-four-hour clock as a circle, a necklace, a string on
which to pin the curses and charms of life. "How strongly
he clings to this life he calls ruined, empty, frightening, a
shred of life," the daughter thinks in one instance.

Isherwood's George shows us a man who drives, even
when and where there is nowhere to go: "Even up here
they are building dozens of new houses. The area is getting
suburban." Bryant's novel gives us a man, Pete, who lives
in suburbia and would drive if only he could get to his test
on time.

> One day wouldn't seem to give an author much to work with, but in these two novels it's enough to present an entire world as it vrooms past right before our reading eyes.
>
> DENNIS BARONE
>
> *Dennis Barone's books include* North Arrow: Stories *and (with James Finnegan) the anthology* Visiting Wallace: Poems Inspired by the Life and Work of Wallace Stevens. *He directs the American Studies Program at Saint Joseph College, in West Hartford, Connecticut.*

Songbirds, Truffles, and Wolves: An American Naturalist in Italy

By Gary Paul Nabhan

1993

On the face of it, this is a memoir of a pilgrimage taken by the author to honor his saint, Francis of Assisi. Yet, because the author is an ecologist, interested in the origins of both plants and animals, his pilgrimage also includes meditations on, and discussions of, the land and its inhabitants. Here is an American who traveled back to Italy, walking from Florence to Assisi while along the way observing the land and the ways it was used, and learning the lore of such exotic beings as truffles, truffle pigs, and tomatoes. The book struck a chord with me, as it might with many Americans who have discovered something of themselves in a foreign land: a sort of reverse exploration, uncovering personal depths rather than expanding imperial boundaries.

SARAH SPENCE

Bio on p. 73

Sorelle Materassi

By Aldo Palazzeschi

1934

Slivers of shuttered light burn shifting patterns on the frayed carpet. Protected from the enervating heat of the Tuscan sun, the Materassi sisters sew fine undergarments for a bride's trousseau. They are the last to practice their painstaking craft, working patiently and mostly silently in the shadowed interior of the house that has been passed down through generations. From within this self-cloistered world, the sisters witness the advent of modernity.

Scarcely the stuff of a racy novel: polite ladies on the margin of aristocratic society with repressed memories of youth and imagined romance, who dress formally for midday Sunday dinner. Aldo Palazzeschi's *Sorelle Materassi* portrays a stultifying society as it fitfully encounters the world of young people, their fast cars, their dreams, and their multiple transgressions—cigarettes, raucous friends, brash behavior, and easy sensuality. Slow-paced and beautifully written, the novel is marvelously evocative of a long-ago Florence suggested by the Tuscan proverb buried at the book's heart: "*Moglie e buoi dei paesi tuoi*" (one's country produces similar wives and oxen); it also suggests that women, like oxen, are born to work, mate, and remain unthinkingly docile.

Modernity has overtaken this world, but not without a sense of loss and a tinge of melancholy. To glimpse lives and attitudes that have not wholly disappeared even today, permit yourself to be transported on the dust motes of time to the sitting room of the Materassi sisters.

WILLIAM E. WALLACE

William E. Wallace is the Barbara Murphy Bryant Distinguished Professor of Art History at Washington University in St. Louis. He has published extensively on Renaissance art and is an internationally recognized authority on Michelangelo. His books include the award winning Michelangelo: The Complete Sculpture, Painting and Architecture, Michelangelo at San Lorenzo: The Genius as Entrepreneur, *and a forthcoming biography,* Michelangelo: The Artist, the Man, and His Times.

Small-Press Gems

Souls of Wind
By John Olson
2008

Army of One
By Janet Sarbanes
2008

It's an old story: a book published by a small literary press astounds the reader, who wonders if anyone else will ever see it over the unavoidable slop of Big Publishing House X, Y, and Z confronting our every turn. At least twice in a single year, I read works of fiction that fascinated me and that I knew multitudes of readers would love but, alas, will never, ever see. They are John Olson's novel *Souls of Wind*, about an imaginary trip by the poet Arthur Rimbaud to St. Louis, Missouri, and then to Wild-West America on a paleontological expedition; and Janet Sarbanes's *Army of One*, an ingenious collection of stories that take various innovative forms and that feature characters that go far beyond the zaniness of any in Nathaniel West's oeuvre. I mention these two books—one from Quale Press and the latter from Seismicity Editions—with the intention of drawing some attention to them, and away from the latest chain-store masterpiece piled so mountain high at the entrances that one shouldn't dare to touch a copy for fear of death by avalanche. Order *Souls of Wind* and *Army of One* from Small Press Distribution, and they'll arrive at your door ready to be read, appreciated, and admired. Now, these, you'll say along with me — these are *books*.

DENNIS BARONE

Bio on p. 302

Sour Sweet

By Timothy Mo

1985

I remember an article written back in the early '90s lamenting Timothy Mo's slide into relative obscurity. Despite having been nominated three times for the Booker Prize, this Sino-British writer might be a household name had he won at least once. (The other two nominees were *An Insular Possession* and *The Redundancy of Courage*. His first novel, *The Monkey King*, is said by some to be the best novel about Hong Kong ever published in the West. It was awarded the Faber Prize in 1979.)

Set in 1960s London, this virtuoso comic novel serves us the Chen family and their kin, lots of them, as they try to make a go of it in the restaurant business. Chinese restaurants, iconic and essential, are omnipresent worldwide, yet they are largely taken for granted. *Sour Sweet* is perhaps the first Western novel to take us back into the steamy, aromatic kitchen and into the living rooms and bedrooms of the people who operate them. One's heart goes out to Mr. Chen, something of an Everyman, something of a sop, something of a man constantly one step behind making that one good success. The descriptions of food alone are worth the price of admission and guaranteed to keep the true foodies salivating:

> . . . sweet black gelatine rolls, formed of layers of transparent film thinner than tissue paper, which gleamed and shivered tantalisingly; cakes of crushed lotus seed paste with fiery, salty egg yolks inside; cold cuts of abalone, chicken, ham, smoked fish, fungus strips, mushrooms so thick and succulent they tasted like meat . . .

Borrowed money, gambling losses, drug money, violence, and vice snake their way into this essentially family-oriented narrative, primarily in the form of the wickedly pragmatic and colorful Hung family, old-school gangsters from the mainland whose sense of entitlement is centuries old, and whose methodology comes straight out of Sun Tzu. They come to plague the Chens like kung fu locusts.

Mo's work anticipates the milieu and artistry of Zadie Smith and many of her contemporaries among the post-colonial British literati. He has the comic cleverness of Martin Amis, but with a heaping (and helping) dollop of his own brand of searing yet gentle wit. Mo remains one of the best and more humane of the lot, and this delicious novel is well worth reading.

RANDALL KENAN

Bio on p. 108

Southland

By Nina Revoyr

2003

I continue to be haunted, on so many levels, by Revoyr's elegantly written novel *Southland*, about a young law student who is led to uncover secrets of her

Japanese-American grandfather's past, as well as the hidden stories of the Los Angeles neighborhood where he once lived and had a small shop.

It still causes me to see the city differently and look more closely at the remnants of forgotten histories as I drive through its neighborhoods—when I see a large old Italian meeting hall in Chinatown; or a bustling Hispanic neighborhood on the former Central Avenue site of the city's once legendary black jazz clubs, where only the Dunbar Hotel remains; and, as in the story of *Southland*, a struggling black community in the Crenshaw district, which erupted in racial tension during the 1965 Watts riots—where there once had been a kind of small town within the big city, a thriving multiethnic oasis of strawberry and barley fields.

The history of a city's neighborhoods is always just under the surface, waiting for someone to be curious enough or to care enough to make sense of it. *Southland*'s journey of discovery takes place just after Los Angeles's 1994 Northridge earthquake and moves in time back to the 1965 Watts riots, as well as to the post–World War II period when a young Japanese-American GI (recruited straight from the internment camps) makes a new life for himself. It's a compelling narrative of past and present, uncovering some sad and beautiful stories of Los Angeles's Japanese- and African-Americans. After reading it, it's difficult to look at the city's neighborhoods without contemplating its hidden stories and their repercussions.

KERRY SLATTERY

Kerry Slattery is the General Manager and Co-Owner of Skylight Books, an independent bookstore in the Los Feliz neighborhood of Los Angeles.

Specimen Days

By Walt Whitman

1892

Specimen Days presents America's greatest poet in an even more informal mode than he allowed himself in *Leaves of Grass*. Fortunately and surprisingly, the result is not slovenly or self-indulgent but energetic, moving, and insightful. What Whitman saw and what he felt are inextricably bound, but the self here is in abeyance; it is not the poet's subject but his lens. He surfaces as a ready responder to a spectrum of situations that present the most dramatic contrasts. He rides the ferry from Manhattan to Brooklyn and describes the excitement he feels in the industry of the port. He rides the horsecar up Broadway, generally sitting on top with the driver. He describes the congestion, the noise, and the motion, but also the stories that the drivers tell and the most notable things he has seen in Manhattan: John Jacob Astor as an old man swathed in furs settling into his carriage, and the actors and actresses in the Broadway theaters.

Moving passages describe events on the periphery of the Civil War: the overconfidence felt by New Yorkers following the secession of South Carolina, shattered by the events at Bull Run. Whitman watches the weary, disorderly troops staggering back to safety in Washington, the weeping women who feed and shelter them, and the half-suppressed grins of Southern sympathizers who look on and say nothing. His descriptions of the field hospitals where he reads to the wounded and writes their letters home are the best-known parts of this book. Its most striking passage may be a late-night description of Lincoln's

White House, heavily guarded and bright with gaslight under a full moon. It is both a place of industry and a dream palace of possibility.

JAMES H. S. McGREGOR

Bio on p. 96

Speedboat

By Renata Adler

1976

Like the work of Borges or Gary Lutz, and maybe a handful of others, Renata Adler's first novel, *Speedboat*, is so perfect—such a surfeit of *this is how it should be done*—that reading more than twenty pages in one go can exhilarate to the point of exhaustion. I'm not saying don't read it. I'm saying take your time. And if you're like me, you'll end up grabbing every copy you see (it's inexplicably out of print) and pressing them on to friends. I'm saying that it's starting to take on the character of a resplendent relic from some mystery cult of Eternally Hot Prose, and to simply call it a novel risks making it sound normal.

Plot is barely present, unless each of the book's many sections—some as short as a line, few longer than two pages—constitutes a story. Does it matter, when everything Adler chooses to describe holds us in deep fascination from first cap to full stop? A scrap of conversation, a memory of a party or prep school or someone else's bad behavior, a joke, an explanation of a superstition; anything is beautiful if you say it is. The spaces separating the sections serve as punctuation.

Put another way: ever attuned to its own motor, *Speedboat* again and again builds up intense lexical velocity before crashing into its own awesome silences.

Put another way: it's not a novel. It's a collection of exquisite prose poems.

But it *is* a novel, with one of the most astonishingly supple voices in modern fiction, by turns confessional and coolly detached. Our nameless narrator, a journalist, has perfect pitch and a set of permanently raised eyebrows, along with a capacity for epigrammatic deadpan: "People who are less happy, I find, are always consoling those who are more." To read it is to let it take up space in your head, let its echo bleed into your own voice. The world-weary note is struck, again and again, but you're allowed to laugh: "There are some days when everyone I see is a lunatic." The anecdotes scan first as whispers, then as screams. The carefully polished fragments amount to a tantalizing portrait of a woman on, or past, the verge, who knows exactly when everybody left the party. The time is the mid '70s, the place mostly New York. The blackout is a couple of years away, but it feels like she's already been through it.

Here's the first sentence: "Nobody died that year." And here's the last: "It could be that the sort of sentence one wants right here is the kind that runs, and laughs, and slides, and stops right on a dime." Don't you want to know what happens in between?

ED PARK

Ed Park is the author of the novel Personal Days and a founding editor of The Believer.

The Spirit Catches You and You Fall Down

By Anne Fadiman

1998

This book should be required reading for anyone about to take a job that involves dealing with people from another culture. It follows the illness of Lia Lee, a little girl born to a family of Hmong refugees in the Central Valley of California in the early eighties. The Hmong are a tribal people, some of whom fought for the CIA in Southeast Asia, and many of whom came to the United States after the Vietnam War. Lia had epilepsy, a condition that is described in the Hmong language with words that translate into "the spirit catches you and you fall down." Her illness resulted in a dreadful clash between people who were, on both sides, well-intentioned. Anne Fadiman unfolds this story with the seemingly effortless inclusion of background—on Lia's medical condition, for instance, and particularly on the history and culture of the Hmong— that's possible only when the author has learned more about her subject than was necessary to write the book. I think of *The Spirit Catches You and You Fall Down* as a model of nonfiction writing.

CALVIN TRILLIN

Bio on p. 76

The Square Sun, by Stefan Knapp

see p. 196

Bruce Jay Friedman

Stern

Bruce Jay Friedman

1962

A Mother's Kisses

By Bruce Jay Friedman

1964

It may seem something of a cheat to choose two books rather than one, but here's why it's fair: you can buy *Stern* and *A Mother's Kisses* bound together in one volume. *Stern* was Bruce Jay Friedman's first published novel; *A Mother's Kisses* came a couple of years later, in 1964.

When these dark and terrifyingly jocular novels were published, Friedman was branded and corralled with the herd of Jewish-American novelists charging through the culture, along with Bellow, Malamud, Roth, and the now shockingly overlooked Wallace Markfield. Friedman is perhaps the most secular of the lot, and page by page the funniest. As a young man, he tried to support himself by grinding out copy for the so-called Men's Magazines, where the elegance and endless attention span of the reader could not be assumed, and in these first two novels (and throughout his career, which is still very much alive), he maintained a kind of gruff directness—a stripped-down style that captured perfectly his protagonists' hapless hedonism, their thirst for life, as well as their dread and their panic.

Part Buster Keaton, part Samuel Beckett—though always careful to maintain their distance from what Terry Southern, Friedman's fellow sojourner in the world of pulp, derisively dubbed "Qual-Lit"—*Stern* and *A Mother's Kisses* are small tragicomic masterpieces, and, though they have been hanging in the culture's closet for nearly half a century, they prove that finely tailored black garments made of first-rate materials never go out of style.

SCOTT SPENCER

Scott Spencer is the author of nine novels, two of which have been nominated for the National Book Award.

Stern

Bruce Jay Friedman
1962

I am always happy when someone asks me what I consider to be the funniest book ever written because it is a question—unlike, say, "How can we achieve peace in the Middle East?" or "What's new?"—to which I have an answer. *Stern*! It is a story that is easy to follow because nothing that can be called "much" happens: a Jewish man named Stern moves to the gentile suburbs with his family and lives his life. However, if you are the eponymous Stern, a world-class paranoiac, this is a lot. The bugs that invade his bushes, the ulcer that invades his stomach, and the neighbor who insults his wife with an anti-Semitic slur and peers between her legs all land him in Nervous Breakdown Country. It is more a tragic tale than a comic one, which, I guess is why it is supremely hilarious (and heartbreaking). As you read along, you think, I'm glad I'm not Stern, and then you think, But maybe I am. And then you laugh because you're either a sadist or a masochist.

PATRICIA MARX

Bio on p. 41

The Stories of Paul Bowles

By Paul Bowles
2001

Many people know Paul Bowles for his novels, but not so many have read his numerous short stories. They pinpoint the clashes between foreigners and the people of the various countries of interest to Bowles, as well as giving the uninitiated a taste of life in Morocco, Latin America, or Sri Lanka. The stories usually end up in tragedy and leave a taste that is often unfamiliar.

In "A Distant Episode," (1947) Bowles explores the failure of communication between a French linguist and Saharan tribesmen. The linguist returns to a desert town where he thinks he knows the innkeeper and where he believes he will be able to study various dialects of Moghrebi. Upon arrival, he goes to the café, only to find a different innkeeper, who takes him out into the desert to look for camel-udder purses. He asks, "Is this a situation or a predicament?" This is a question that Bowles asks in many of his stories. Instead of buying a purse, the linguist is attacked by Reguibat bandits, beaten, robbed, and left unconscious. In the morning, a robber wakes him, squeezes his nose, then pulls out and cuts off his tongue. The linguist goes into shock, where he remains for a year or so, dressed in tin cans and made to dance and make sounds for the amusement of the Reguibat. Some time later, the Reguibat decide to sell him to the Tuareg. After he is sold, the linguist hears some Tuareg speaking Arabic, the first language he has understood in more than a year. He refuses to perform, and eventually breaks out of the house where he is being held. As the story ends, a French guard sees him run by, and remarks that "a holy maniac" is running into the desert. This sort of tragic failure to understand where a person is and how the people there act is a recurring theme in Bowles's short stories.

"He of the Assembly" (1960) recounts the nocturnal ravings of a young kif smoker and his chance encounter with a man whom he befriends and then robs. It ends with the Nchaioui proverb "A pipe of kif before breakfast gives the strength of a hundred camels in the courtyard." Bowles has a series of these stories describing the debate between kif smokers and alcohol drinkers as to who is superior.

Anyone interested in the obscure, odd, or just different should read *The Stories of Paul Bowles*.

STEVE BERCU

Steven Bercu is the president of the BookPeople bookstore in Austin, Texas. He practiced law for twenty-five years before entering the book business. He is an American Booksellers Association (ABA) board member and president of the Independent Booksellers Consortium.

Straight Life: The Story of Art Pepper

By Art and Laurie Pepper

1979

"*Straight Life*, by Art and Laurie Pepper"—even the word "by" on the book's cover has a special, bewildering, and exciting meaning: a *jazz* meaning.

Laurie Pepper gives an elegant, three-sentence preface:

> This is a true story, a tape recorded narrative by Art Pepper (and those who've known him) which I have transcribed and edited. In order to avoid embarrassing a number of people, some details have been changed and pseudonyms are occasionally used. Attitudes, intentions and feelings attributed by Art Pepper to anyone besides himself should be understood by the reader to be Art's impressions, not fact.

The emphasis on truth, and on the subjectivity of truth; the sleek plainness of the statement introducing a furious, wild set of variations and evolutions; the spontaneity and calculation of spoken, recorded

narrative, the collaboration and the idiosyncrasy; the
laconic irony and the implicit passion: all these have a
jazz quality, emphasized and deepened by *Straight
Life*'s epigraph:

> What is the use of talking and there is no end of
> talking.
> There is no end of things in the heart.
>   —Ezra Pound

The book is talked and it is composed, from Art
Pepper's heart and in his voice. It has the qualities I
admire in writing, though it was not literally "written"
but spoken by its main author.

The material of this life story is mostly hard drugs
and jazz music, and its action is the agony of self-
destruction and self-preservation. The way I remember
passages in Dickens, Joyce, and Dostoyevsky, I
remember Pepper's account of the first time he takes
heroin and his account of making his historic recording
Art Pepper Meets the Rhythm Section with Miles
Davis's rhythm section—Pepper playing with those
master sidemen while he was strung out, with a horn
needing repair, the instrument neglected because he
hadn't practiced for six months. Having been either in
prison or stoned, Pepper hadn't heard current tunes
like "Imagination"; Red Garland played the head
melody once, and Art Pepper played an approximate
version of it, later (rightly) praised by critics for its
inventive quality.

Art Pepper has no interest in making jazz or drugs
romantic. There is no glamorous bullshit here—though
there are heroes, like the producer Les Koenig, who
defied the Loyalty Oath and the HUAC scoundrels,
leaving movies for music. Pepper hates hypocrisy and
complacency. The style of his book, like the style of

real poetry, disrupts ease with discovery. Pepper's
description of the night he dueled with his rival Sonny
Stitt, the two saxophone players challenging one
another with multiple choruses of improvisation, is
exciting—but the narrative of that cutting session is as
grim and doomed and realistic as battles in *The Iliad*.

ROBERT PINSKY

*Robert Pinsky's many books of poetry include Gulf Music. His
best-selling translation The Inferno of Dante received the Los
Angeles Times Book Award. He is among the few members of the
American Academy of Arts and Letters to appear on both The
Simpsons and The Colbert Report.*

The Street of Crocodiles

By Bruno Schulz
1934; first published in English, 1963

A slim book of hallucinatory stories in which the writer
recaptures the weirdness of the world when you were a
boy, before the black lines were drawn between now
and later, you and me. Two steps from the door, he's in
another country. Most of these stories are about simple
family things, a trip to the market, a walk to town, the
first snow, but are wildly abstracted in a heroic attempt
to get back the weirdness of that first world, the deep
knowledge taken from everyone, even the craziest
street visionary, by the passage of time. Your toddler
nephew is dreamy because he was with God a minute
ago—that's what Schulz was after in these stories. In
the end, the otherworldly quality of these stories,
which began as letters to a friend, cannot be untangled
from the otherworldly quality of the author's life: he
was a would-be painter and high-school art teacher in
a Galacian town, one of those burgs in distant orbit
around Vienna. When his stories were published in the

'30s, he was famous, but just for a moment. By the end
of the decade, his country had been overrun by Nazis,
its Jews closed in ghettos. Schulz, taken as a kind of
mascot by a Sturmführer, was allowed to live in town,
where, among other things, he painted illustrations of
Grimm's fairy tales on the walls of the Sturmführer's
baby nursery. But when the Sturmführer got in a fight
with a competing Sturmführer, that competitor,
knowing Schulz to be his rival's mascot, a trained dog,
shot him dead in town. Schulz, the tether connecting
him to our world finally cut, lay in the street for hours
before his body was taken to the graveyard. A few years
ago, a family living in what they took to be an ordinary
house in an ordinary village in Poland, discovered, while
stripping paint in a pantry, Schulz's illustrations. While
the authorities were deciding what to do, a few Israelis,
disguised as tourists, paid off the family, cut the wall
into pieces, and carried them back to Israel, where the
wall has been rebuilt and is on display at the Jewish
Museum. In this one man, you therefore have the entire
story of the Jews at the end of Jewish Europe: the
mysticism and flight from the real forced on the brain
by centuries in the ghetto, the art made in the land of
the enemy—songs of Zion sung in a strange land; the
whitewash; the rediscovery; then the sudden, presump-
tuous, late-game appearance of the Jewish State, which
spirits off and redefines a weird idiosyncratic work as
the expression of the exile. If there is ever a new Jewish
Bible, Schulz's book will be canonized along with the
works of Primo Levi and Sigmund Freud, as slender and
picked over and mesmerizing as the Book of Job.

Rich Cohen

*Rich Cohen is the author of, among other books, Tough Jews,
Sweet and Low, and Israel Is Real: An Obsessive Quest to*

Understand the Jewish Nation and Its History. He is a contributing editor at Vanity Fair, and lives in the north country of Connecticut, in the hills, with his wife and many sons.

The Summer Book

By Tove Jansson

1972

Like most English-language readers, I was introduced as a child to Tove Jansson through her exceptional Moomin series. Many years later, I came upon a secondhand copy of *The Summer Book*, thrilled to find that she also wrote for adults.

Set on a tiny island in the Gulf of Finland, the novel consists of vignettes, postcards from summers shared by Sophia, a motherless six-year-old, and her artist grandmother. Sophia's father is also present, though only just, since interaction and dialogue are limited to the two females. I know this all sounds perilously twee; fortunately, *The Summer Book* is as bracing as the chilly Baltic Sea water.

Carefully observing the natural world, Sophia and her grandmother also observe each other. The hardscrabble setting contributes to a timeless, unsentimental feel: "On an island, the grandmother thinks, everything is complete."

Jansson based the characters on her own recently deceased mother and on her niece. They often bicker but never discuss the dead mother, though death figures in more than a few of their conversations. Sophia and her grandmother draw "awful things," build Venice in a marsh pool, row to other islands, swim, and sleep. It's a rare picture of non-romantic love, of two individuals, decades apart, attempting to figure out who the other one is. Jansson leavens the tenderness with a great deal of pragmatism, even toughness. "It was a dreadful disappointment," the grandmother admits as Sophia wails after being left out of her father's excursion to a passing ocean liner, "but blow your nose anyway. You look awful."

The Summer Book is delicate but not precious. Jansson's plain language plumbs emotional depths without resorting to bromides, the memorable result as enchanting as childhood itself.

MEGAN RATNER

Bio on p. 113

The Sword of Honour Trilogy *(Men at Arms, 1952; Officers and Gentlemen, 1955; Unconditional Surrender, 1961)*

By Evelyn Waugh

1994

Evelyn Waugh is probably best known in the United States as the author of *Brideshead Revisited*. In the U.K., he is renowned as the author of *Scoop*, *Decline and Fall*, and a handful of other novels satirizing the decadent, debauched, frequently penniless, but still witty and amusing, Britain of the 1920s and 1930s. Less well known is his work on the 1940s, namely, his war trilogy, *The Sword of Honour*. It consists of three short books—*Men at Arms*, *Officers and Gentlemen*, and *Unconditional Surrender*—whose characters are the incompetent officers, disinterested enlisted men, and indifferent civilians of the wartime army, and whose themes are the ridiculous rituals, pointless tasks, and mindless cruelty of military life. He describes the ludicrous training camps and the chaotic administration which he himself experienced in the army. He also describes the panicked British abandonment of Crete, as well as its army's deeply cynical arrest and deportation of thousands of White Russians—which Waugh had also witnessed—to the Soviet Union, where most were killed.

The books are pessimistic, despairing, and tragic. They are also hilarious. Though their real theme is the death of idealism, they read as if they were purely comic. Waugh clearly set out to paint a devastating picture of mid-century Britain—but he can't stop himself from making jokes at the same time.

Anne Applebaum

Anne Applebaum is a columnist for the Washington Post and Slate magazine, writing about history, politics, and foreign policy, particularly European and Russian. Her most recent book, Gulag: A History, won the 2004 Pulitzer Prize for nonfiction.

T

The Telephone Booth Indian

By A. J. Liebling

1942

What book would you choose to epitomize New York? Which book speaks directly to the delightfully dark heart of the city, as *Taxi Driver* or *The Sweet Smell of Success* might in film? To me, a lifelong Manhattanite, that book is A. J. Liebling's *The Telephone Booth Indian*, his love poem to the petty con men, boskos, chorines, and gozzlers who comprise the midtown stew.

The Telephone Booth Indian chronicles the labyrinth hierarchy of the Jollity Building on Broadway in the upper forties, a cubicled souk of small-time swindlers and various sharpies whose fortunes fall and fall harder in the eternal quest for pastrami sandwiches and two dollars to lose at the racetrack. Those in the social catbird seat—bookies, orchestra leaders, burlesque promoters—rent time-shares in the upper-floor desks so prospective suckers can be greeted between, say, 2 and 4 P.M. in a semi-legitimate office surrounding. But the bons vivants without a dollar are forced to huddle in the lobby, near the bank of telephone booths, having earlier given out that phone number as the world headquarters of their no-account enterprise.

It's a tricky thing to squat in a telephone booth all afternoon, awaiting the ring of an elusive mark, but Liebling's boys ground the system of looking busy into a science, shouting into the mouthpiece with the receiver cupped urgently to their ear and the hinged door slammed tight.

Liebling's reverence for these chiselers and their quest for the soft dollar is jumbo-sized. He not only devours their flimflam artistry like a fat man at the hot-cold buffet table, but he also loves describing them, *writing* them. Meet Jerry Rex, for instance, "a swarthy, discouraged man who used to be a ventriloquist," or Jack McGuire, fall-guy boxer who puts the "stiff" in stiff opposition. Jack's main source of income derives from his services as middleman between the various entertainers who wander into the Jollity Building—the dog-and-plate acts, the balloon-twisting twins—and the big-timers with desks upstairs who might book them for "a week in a Chink joint in Yonkers." Liebling soberly describes Jack's particular problem as follows: "When he drinks he sometimes threatens to put the muscle on strangers who refuse to pay for his liquor. This detracts from his popularity at the neighborhood bars."

Liebling has a particular affection for pugilists, as enumerated in his brilliant twin volumes of boxiana, *A Neutral Corner* and *The Sweet Science*, the latter of which *Sports Illustrated* deservedly named the greatest sports book ever. In addition to Jack McGuire, the Jollity Building welcomed into its demimonde the aspirant pickpocket Marty the Clutch. "He used to be a prize fighter, but, he says, he worked with a group of hijackers several nights a week and this interfered with his training, because he was always getting shot." At the time of *The Telephone Booth Indian*'s publication, Marty was augmenting his pickpocketing vocation with occasional work as a gozzler, one who mugs others through the motivational enhancement of strangulation. But, as Liebling notes, "The gozzling business cannot be very good, because Marty is

customarily as broke as most other patrons of the
lunch counter."

You get the idea. And I haven't even recounted the
august tales of Hockticket Charlie, Judge Horumph,
Hy Sky, or Maxwell C. Bimberg, a.k.a. the Count de
Pennies, revered throughout Times Square as the sine
qua non of heeldom, the heel's heel. So why, then, does
Liebling's book capture the essence of Manhattan like
none other? Why is the snake charmed by the charmer?
Because his music swings at a pitch and a rhythm equal
to the undulations of the snake itself. It is worthy, and,
like the offer of extensive real-estate holdings in
Florida, seems real.

MATTHEW HOROVITZ

Matthew Horovitz is a television producer whose work has
appeared on PBS, NBC, ABC, ESPN, The History Channel, Food
Network, and Travel Channel, among other networks.

Ten Days in the Hills, by Jane Smiley

see p. 94

A Terrible Love of War

By James Hillman
2004

Among the writers of the various schools of depth
psychology, James Hillman is the one with a true
writer's prose. Freud's writing impresses with the
brilliance and wit of his mind. Jung made an almost
heroic effort to forget his brilliant conversation and
write a scholar's and scientist's prose, as if to keep his
thought exact and pure — were that possible. Laing's
prose is closer to my heart, with its often supple,
contemporary directness. James Hillman, however, is

one who has always written from inside language. He likes to explore the sound and the meanings of words, and their etymological connotations, as he progresses. He treasures the ideas they yield, and the etymologies and associations are enriched by his mastery and love of languages: ancient Greek, Latin, Italian, French, and German. Yet he is no pedant and no snob. He moves and lives as naturally in the medium of languages as in his professional medium, the psyche, which he prefers to call the soul. He has a natural ease and appreciation in the medium of contemporary art and writing, again unique among the masters of personal psychology.

These qualities in his writing are what first captured me when, in 1991, in my lasting enthusiasm, I translated into Hungarian a chapter from his *Suicide and the Soul.* As a psychologist, Dr. Hillman captures the reader with the broadness and equilibrium of his vision of the human soul, and the warmth and understanding for the mundane in our lives, laden with meanings not to be hidden in shame. He has revived in us the archaic foundations of the Atlantic soul, the ancient Greek gods and goddesses, and the thinkers of classical Greece. While he sees deep into the ravines of the soul, the pioneering discoveries of psychoanalysis are seen by him as a natural part of human existence as it courses its way between patches of light and darkness. Depressions are natural, he thinks—to be lived with and understood. Dr. Hillman is clearly a postmodernist who shares his visions about human life with those of Plato and Plotinus.

Beginning with the best-selling *The Soul's Code*, his work has conquered new ground and taken on new qualities. The new books directly address our contemporary anxieties in a sensitive, almost nervous style. He exposes his healer's wisdom to tough tests: he discusses the vicissitudes of the growing personality and the fallacies that psychology has built around it, the challenges and charms of aging, and most recently the warring instinct. In 2004, at the height of the war in Iraq, he published a book about the modern Mars, the Martian instinct in all humans, the terrible love of war. On page one, in the second paragraph, he writes: "We can never prevent war or speak sensibly of peace and disarmament unless we enter this love of war." No doubt, he again sought out the sore point in our souls with the bravery of a young iconoclast. As he wrote to me at the time, with some resignation, the book met with a reserved reception.

GYULA KODOLÁNYI

Bio on p. 98

The Test, by Dorothy Bryant

see p. 301

They Came Like Swallows

By William Maxwell

1937

I wish I knew this little book by heart. It isn't forgotten, but it is surely undervalued. Published in the same year Maxwell became a fiction editor at *The New Yorker* (a job he held for the next forty years), it fictionalizes the defining moment of Maxwell's life, his mother's death in the flu epidemic of 1918, when he was ten.

The Morison family, father James, mother Elizabeth, older son Robert, thirteen, and younger son Peter (nicknamed Bunny), age eight, live in harmony in a small central Illinois town. In the autumn of 1918, as the Great War concludes and family life is full of its usual seasonal upheavals, Elizabeth succumbs to the flu just after giving birth to her third child. Maxwell's acute sense of physical detail combined with short, self-contained scenes give the book a film-like clarity. This is carried further by his dividing the book into three sections, each told from a different point of view.

The first ("Whose Angel Child") is told through the eyes of Bunny. Maxwell uses simple scenes of effortless tenderness to reveal a profound love and happiness between the mother and her "delicate" son. The second section gives us the older, more seemingly confident son ("Robert"), who, we discover, will forever carry the burden of letting his mother enter Bunny's sickroom earlier in the fall. The final section ("Upon a Compass Point") is a breathtaking imaginative journey as we follow James through the days before the funeral. These pages are unforgettable in their love, grief, and struggle toward understanding.

For Maxwell, the book is an act of devotion and forgiveness. For the rest of us, it is a rare glimpse into the deepest heart of life.

JAMES BOHNEN

James Bohnen co-founded the Remy Bumppo Theatre Company in Chicago, and is currently its Artistic Director; every summer, he directs at American Players Theatre, a Shakespeare festival in Spring Green, Wisconsin.

The Third Kind of Knowledge

By Robert Fitzgerald

1952

One of the most moving books I know about the life of writing is Robert Fitzgerald's *The Third Kind of Knowledge*. The title refers to Spinoza's idea that beyond sense perception and reasoning, a "third kind of knowledge," which he called "scientia intuitive," allows glimpses of the Real, and perhaps even aspects of the divine. Fitzgerald ran across this notion as a student of classics and philosophy at Trinity College, Cambridge, and it helped him make sense of certain states of intensified, glowing, almost trancelike awareness into which he fell from time to time.

Fitzgerald's book is a lovely composite of memoir, literary portraiture, and critical essays. It begins with evocations of his boyhood in Springfield, Illinois, a life shared with his crippled and bedridden father after the deaths of both his mother and his younger brother; it moves into portraits of his close friends James Agee and Flannery O'Connor; and it continues into a sequence of studies of Homer, Virgil, and Dante. Fitzgerald's soul and intelligence are mobilized as eloquently in the literary essays as in the autobiography and memoir, and all the pieces are integrated into a rare, unself-centered wholeness. His prose has the pace, texture, and density of life observed in unusual keenness and sympathy.

Agee and O'Connor quicken Fitzgerald's subtlest instincts in style. He and Agee had been undergraduates together at Harvard, and they battled the Depression as young journalists in New York City, comrades in literature, art, and dreams of justice. Fitzgerald sets his friend squarely before us: "He would come at his fast loose long-legged walk, springing on the balls of his feet, with his open overcoat flapping." Sometimes a single verb lights up the sentence, as in Fitzgerald's description of himself, the reporter who "all day long spanieled back and forth" in the city. He composes his memoir of Agee under the aegis of the word *veritas*, which was carved over the gate in Harvard Yard and which was, he says, "destined to haunt us like a Fury." In his poems, in his fiction, his journalism, his film reviews, Agee scrabbled away at the English language to make a truth newly visible—hurtfully visible. I keep Fitzgerald's description of Agee on my desk to remind me of the larger goal: "He was after the truth, the truth about specific events or things, and the truth about his own impressions and feelings. By truth I mean what he would chiefly mean: correspondence between what is said and what is the case—but what is the case at the utmost reach of consciousness." Agee also had an almost mad streak of generosity, in the depths of the Depression sending Fitzgerald one hundred precious dollars a month from his meager journalist's paycheck so that Fitzgerald and his wife could live for a year out West, where he worked on his poetry and literary translations, turning himself into the writer he dreamed of being.

Fitzgerald's portrait of Flannery O'Connor has the same intensity. The two were as close in their way as Fitzgerald and Agee. In 1949, O'Connor boarded with Fitzgerald and his wife and young children in their Connecticut farmhouse, and throughout that year the conversation each evening, after the day's writing, stood in for all other entertainment: "they were our movies, our concerts, and our theater." "She kept going deeper," Fitzgerald writes of O'Connor's fiction, quoting the phrase she used about herself, but it applies equally to Fitzgerald. His narrative of their friendship, so soon truncated by the disease—lupus—that would disable and eventually kill her, is one powerful writer's tribute to another. In his descriptions of the sleety white peacock droppings on O'Connor's lawn in Georgia, and the metal crutches still in her bedroom after her death, and her narrow girlhood bed, he builds in our mind's eye the world from which O'Connor drew her vision, and which she had made real. O'Connor, too, was privileged with that third kind of knowledge, which is nowhere better described than in her own words: "The fiction writer presents mystery through manners, grace through nature, but when he finishes, there always has to be left over that sense of Mystery which cannot be accounted for by any human formula."

Robert Fitzgerald's book has that clarity and that margin of Mystery. For that reason, it remains inexhaustible and alive.

Rosanna Warren

Rosanna Warren is the author of Departure; Stained Glass, *which was named the Lamont Poetry Selection by the Academy of American Poets;* Each Leaf Shines Separate; *and* Snow Day. *She has received the Pushcart Prize, the American Academy of Arts and Letters Award of Merit in Poetry, and the Witter Bynner Poetry Prize, as well as a Guggenheim Fellowship. Warren is currently the Emma MacLachlan Metcalf Professor of the Humanities and professor of English and Romance Studies at Boston University.*

The Tramp Steamer's Last Port of Call

(from *The Adventures and Misadventures of Maqroll*)

By Alvaro Mutis

Translated from the Spanish by Edith Grossman

1988

There is a line of James Wright I have always loved: "Where is the sea, that once solved the whole loneliness of the Midwest?"

Rereading one of the great modern novellas of the sea, *The Tramp Steamer's Last Port of Call*, by the Columbian writer Alvaro Mutis, I thought of this line of Wright's. As if loneliness was a problem to be solved. And yet this is the ultimate truth, isn't it? Aren't we perpetually trying to solve this problem?

The Tramp Steamer is a sea story. It is the story of an old dilapidated wandering boat that the narrator—an oil company executive who travels around the world—coincidentally sees limping into various harbors at different times in his life. Helsinki; Costa Rica; Kingston, Jamaica. He becomes, for years, haunted by the image of this tramp steamer: "This nomadic piece of sea trash bore a kind of witness to our destiny on earth. . . ." A sea story, but also, like any great story maybe, it is a love story. Years after his last encounter with that strange, memorable boat, the narrator (again coincidentally, but as Mutis suggests, our lives are made up of these sorts of coincidences) meets the captain of it and becomes privy to the story behind the image.

"Life often renders its accounts," Mutis writes. "And it is advisable not to ignore them."

The story within the story is about a middle-aged Basque ship captain named Jon Iturri who falls for a beautiful young Lebanese woman named Warda. As the captain begins to talk—on the deck of a different boat, long after the love affair that has come to characterize his life has ended—he says, "This is the first and last time I'm talking about this. You can repeat it to anyone you like later on. That isn't important; it doesn't concern me. Jon Iturri has really ceased to exist. Nothing can affect the shadow that walks the world now and bears his name."

And he proceeds to recount the single most important event in his life. A simple story, really. In the course of wandering from port to port, love is found, love is lost. But what is more calamitous?

PETER ORNER

Peter Orner is the author of Esther Stories, a New York Times Notable Book, and the novel The Second Coming of Mavala Shikongo, a finalist for the Los Angeles Times Book Prize. He is the recipient of fellowships from the Guggenheim and Lannan Foundations, and the winner of the Rome Prize in Literature from the American Academy in Rome.

The Transit of Venus

By Shirley Hazzard

1980

I read *The Transit of Venus* when it was first published, long before I had published a book of my own, and for nearly thirty years, whenever people mentioned the novel, I would nod appreciatively; yes, it was wonderful. But neither my early reading nor subsequent conversations had prepared me for the shock of reading the novel again in the autumn of 2008. From the opening page, I recognized that here was a novel that demanded and repaid the best attention I could give it. Indeed, I wasn't even sure what was happening on the opening page and had to read it several times to figure it out, but I did know, immediately, unmistakably, that I was in the presence of someone making art at the highest level.

The novel is about two Australian sisters and love on three continents, and it covers several decades in a highly economical fashion. Hazzard can pinpoint even a relatively minor character in a few sentences: "Charmian Thrale's own reclusive self, by now quite free of yearning, merely cherished a few pure secrets—she had once pulled a potato from a boiling pot because it showed a living sprout; and had turned back, on her way to an imperative appointment, to look up a line of Meredith."

But even more striking, I think, than Hazzard's remarkable characters is her remarkable and sweepingly omniscient narrator—a narrator of such keen intelligence, such dazzling wit, such deft turns of phrase, such psychological insight, such historical awareness, and such an unwavering sense of the British class system that I can only identify her as being a version of the highly cosmopolitan Hazzard. Here is a breathtaking novel in which beauty and intelligence go hand in hand, and which achieves moments of the utmost emotion.

MARGOT LIVESEY

Margot Livesey has taught in writing programs at the Iowa Writers' Workshop, Boston University, and the University of California at Irvine, and has received grants from the NEA and the Guggenheim Foundation. The author of a collection of stories and six novels, including Eva Moves the Furniture and The House on Fortune Street, she is a distinguished writer-in-residence at Emerson College and a visiting writer at Bowdoin College.

The Transylvanian Trilogy

By Miklós Bánffy

*Translated from the Hungarian by Patrick Thursfield
and Katalin Bánffy-Jelen*

1934–1940; first published in English, 1999–2001

The most remarkable novel I've read in the past few years is *The Transylvanian Trilogy*, by Miklós Bánffy. No, it's not a vampire novel but, rather, a magisterial work about life in Hungary between 1904 and 1914, concluding with World War I and the destruction of a way of life that's hard to believe existed a mere hundred years ago. Published to great acclaim in Hungary, the novel makes alarmingly clear, in the most passionately human of terms, the forces that led to World War I—and World War II—and to where we are now, a century later. Subsequent history caused the book to be forgotten until Bánffy's daughter, Katalin, and her collaborator, Patrick Thursfield, did the world a great honor by translating its three volumes—*They Were Counted*, *They Were Found Wanting*, and *They Were Divided*—into English. *The Times Literary Supplement* hailed it as "a genuine case of a rediscovered classic." *London Magazine* wrote that "Bánffy's masterpiece resembles Proust's, [yet] he writes with all the psychological acumen of Dostoyevsky." For me, the infusion of Trollope makes the book all the more irresistible and original—not to forget a scope that rivals Tolstoy's. But I swear this revelatory novel is the fastest seventeen hundred pages you'll ever read.

JOHN GUARE

John Guare was awarded the Gold Medal in Drama by the American Academy of Arts and Letters for his Obie-, New York

Drama Critics' Circle–, and Tony-winning plays, including House of Blue Leaves, Six Degrees of Separation, Landscape of the Body, and A Few Stout Individuals. His screenplay for Atlantic City received an Oscar nomination. He teaches playwriting at the Yale School of Drama.

Traps

By Friedrich Dürrenmatt

1956

Friedrich Dürrenmatt has been called one of the most important literary figures of the second half of the twentieth century, but he's seldom read in the United States. Outside of Europe he is best known for his play *The Visit*, a sort of tragic comedy that was produced first on Broadway and then as a film starring Ingrid Bergman and Anthony Quinn.

Traps is a quick and capturing read, at once smart and insidious. It is the story of Alfredo Traps, a traveling salesman drawn into an innocent parlor game at a hotel where he is staying after his Studebaker breaks down and he is put up for the night by a former judge. The dining room where he finds himself plays host to a group of old men retired from the judiciary: two lawyers, a hangman, and the judge. To pass the time, hone old skills, and amuse themselves, they hold mock trials. Traps eagerly accepts the role of defendant. But as the trial deftly proceeds, he begins to feel that the prosecution has uncovered an essential truth about his nature—a truth previously suppressed. As a consequence of the verdict, Traps hangs himself.

Part dark fairy tale and part existential thriller, the novella masterfully elevates a simple story to an existential revelation. It reads more as a poem in which the moral landscape and the judgment of self illuminates a truth so profound that death by hanging is the appropriate end to the travesty of living wrong.

JOSHUA SAPAN

Joshua Sapan is the CEO of Rainbow Media, the company that operates the cable channels AMC, IFC, WEtv, and the Sundance Channel. He serves on the board of trustees of the New School, People for the American Way, and the Museum of the Moving Image. He is the author of one book, and his poetry has appeared in many literary journals.

Travelling in the Family: Selected Poems

By Carlos Drummond de Andrade
Edited by Thomas Colchie and Mark Strand, with additional translations by Elizabeth Bishop and Gregory Rabassa
1986

Emerson wrote, "In every work of genius we recognize our own rejected thoughts. They come back to us with a certain alienated majesty." So it is with Carlos Drummond de Andrade, a Brazilian poet born in 1902, witness to the modernist movement of the 1920s, which began in Europe and affected much of the world. *Travelling in the Family* contains poems written early and late in his career. As with all great books, this one reveals a life, however remote, that becomes our own. In his thoughts we can find our own ruminations.

In this collection, beautifully translated, Drummond writes of his origins in Itabira, of his dead father, of art, love, death, and survival. His work is accessible, but he is hard on himself: he considers nothing less than the heart's deep truths. Sometimes he is witty and ironic, in a kind of helpless but involved observation of the world's ills. Often, the deeper and sadder Drummond's subject the more buoyant his tone. I think of "The Elephant," one of my favorites in this collection. He

tells of making an elephant filled "with cotton, silk /
and sweetness," who then goes out

> to find friends
> in a tired world
> that no longer believes
> in animals and doesn't trust
> in things.

Late at night he sees his elephant return, disillusioned, and it collapses in fatigue:

> all of his contents,
> forgiveness, sweetness,
> feathers, cotton
> burst[s] out on the rug
> like a myth torn apart.
> Tomorrow I begin again.

Whether he is whimsical, wry, or deadpan,
Drummond continually grapples with a world that
we soon recognize as completely familiar.

GRACE SCHULMAN

Bio see p. 269

True Tales from the Annals of Crime and Rascality

By St. Clair McKelway

1950

My first job out of college was as an editorial messenger
at *The New Yorker*. I had already read many of its
legendary writers, but within hours of my first day at
work, writers, editors, and receptionists were telling me
about contributors I'd never heard of. "You mean
you've never read William Maxwell?" some editor
would say, and within twenty-four hours I would have.

At Mark Singer's suggestion, I read John Bainbridge; at
Nancy Franklin's, Kenneth Tynan. At everybody's
urging, I read Joseph Mitchell. But the writer I became
most enamored of was one whom nobody told me
about. I discovered him myself, in the magazine's
library. And how could I not? Next to the poet Edna
St. Vincent Millay and the novelist W. Somerset
Maugham, he had the most awesome writer's name I'd
ever come across: St. Clair McKelway. And the title of
his best book, a collection of profiles published in 1950
and now long out of print, was no less wonderful: *True
Tales from the Annals of Crime and Rascality*.

"Rascality"—now there was a word I'd never used
before. If you take a journalism class in college, you're
taught to treat the commission of a crime, any crime,
as a serious thing. McKelway (1905–1980) certainly
took his subjects seriously, but he made no bones about
the fact that many criminals are endearing, even
admirable. They may have ethical shortcomings, but
they also have the virtues of pluck and imagination.
Short of cash, they don't go on the dole; they turn to
counterfeiting. Caught embezzling, they don't see the
error of their ways; they steal another man's identity
and try again. McKelway steers clear of thugs and
violent offenders, yet he speaks with equal affection of
pyromaniacs ("a rather sexy and perverted mania on
the whole") as of the dogged men assigned to catch
them. His affection runs from wily craftsmen to
two-bit hacks. "The city of New York," he writes,
"was composed of some seven million suspicious
characters, most of them stupid, a few of them clever,
and all of them capable of vicious and dishonest
behavior." But that's not meant as a put-down. It's
their flaws that make people compelling.

I suspect McKelway's fondness for human foibles, even when they run to the criminal, has a lot to do with his own well-documented difficulties. He was bipolar, frequently delusional, occasionally paranoid. "I have pretty much come to the conclusion that I have a great many heads," he once wrote. "I've counted and identified twelve separate and distinct heads, or identities, that I know and possess." While serving in Guam during World War II, he sent off telegrams to the Pentagon accusing the commander of the Pacific forces of high treason. Years later, in Scotland, he became convinced that the CIA was sending him urgent messages via license plates. The wonder of these lunatic episodes is that McKelway was able to recount them with the same understated lucidity and good humor that he brought to the misadventures of other men enthralled to obscure, quixotic proclivities.

I have never committed a crime. Nor have I taken leave of my faculties. But if ever I should, I hope that my travails would make for the kind of tale that a writer of McKelway's sensibility would want to tell.

THOMAS HACKETT

Thomas Hackett has been a newspaper reporter in New York and North Carolina, and has written features for The New Yorker, The New York Times Magazine, Rolling Stone, and many other magazines. He is the author of Slaphappy: Pride, Prejudices, and Professional Wrestling. He presently lives in Austin, Texas, where he makes documentary films and teaches journalism at the University of Texas.

Dalton Trumbo

Additional Dialogue: The Letters of Dalton Trumbo

Edited by Helen Mafull

1970

Dalton Trumbo was an acerbic wit with a bristly moustache who was one of the most successful screenwriters in Hollywood (*A Guy Named Joe, Kitty Foyle, 30 Seconds Over Tokyo*), and a member of the Communist Party who refused to name names when commanded to by the House Un-American Activities Committee.

I will leave his literary reputation to film scholars (many point out that somehow he wrote his best films—*Roman Holiday, Spartacus, Lonely Are the Brave*—under the pseudonyms he had to adopt during the blacklist). But this collection of letters establishes Trumbo as the most extraordinary and entertaining correspondent of all time.

He spent most of his best creative years living in a ranch many miles from the film factories of southern California, in exile in Mexico after he was blacklisted, and even in prison, where he spent eleven months for refusing to testify to the HUAC. The kind of creative effort other Hollywood writers might apply to studio meetings, lunches, and, for that matter, scripts they knew from experience would be substantially rewritten by others, Trumbo poured into magnificent letters that only he could send, to family, friends, contractors—even, at one point, to the man repairing his kitchen.

Some highlights: a missive sent to a hotel manager on why Trumbo felt entitled to swipe a room service coffeepot; a travel manual of sorts sent to his daughter, Melissa, about to embark on a trip to Europe, about the romantic dispositions of various European nationalities; and a hilariously detailed epistle to his son, Christopher, about to depart for college, on onanism and other solitary pursuits. There is a little lefty politics among the letters, which can now seem dated or naïve. But they are mostly letters written by a tenderhearted parent, husband, and friend to the people he cherishes most, and who cherish his wit and strength in adversity.

SCOTT SIMON

Bio see p. 156

Twelve Against the Gods

By William Bolitho

1929

If William Bolitho were alive today, he'd probably be dead. Sad but true. Bolitho's need to rearrange history's furniture would have made him a sitting duck for our current brand of fanatic and talk-show thug. Consider: in this collection of twelve portraits of adventurers—in this case, individuals who, through sheer will, force of personality, obsession, greed, insanity, or sometimes a combination of all these traits, irrevocably changed the world or our perception of it—Bolitho paints Mahomet as the world's most successful tout, creating a visionary religion for the sole purpose of bringing tourism to a drab and desolate spot; Columbus as a third-rate cheese merchant with a talent for sadism, cruelty, and mismanagement; and Casanova as one of the only men of his or any time who truly understood and honored women, and who paid them in the currency of their realm.

Born in South Africa in 1890, Bolitho was buried alive by German bombs while fighting in the Somme in 1917, and died in 1930 through the incompetence of a French doctor who misdiagnosed his appendicitis. In the years between, Bolitho was an inveterate roustabout, troublemaker, and journalist; he was one of the first to condemn Mussolini as a hooligan (convincing Hemingway, who, from a distance, saw the dictator as a visionary); he chronicled the rise of the Mafia, and he wrote convincingly about magic and movies. But it is this strange and astonishing book that is his tour de force.

Having cheated death once, at an early age, Bolitho looked at life as if he were already a ghost, unimpressed by reputation or statues in the park, incapable of seeing the past as distant or separate from the life and the world around us. It's hard to imagine a more passionate or amusing companion, especially one whose vision was so hard-won. If *Twelve Against the Gods* is little read these days, it's due in part to the gnarled rhythm of Bolitho's writing, an odd mix of the classical, the lurid, and the whoops-a-daisy. As an aphorist, Bolitho is almost the equal of Oscar Wilde ("It's when the pirates count their booty that they become mere thieves"; "Adventure must start with running away from home"), but his prose can be overheated by the swirl of ideas and visions. Bolitho is incapable of going across the street for a pack of smokes without stopping to buy a goat, rewire the streetlight, investigate the provenance of manhole covers, borrow a quarter from a policeman, and buy a beer for a homeless gent. Most sentences end miles from where they began, but it's a marvelous journey and well worth the effort.

BRIAN CULLMAN

Bio on p. 82

The Twilight of the Elephant

By Elio Vittorini

1951

The Twilight of the Elephant is a loud and funny book. It takes the form of a sustained rant leveled against the patriarch of a family struggling to survive on the outskirts of Milan. The patriarch, referred to as the "elephant," is the narrator's grandfather. In his younger years, he was a wage earner with the strength of three men, but now, in his "twilight," he is a food-consuming, space-occupying, resource-disposing monster. He doesn't say a thing the whole book and doesn't need to, oppressive with his presence that recalls the way things were and are no longer. His daughter struggles with her deference to the power of the past, fury at her impoverished present, at her "small blond husband," and at her children, only one of whom has a job, and who supports them all—the elephant included—with his work as a bicycle repairman. The narrator, with a sort of patient longing, tells of their hopeless existence, never out of the shadow of his grandfather, nor out of earshot of his mother and her gloriously delivered, obscenity-laced frustrations.

Vittorini had a thing for opera: he wanted his books to hit all the same buttons as opera did, and although he's best known as an anti-fascist radical socialist, he wrote as a humanist, a quality that made his work peripheral to much of what was influential at the time (his books appeared from 1931 to 1956) yet also made it timeless. Whatever mention of *The Twilight of the Elephant* exists in print is dismissive. The book is "plotless," a "Marxist allegory," a "lesser work"; maybe it's true. Shoulder-to-shoulder with Vittorini's masterpiece, *Conversation in Sicily* (1941), with its "abstract furies," *The Twilight of the Elephant* instead presents us with hunger: constant, deep, and concrete. Not abstract at all. Against the ambitious, flawed, and much reworked (and therefore extant in several forms) *Women of Messina* (1949), *The Twilight of the*

Elephant is limited in scope, presenting—much of the time—just the interior of a rough cottage and the family existing there. It is a small book about a large man, an angry woman, and her hungry son. But its pleasures exist in these very simplicities. From such uncomplicated elements, Vittorini wrings humor, compassion, awe, desire, a dozen varieties of frustration, tension born of empathy, and even a swirling cinematic sort of food chase, where we pursue a waxy paper round and round a table—heart in throat—to see who will get to eat the anchovy hidden in its folds. I return to this book for its dark humor, its eloquent address of poverty, its pure glimpse of humanity. There is truthfulness in the characters that demands sympathy. After all, who has not been hungry?

Sabina Murray

Sabina Murray is the author of the novels A Carnivore's Inquiry, Slow Burn, and Forgery. Her short story collection, The Caprices, received the 2002 PEN/Faulkner Award. Her stories are anthologized in The Norton Anthology of Short Fiction and Charlie Chan Is Dead II. She has held fellowships from the Guggenheim Foundation and the Radcliffe Institute. She teaches at UMass Amherst.

V

The Violins of Saint-Jacques: A Tale of the Antilles

By Patrick Leigh Fermor

1953

Patrick Leigh Fermor, the British author, scholar, traveler, and war hero, is justly famous for his dazzling travel writing, but his only novel is often overlooked, even though it has all the qualities that make his other books so admired.

Set on an imaginary Caribbean island at the beginning of the twentieth century, the novel grew out of an account that Leigh Fermor was planning to write, about a ball held in Martinique in 1902 on the eve of the terrible volcanic eruption of Mount Pelée, which destroyed the town of Saint-Pierre and all but two of its inhabitants. Few facts are known about that fateful ball, so Leigh Fermor decided to turn it into fiction. He says that the novel "blossomed and wrote itself," an enjoyable process for an author who is legendary for working and reworking his prose, and for the snail-like speed at which his books appear.

The story, a romantic intrigue, is told to the narrator many years after the event by Berthe, a mysterious Frenchwoman, who goes out to Saint-Jacques as an impoverished eighteen-year-old to act as governess to the children of a distant Creole cousin. The six happy years she spent on the island come to a tragic end on the night of a lavish Mardi Gras party given at her cousin's house.

The action of the novel is straightforward, the plot slender, the characters uncomplicated, but the richness and beauty of Leigh Fermor's writing is intoxicating. Such is his ability to evoke the exuberant colors, scents, and sounds of the tropical island; the lavish, indolent way of life of its fading French aristocracy; the menacing heat, evil portents, and final horrific cataclysm, that he holds you spellbound by the power of his descriptions. Short enough to be read in one sitting, *The Violins of Saint-Jacques* is a heady experience not to be missed.

CHARLOTTE MOSLEY

Charlotte Mosley lives in Paris, where she has worked as a publisher and journalist. She is the editor of The Mitfords: Letters Between Six Sisters and In Tearing Haste: Letters Between Deborah Devonshire and Patrick Leigh Fermor.

Voices of the Old Sea

By Norman Lewis
1984

First-rate travel writing requires near-anonymity. Norman Lewis, whose natural gifts were no doubt intensified by a stint in the British intelligence service, knew how to weave himself into a community yet remain virtually undercover. A combination of fearlessness and bottomless curiosity often led him to societies on the verge of modernization, collapse, or even war, from postwar Europe to South America and Asia. Graham Greene called him "one of the best writers, not of any particular decade, but of our century."

It's tough to choose just one of Lewis's excellent books, but *Voices of the Old Sea* is my favorite (with *Naples '44* and *The Honored Society* very close seconds). This seamless chronicle details the three summers Lewis spent in Farol, along Spain's Costa Brava. A tiny fishing village chosen, he alleges, for lack of access, it is more likely Lewis's own invention: it appears on no map. Through individual encounters, he outlines the relatively rapid loss of long-standing traditions, as Farol's fishing-based economy gives way to developers and vacationers.

Lewis clearly has little use for the changes he witnesses. His reporter's detachment portrays the slide into modern homogeneity—beginning with the food, which Muga, a former Farol black-marketer, insists will appeal to tourists only if made "tasteless"—as poignantly unavoidable. Yet Lewis seems to virtually disappear within the narrative, his elegant, deceptively straightforward prose personal without a trace of confession.

Of his approach, Lewis said: "I am looking for the people who have always been there, and belong to the places they live. The others I do not wish to see." By temporarily belonging to Farol, he captures in *Voices of the Old Sea* the moment, repeated in so much of Europe, when distinctions began to blur and tourism became the only game in town.

MEGAN RATNER

Bio on p. 113

The Warden

By Anthony Trollope

1855

Although Trollope definitely has a following, it never fails to surprise me how few people I meet have read him. While many of his books may be a little daunting by virtue of their size, *The Warden* is a relatively modest 284 pages, and is my favorite among his books. The story is centered on the Church of England, a subject that today might seem as remote as the Stone Age. However, at its core it is an old-fashioned morality tale, as valid today as when Trollope wrote it.

In a victory of principle over expediency, a good man sticks to his beliefs, despite intense pressure. While it is not a Dickensian triumph of good over evil, it is still a triumph. Unlike Dickens, his celebrated contemporary, Trollope was aware that people, events, and emotions are rarely straightforward, and his nuanced approach to things, sharply drawn characters, well-contrived plots, and ability to tell a story are more relevant than ever in today's complex world.

PETER KRAUS

Peter Kraus is the owner and founder of Ursus Books, specializing in art books and illustrated books of all periods.

The Way of a Transgressor

By Negley Farson

1936

The Way of a Transgressor is on my personal list of must-reads not because it's superbly well written or particularly relevant to our time but because it is without a doubt that rare, one-of-a-kind monument that, like Mount Rushmore, has an important and transcendent appeal. The writing, which sometimes rises to surprising poetic heights, brushed onto the page with the deft strokes of a master colorist, is at other times mundane, the stuff of diary entries and old journalistic writings bound together for continuity. Its one all-transcendent saving grace is that Farson wrote it as he lived it, and, given the panoramic scope of his life, that is an achievement few other authors can match or surpass. You've heard the expression "You can't make this up"? Well, whoever coined it might have been thinking of Farson's book. In short, this is reality, long before reality hit the tube; it's extreme, way before "extreme" described a cellophane-wrapped spicy supermarket burrito.

Part biography, part travelogue, and part history, the book chronicles the life of its author from late childhood, at the turn of the twentieth century, to middle age, in the early 1930s. Its locales span turn-of-the-century Chicago; Russia immediately before, during, and right after the Bolshevik Revolution; Egypt in World War I; and the still-unspoiled backwoods of British Columbia, where the author spent a two-year idyll. It effectively concludes with an astounding odyssey on a twenty-six-foot, two-and-a-half-ton yawl, dubbed *Flame*, sailing from the Lower Rhine in Holland to the Black Sea coast of Romania—a trip that took Farson and his wife, Eve, three thousand miles across Europe in an era without GPS, sonar, or maritime radar, and apparently without even a long-range radio aboard—inland along rivers passing through countries already benighted in the gathering darkness of Nazism and Fascism. There's more beyond this, including a sojourn amid the moors and lochs of the Scottish Shetlands, travels in Ireland, and an engrossing narrative about a trip from London to India to interview Gandhi, notable for its descriptions of the perils and pleasures of early commercial air travel, as well as Farson's emotionally charged return to Russia, in 1928.

The Way of a Transgressor begins to steamroll with an account of Farson's escapades in pre-Revolutionary Russia in the approximate half decade preceding and encompassing the start of World War I. Based in St. Petersburg, he was one of many American and British entrepreneurs bent on making their fortunes in a hospitable foreign country that, like many of its European neighbors, was already in the process of building its military capacity to fight the next big land war on the Continent. As war broke out, Farson and like-minded operators from the U.S. and Great Britain were pumping arms and war matériel to the Czarist army as fast as shiploads of it could dock. Farson's counterparts were doing the same in Germany, Austria, France, and Italy—the other contenders in the Great War before the involvement of the U.S. According to Farson, in the months prior to the outbreak of war, "half the U.S. had gone overseas," an exaggeration that's close to the truth, in that staggering numbers of Americans had moved to Europe and would form the core of an expatriate community that was later to give rise to the Lost Generation of the 1920s.

Farson, who had befriended the American Communist and Russophile journalist John Reed, was present at the birth of the Russian Revolution, watching it coalesce as strikes and marches materialized into a rampage of violence by the Russian working and peasant classes. Also compelling is Farson's account of joining the British Royal Air Force after being declared medically unfit to serve for the U.S. Farson is sometimes strained in his attempts to fashion himself in the mold of a Hemingwayesque antihero. But his earliest period was one in which he was, in fact, acting out—or trying to act out—some sort of prototypical Jazz Age role as tragic icon, which, by the time of *Transgressor's* appearance, in 1936, wouldn't have been a bad gimmick, considering the commercial success of works by Hemingway and Fitzgerald.

The first quarter of the book, chronicling Farson's early adulthood, is considerably different from its latter portions, but, then, so apparently is the author, whose crash over an airfield in Egypt—the result of a dumbass stunt performed as a callow young flier pushing a Nieuport trainer far beyond the aircraft's known performance limits in order to show off—marked a turning point in his life. Farson shattered his already damaged right leg and broke many other bones in his body. Owing to poor treatment and lack of modern antibiotics, he was left with a chronically recurring bone condition that plagued him for the rest of his life. As Farson puts it, "Before the accident it was all about brawn. Afterward it was brain that mattered."

The story of how Farson was forced to undergo painful operations in odd corners of the earth figures strongly in the latter part of the book. In some ways, it also serves as a key to understanding its title. Though he never says it outright, Farson's transgression seems linked to his injuries—part of an early life lived large but recklessly—for which he paid in later decades with what he estimates as some three years total spent recuperating in hospital beds. Another transgression is Farson's loss of the small fortune he made in his early Russian days—and of the plush-upholstered life it might have continued to make possible after he'd left the country. But the "Way" part of the title says that if Farson is a mutinous existential renegade to at least certain aspects of the System, he's content to have lived his life as such.

Today, this might not exactly sound like the outer limits, but in the mid-1930s, Farson's story of going from expatriate high roller in Russia to expatriate flier for the RAF in Egypt to reclusive backwoods-cabin dweller in Canada to high-powered Mack-truck salesman in Chicago—and then back again to expatriate, drop-out sailor, and on to become a game-legged, globe-trotting feature writer for the *Chicago Daily News*—makes him sound a little like Marco Polo with some fashionable psychiatric disorder. Since today they make you swallow Prozac for wanting to do many of the things Farson lived to experience, reading the admittedly sometimes rambling *The Way of a Transgressor* might be what some sufferers need to toss the antidepressants and exchange reality TV for reality itself.

DAVID ALEXANDER

David Alexander is an author of fiction and nonfiction. He has written and published in virtually every literary category, including novels, novelettes, short stories, poetry, essays, and film scripts, and a miscellany of other forms, some of them unclassifiable. His most recent book is The Building: A Biography of the Pentagon.

When the Mountain Fell

By C. F. Ramuz

Translated from the French by Sarah Fisher Scott

1947

At the beginning of his essay "Nature," Ralph Waldo Emerson writes, "Embosomed for a season in nature, whose floods of life stream around and through us, and invite us by the powers they supply, to action proportioned to nature, why should we grope among the dry bones of the past?" While acknowledging that "Nature always wears the colors of the spirit," Emerson's writing reveals an irresistible optimism and confidence, and in his Romantic and transcendentalist world view "Nature is thoroughly mediate. It is made to serve. It receives the dominion of man as meekly as the ass on which the Saviour rode."

It is a matter of historical record that the hamlet of Derborence, in the French-Swiss Alps, suffered two devastating rock falls from the mountains above, the first in 1714 and the second, on June 23, 1749, sufficient to obliterate the settlement altogether and give rise to a lake. The second rock fall was in fact the largest ever recorded in Switzerland in historical time, with a volume of fifty million cubic meters of rock. And it is also recorded that one cowherd, Antoine Pont, whose hut was buried that summer night when the mountain called St. Martin's Tower fell, actually managed to claw his way out from under the rocks and stumble back into the village below many weeks later, like a resurrected Lazarus, having survived on a trickle of water and a bit of stale bread.

In 1934, the Swiss writer C. F. Ramuz (1878–1947) published a novella entitled *Derborence*, taking its title

from the name of the unlucky hamlet in the Canton of
Valais. In 1947, an English translation was published
with the bafflingly mundane title *When the Mountain
Fell*. In her back-cover blather, Dorothy Canfield Fisher
writes, "In the cataclysm of our times, with old, stable
human institutions tottering to ruin around us, there is
something almost magically reassuring, strengthening,
stimulating, ennobling about this true story . . ." And
there is, in truth, a kind of mythic lyricism in Ramuz's
book that is crossed with a deep and sometimes
portentous fatalism. This amalgam sits uneasily with a
contemporary reader.

As it happens, Derborence lies one valley over from
the mountain village of Chesières, where for two years
I attended a boarding school modeled partly on the
American Outward Bound program. There I came to
know the Diablerets Massif that had twice buried
Derborence. The Christological elements in Ramuz's
novella are obvious, even labored: upon his return,
Antoine Pont's wife, pregnant, says to him, "A son of
man is coming." But what I cherish in the book are its
authentic descriptions of the mountains and of the
people whose lives were brutally shaped by those
mountains, in a world of hard labor, simple food, and
soot-blackened beams that corresponded to what I,
even as a schoolboy and a foreigner, observed when I
was there.

And something else: there is a sense of brooding in
the landscape as Ramuz describes it, a sense of
malignancy that I recognize also as true, and that
absolutely refutes, with its Old World pessimism, all
the New World visionary nonsense I found when, as a
college student back in the United States, I read
Emerson. "Silence," writes Ramuz, "A silence of the

high mountains, a silence of unpeopled spaces, where man comes but rarely, and where, if by chance he falls silent himself, he may listen all he will, but all that he can hear is that there is nothing to hear. . . . Nothing, the abyss, the void; the annihilation of self; as if the world were not yet created, or had ceased to exist."

Strange stories are bred by such silences. The devil and his wife and children live up on the mountain; the occasional tortured heavings of rock and glacial ice are part of a game: "The Devil's Pin . . . They aim at the pin with their balls. And good-looking ones too, I tell you! All made out of precious stones. They're blue, they're green, they're transparent." The beauty of the mountains is delusive, because it is fatal: "Something up there was shining softly: a luminous fringe, faintly transparent, with gleams of blue and green and a sheen like phosphorescence—it was the broken edge of the ice, and in that enchanted hour of the night it too was filled with infinite silence and infinite peace." The French-Swiss Alps are unchanged in my imagination, now almost forty years since I came to know them, though I have lived my life in America. And Ramuz's novel gets them right.

KARL KIRCHWEY

Bio on p. 46

The White Rose: Munich 1942–1943
By Inge Scholl (Introduction by Dorothee Soelle)
Translated from the German by Arthur R. Schultz
1952

Inge Scholl, the surviving sister of Hans and Sophie Scholl, transcribed the resistance and courage that defined the tiny, short-lived movement known as the

White Rose. Hans Scholl, Christopher Probst, and Sophie Scholl, all in their young twenties, along with Professor Kurt Huber, Willie Graf, and others, were all executed by the Nazi regime in 1943. Today, Sophie Scholl, one of the martyrs beheaded for encouraging opposition to Hitler and his party, is considered among the most heroic Germans of all time. This posthumous elevation was in part the consequence of the de-Nazification process after the war, which sought to identify "good" Germans.

Appearing in 1952, the first German edition of *The White Rose*, written in clear, simple language, was originally meant for use in schools. The book provides an inside view of a specific group of youngsters who, after 1933, were caught up in the early optimism and patriotic frenzy of prewar Germany. As soon as they were strong enough to walk tall, they joined the Hitler Youth. However, under the influence of a humanistic liberal education at the University of Munich, they became dissenters, provocateurs, and then would-be assassins, all within a decade. Through Inge Scholl's eyes we see how Hans gradually woke up to the horrors of Nazism just as he was waking up to the world. When a book by Stephan Zweig was snatched away by the fascist state, it proved to be a turning point, although Hans was already questioning political disappearances and the treatment of Jews.

The book is one individual's record of history, and its subjectivity is not surprising, coming as it does from a survivor of the German nightmare. Following the short narrative text are reprinted the actual leaflets spread by the White Rose organization—determined words used as weapons in the resistance to Hitler. After concluding remarks by the author, written as an afterword in 1969, there are also other historical documents: the smug prose of the indictments, the sentences, various letters concerning the case, and hard-to-stomach newspaper articles such as "Just Punishment of Traitors" from *Völkischer Beobachter*.

Among the most interesting and relevant revelations is how "life went on as before," despite murderous nationalism and the tightening circle of fear. Beneath the surface, we are made to note, rebellion, however ineffectual, did occur.

Inge Scholl's narrative mixes direct reportage with a sometimes sentimental elegiac presentation, and by the end of her story, the book reads as propaganda for resistance and for a left-leaning response to history. However, this book, like *Notes from the Gallows*, by the Czech journalist Julius Fuchik, who was also killed in 1943 by Hitler's Gestapo, should be required reading for anyone even slightly interested in the period of the Holocaust. Today this story remains as essential as ever.

BARRY WALLENSTEIN

Bio on p. 283

Who Sleeps with Katz

By Todd McEwen

2003

In the few years since it was published, Todd McEwen's *Who Sleeps with Katz* has quickly met two of the key requirements for achieving cult-favorite status, having first been critically acclaimed and then going out of print. This unfortunate combination may be related to the peculiar implications of the word "Joycean," found in the blurb on the hardcover edition's dust jacket.

Meant to convey praise of artistry, it is in fact commercially lethal. But it also serves as a kind of password to the intrepid reader: the promise of a dare worth taking. In McEwen's case, it accurately advertises a writer unafraid to meddle with the mechanics of language—not one who diffuses meaning beyond comprehension or makes puzzles for the sake of being puzzling but instead one who strives to enhance expressiveness and to enrich every page with harmonizing syllables.

MacK and Isidor drink and smoke in New York City, and they do both very well, demonstrating a remarkable attention to detail and a long memory for the perfect moments they sometimes find in cocktail glasses, cardboard packets, and well-framed views of the urban landscape. The narrative takes place both in the abundant present and in the multiple pasts that intrude into that present with spontaneous sensations and visions. McEwen doesn't make the city live so much as he reveals it as lived in, as a collection of remembered places all animated through his characters' sense of history. A particular building inspires, traffic and weather demand their own soundtrack, and imagined stories tumble from the grade-school photograph of an almost perfect stranger. Time doesn't flow as much as it breathes, moving back and forth, pausing for moments of sentiment and speculation.

It is impossible to read this book and not wonder at the accomplished style in which it is composed. Deft but subtle, McEwen has perfect rhythm and pitch, maintaining a sense of humor throughout despite a somewhat dire undertone, and demonstrating a knack for the artful arrangement of material in addition to just plain remarkable and consistent invention. His rants live on the page: just look at the first paragraph, and then double-check the opening epigraph. He can retrospectively alter the tone of a passage, recasting the texture as if with new light. His use of italics is almost physical yet completely natural, like a close friend leaning in to say the right thing. Like Joyce, McEwen also appreciates the importance of a good adverb, even when he has to make one up. At ease in its perfection and unique in its accomplishment, *Who Sleeps with Katz* is an underappreciated treasure deserving of a wider readership.

MICHAEL F. RUSSO

Michael F. Russo is the manager of St. Mark's Bookshop in New York City.

Wide Sargasso Sea

By Jean Rhys
1966

People think I exaggerate when I tell them that Jean Rhys's 1966 literary masterpiece, *Wide Sargasso Sea*, sent me into a weeks-long depression the first time I read it. I'm almost embarrassed to admit how true that is. I was an English-literature major at UCLA, taking a course in the Women's Studies program. I have forgotten the title of the class, but its syllabus was, for lack of a better word, gorgeous: Rhys's *Wide Sargasso Sea*, Charlotte Brontë's *Jane Eyre*, Charlotte Perkins Gilman's "The Yellow Wallpaper," Zora Neale Hurston's *Their Eyes Were Watching God*. Some of the books I'd already read, but *Wide* was new to me, which may partially explain why its effect was so devastating.

Wide Sargasso Sea is Rhys's brilliant dismantling of Brontë's *Jane Eyre*. Rhys takes us into the attic of

Brontë's Byronic hero, Rochester; sits us right across from Bertha, the madwoman whose existence thwarts Jane's dreams; and tells the madwoman's tale. Through the use of brutally poetic (never flowery) language and insightful conceptualizing and craftsmanship, Rhys forces the reader to consider the impact of history on the individual, particularly when that history is a fusion of racism and colonialism. She forces the reader to consider on whose backs everything from material wealth to romantic option and possibility might be balanced. And she does this all while taking full and powerful measure of the roles that sexuality and eroticism play in the macro- and micropolitics of our daily lives.

Antoinette is a white-skinned Creole who lives on an island in the West Indies. A shift in fortunes (literal, metaphorical) has stripped her once esteemed family of status, but her fair skin, Euro features, and former class standing are charged, complex testaments to the presence and values of Europe as imposed on the island. Her misfortune is compounded when she falls in love with and marries Rochester, a spoiled, racist young British man who feels tricked into being on the island. Antoinette's betrayal by Rochester (who will rename her Bertha and cart her back home to live in his attic) and her subsequent madness are depicted sans didacticism but with unflinching candor. Their relationship and its fallout—and the relationships between the dark-skinned islanders and their humbled Creole "superiors"—unfold to heartbreaking effect, resonating larger social, political, and cultural commentary that is as relevant today as when the book was written, and will likely be relevant for generations to come.

Reading *Wide Sargasso Sea* left me wounded, open. It's one of the reasons I am now obsessed with backstory—that I am hesitant to simply accept anyone (in the arts, in life) as pure villain. The impact of the book on my own politics, worldview, and writing is incalculable. It is one of my all-time favorites. And I still can't bear to reread it.

Ernest Hardy

Ernest Hardy is a Sundance Fellow whose music and film criticism has appeared in The New York Times, The Village Voice, LA Weekly, Rolling Stone, The Los Angeles Times, and Flaunt. His first collection of criticism, Blood Beats: Vol. 1: Demos, Remixes & Extended Versions, was a recipient of the PEN/Beyond Margins Award, and was followed by Blood Beats: Vol. 2: The Bootleg Joints.

The Winshaw Legacy; or, What a Carve Up!

By Jonathan Coe

1994

Set in the 1980s in the form of a family saga, this is the story of the Winshaws—arms dealers, bankers, farmers, art dealers, politicians, and tabloid journalists of the most corrupt and ruthless kind. Reclusive novelist (and narrator) Michael Owen is commissioned to write a biography of the clan. He's less than successful, but his own story becomes a tale within a tale, a sharp and sobering contrast to the life of the gruesome Winshaws.

This is a brilliant social commentary, a sort of detective story, and a rollicking caper that manages to be laugh-out-loud funny, thought-provoking, and sad. One or two outrageous characters have stuck in the mind for years. And although the book was adored and admired when first published, many wondered whether it would stand the test of time. Happily, it reads just as well now as it did then, and, strangely, feels just as relevant.

LUCINDA SEBAG-MONTEFIORE AND ROBERT DYE

Lucinda Sebag-Montefiore is a producer at BBC Radio 4. Previously, she was an editor at Virago Press. Robert Dye is an architect who teaches Urban Design at UCL London.

Within the Context of No Context

By George W. S. Trow

1981

Within the Context of No Context is a small yet disturbing book. It was originally published as a *New Yorker* essay, in one of only four *New Yorker* issues dedicated to a single piece of writing. It was reissued in 1997, along with a new foreword also written by its author, George W. S. Trow. Both its subject matter and its very tripped-out writing style make it an uneasy read, and like any inspired journey it requires some willingness to just get in and go along for the ride.

This book provides a strange and challenging experience on at least two levels. One is very intimate and regards the experiential sadness of some of our peculiar American rituals. The other seems to be about the weird stuff in the air, installed there by various forms of media, that makes us feel the way we do. Trow speaks of two "grids," one intimate, on the scale of the individual, the other the grid of two hundred million (the population at the time), and the "middle distance" between them expanding as these two "grids" become farther apart. There was a "shimmer of national life," but only a shimmer, on this large and expanding national grid. There was a rather lonely, intimate place on the grid of one. Then there was the "middle distance, where comfort used to be," like home. The distance, now too great to provide comfort, is bridged with the help of television. Something had to fill this space; Nature says so. "Television provides comfort, provides home and people reached out for it." It provides a synthetic context for living. As observed by Trow, celebrities, on the other hand, have collapsed this distance; their two grids of American life are one. "Of all Americans, only they are complete." We are not, and we need to be reassured.

Scared yet?

This book touches on so much in so few pages. Aphorisms and conjecture hang like shiny-bright pieces of metal, tied with thread, from tree branches. They beckon, frighten birds, and can draw blood. They are reflective and pretty and kind of sad. This book is sad. It is about loss and loneliness. It is about the cult of celebrity and gossip and the made-up world that we swim in. It is about the absence of fact, seeking the average, and the trick, the American con, where "you make it easy for people to *think* they've got it right." Shudder.

Thankfully, Trow will also make you laugh. In the foreward, "Collapsing Dominant," he writes: "Gerlado Rivera (world's most culpable man; I have been drawing back from writing this just to avoid the pain of mentioning his name) is interviewing a panel of Teenage Satanists. As you know in addition to being the worst person on the face of the earth, Geraldo is just about the nicest." He dissects the abandoned TV show "Family Feud," *Life* magazine covers, *People* magazine, the '64 World's Fair, and talk shows. In Trow's snow globe, magazines dispense authority and the inside dope without actually having any, because we agree to let them; television empowers the trivial while "the power is lowered towards the trivial" and "a fedora hat worn by me without the necessary protective irony would eat though my head and kill me."

Today, authenticity has become something rare and unusual and therefore highly sought after. This articulate book helps identify how meaning and truth and dignity have become equally elusive. It is harsh. Is our culture doomed to the "terminal silliness" that John Irving mentions in his review of this book? It sure seems that way. The description of the popular ride at the Ford Pavilion ('64 World's Fair) hits a familiar note: we are alone. "You got in a car, a Ford car, and the car drove itself along a track. A voice came out of the radio. Then you saw the history of the world shown by Walt Disney automatons. It was not complete. The Future was shown as an empty highway. Suddenly, there was just nothing."

Think of this book as something useful to own, like one of those small, red-handled screwdrivers with a pocket clip. It does many things other than turn a screw. Like a good car, *Within the Context of No Context* takes you places that need to be seen, places that are off the map and a bit inconvenient. It was powerful then, but today the "grids" are farther apart, television has more channels, magazines are thinner but abundant, and this book has become a disturbing classic.

ROSS ANDERSON

Ross Anderson is the founder of the award-winning design firm Anderson Architects. Previously, he was a founding partner (with Frederic Schwartz) of Anderson/Schwartz Architects. A recipient of the Rome Prize in architecture from the American Academy in

Rome, Anderson has won many awards from Architectural Record and the New York Chapter of the American Institute of Architects (AIA), where he is a member of the College of Fellows. He has taught at Yale, Columbia, and Carnegie Mellon universities, and at the Parsons School of Design.

The Women's Decameron, By Julia Voznesenskaya

see p. 94

Woodbrook

By David Thompson

1974

In *Woodbrook*, David Thompson charts his struggle toward a definition of his own reality and the acceptance of his aleatoric young life, weaving a personal history of desolation, bereavement, and tenderness into the larger history of a lost Ireland—ravaged, incurable, and indomitable.

At first glance, it's a simple book. Written in 1974, when Thompson was sixty years old, the brilliant text is about his years in the 1930s as a tutor to the young Phoebe (she is twelve when he first arrives) at Woodbrook, home of an Anglo-Irish family in Sligo, where he would spend his summers from the age of eighteen to age twenty-eight. Thompson never got over these formative years, and it is because of the infection of Ireland and Phoebe into his bloodstream that we have this gift of a book.

It is on every page a love story, a history, a lament, and a paean. The subtext gives it its magic—a palimpsest that reveals a turbulent, hidden Ireland; but perhaps most of all it is a romance, one with a haunted Ireland and a dreamlike unsullied childlike love. Here is what he observes as Phoebe leans to drink from the "Boiling Well," which Thompson observes, "boiled very cold." (This is what is known as an Irishism, but Thompson was an Englishman, and his is one of the few books I have read that acknowledges the dreadful history of Ireland and recognizes fully the wrongs done to her by England.)

> She was wearing light jodhpurs and a sleeveless shirt, the one I liked her best in at that time, the one I always think of as the 'strawberry' shirt, not only because of its colour but because the material was puckered into small pointed sections rounded at the base, each with a fleck of yellow in it, like a segment of a strawberry. In sunlight the colour glowed faintly on her cheek. It had a round neck rather low, no collar, no buttons. It left the whole of her shoulders bare except a piece two inches wide, and was close and fragile enough to show the full outline of her growing breasts.

This simplicity is, like all simplicity, an artful thing. There is one amazing set piece—Phoebe's dance of death—which lovers of the book can quote instantly. Thompson is deprecating about himself ("even in England strangers think I look odd"), but it is obvious that he was loved by the native Irish with whom he worked on the farm as well as by the family with whom he lived as half-servant, complete friend.

I was born in Ireland ten years after Thompson first rounded a bend in a narrow road in Sligo and was seduced by the sight of Woodbrook lying low in the fallow greenness around him. I know what he describes viscerally; it has now utterly vanished, yet it was exactly as he tells it. But how he tells it is the thing. *Woodbrook* is felicitously written in pellucid

prose, illuminated with the spotlight of his humor
and intelligence. It is enchanting in the truest sense
of the word.

POLLY DEVLIN

*Polly Devlin's first book, All of Us There, has been republished by
Virago as a Modern Classic. She was awarded an OBE for services
to literature in 1994 and teaches at Barnard College.*

INDEXES

INDEX OF CONTRIBUTORS

CHRONOLOGICAL INDEX

BIOGRAPHIES

MARK STRAND is the author of numerous collections of poetry, including *Man and Camel* (2006); *The Continuous Life* (1990); and *Blizzard of One* (1998), which won the Pulitzer Prize. His many honors include the Gold Medal for Poetry from the American Academy of Arts and Letters, the Bollingen Prize, three grants from the National Endowment for the Arts, a National Institute of Arts and Letters Award, the 1974 Edgar Allen Poe Prize from the Academy of American Poets, and a Rockefeller Foundation award, as well as fellowships from the Academy of American Poets, the MacArthur Foundation, and the Ingram Merrill Foundation. He has served as Poet Laureate of the United States and is a former Chancellor of the Academy of American Poets. He currently teaches English and Comparative Literature at Columbia University.

ROBERT KAHN, creator and editor of the *City Secrets* series, is an architect in private practice. A recipient of the Rome Prize in Architecture from the American Academy in Rome, Kahn has received numerous awards from the New York chapter of the American Institute of Architects (AIA). His work has been featured in *Architectural Digest*, *House & Garden*, *Metropolitan Home*, *The New York Times Magazine* and in *The New York Times*, among other publications. He has taught design at Columbia University, Ohio State University, and Yale University, where he held a Davenport Chair Professorship from 1985–1986. Kahn founded Fang Duff Kahn Publishers in 2009. He lives in New York City and Shelter Island, N.Y. with his wife and daughter.

A portion of the proceeds from *Books: The Essential Insider's Guide* will be donated to FIRST BOOK, a national organization that gives children from low-income families the opportunity to read and own their first new books. To date, First Book has distributed more than fifty million books to children in over 1,300 communities around the country.

For more information, please visit www.firstbook.org.

ACKNOWLEDGMENTS

I am deeply grateful to my friend Mark Strand for sharing the remarkable depth of his knowledge. I would also like to thank Charles Miers, Ingrid Bromberg Kennedy, Robert Grover, Caitlin Leffel, and Sarah Larson for making the process of putting this book together a terrifically enjoyable experience. Special thanks to my wife Fiona Duff Kahn for her patience and fortitude (yes, like the lions) and her sense of humor throughout this whole process.

I extend my heartfelt thanks to all the contributors who have so generously and eloquently shared their insights, expertise, and love of books with the rest of us. It has been a privilege and an honor to receive each one of your entries.

ROBERT KAHN

City Secrets Movies

Always in pursuit of the best and most obscure movies, filmmakers, artists, and writers are the ideal guides to film. With over two hundred and fifty films to choose from, this unique guide will help you discover great but little-known gems.

Contributors include Wes Anderson, David Ansen, Alec Baldwin, Milos Forman, John Guare, Anjelica Huston, Jim Jarmusch, Barbara Kopple, Sidney Lumet, Simon Schama, Martin Scorsese, and Kenneth Turan, among many other film experts.

"A wonderfully subjective little guide to the best films of all time." —Graydon Carter, Editor, *Vanity Fair*

"I want to spend a weekend hidden away in some idyllic place, watching all the wonderful movies I have never heard of. To prepare for this weekend, I have this book." —Mary-Louise Parker

"*Movies: The Ultimate Insider's Guide* is an offbeat, expertly curated compendium of hundreds of movies you may have missed." —*VeryShortList.com*

THE CITY SECRETS TRAVEL SERIES:

"The best literary gift to travelers since the Baedeker and Henry James." —*Financial Times* (London)

Artists, writers, architects, curators, restaurateurs, and historians reveal their favorite discoveries in these ultimate insider's guides to the world's most fascinating cities.

Contributors include journalists Anna Quindlen and Kurt Andersen; architects Michael Graves and Richard Meier; artists Frank Stella and Brice Marden; playwrights David Hare and John Guare; novelists Michael Cunningham and Rick Moody; gourmets Danny Meyer and Marcella Hazan; poet laureate Mark Strand; author and neurologist Oliver Sacks; Museum of Modern Art director Glenn Lowry; as well as historians, urban archaeologists, curators, actors, and filmmakers.

The travel series currently includes:
City Secrets Rome
City Secrets Florence, Venice & the Towns of Italy
City Secrets London
City Secrets New York City

For more information please visit www.citysecrets.com.

PRAISE FOR CITY SECRETS:

"Escape from the crowds and chaos can be a challenge in Rome, but help comes in the form of *City Secrets Rome*. Architect and former resident Robert Kahn has collected the wisdom of his artist and writer friends in a guide that peels back the layers of the city's charms." — *Condé Nast Traveler*

"Architect Robert Kahn's *City Secrets Rome* and *City Secrets Florence, Venice & the Towns of Italy* are full of interesting finds, even for those who know Italy well." — *Town & Country*

"*City Secrets* guides are unlike any others on the market . . . in this case, a formidable cross section of London's intelligentsia . . . share their inside information on the parts of London they know best, the sorts of places that they might reveal to visiting friends, the keys that might unlock some of the city's meaning." — *The Sunday Times* (London)

"*City Secrets New York City*, the latest installment in architect Robert Kahn's invaluable series of insider guides for travelers, comprises recommendations from more than 300 writers, artists, historians, gourmands, and other notables . . . who live and work in New York. Entries in the form of personal vignettes explore everything from art to food, architecture to shopping, and music to landmarks, in all five boroughs." — *New York Magazine*

"The future of guidebooks." — *Good Magazine*